Built from Stone
The Westerly Granite Story

BUILT FROM STONE
THE WESTERLY GRANITE STORY

Second Printing, January 2012

Front Cover Picture: Smith quarry gang circa 1904

Back Cover Picture: Lion at Coduri Mausoleum 1938

Endpaper Picture: a photograph of Quarry Hill taken from Pawcatuck, CT
from the Burke Glass Negative Collection of the Westerly Historical Society

Babcock-Smith House Museum
124 Granite Street
Westerly, RI 02891

www.babcocksmithhouse.org

AUTHORS

A hometown flavor permeates this book. The authors and the technical advisor are all Westerly natives, products of the local school system, and trustees of the Babcock-Smith House Museum, who share a passion for preserving local history.

Linda Smith Chaffee, a graduate of Brown University, is the great-great-granddaughter of Orlando Smith, the founder of Smith Granite Company. She retired as a physics teacher and head of the science department after 26 years in the Westerly School System. A grandmother of thirteen and great-grandmother of one, she is active in the ministries of the Dunn's Corners Community Church, Presbyterian and is an avid quilter.

John B. Coduri, a graduate of the University of Rhode Island, is the grandson of Joseph Coduri, founder of the Joseph Coduri Granite Company in 1916. His father, Richard Coduri, served as company president from 1940 until its closing in the early 1960's. John retired in 2010 after a 40-year YMCA career that included 16 years as President/CEO of the Westerly-Pawcatuck YMCA and 10 years as the National Executive Director/CEO of the Association of YMCA Professionals. John and his wife Julie have one daughter, Jennifer, and a granddaughter, Hannah. He currently serves as the chair of the Board of Trustees of the Babcock-Smith House Museum.

Ellen L. Madison, Ph.D., a graduate of RIC, NYU, and URI, is the great-granddaughter of Richard Opie, owner of a small quarry and granite works. She retired after 33 years as an English teacher at Ledyard (CT) High School and has operated Woody Hill Bed and Breakfast since 1973. She has visited quarries in Egypt and China and struggled with stones in her gardens.

Granite industry technical advisor

Isaac G. Smith, Jr., a journeyman stonecutter and great-grandson of Orlando Smith, helped clarify the technical aspects of production processes of the granite industry. He retired from Electric Boat as maintenance superintendent.

Book Design and Production

Andrew Burris of Sun Graphics, Westerly, RI.

The BUILT FROM STONE book team included Ellen L. Madison, Ph. D., John B. Coduri, and Linda Smith Chaffee, authors; Betty-Jo Cugini Greene, director of marketing; and Susan Sullivan Brocato, coordinator of the list of granite workers and preorders.

TABLE OF CONTENTS

HISTORY

COMMUNITY

PRODUCTION

MONUMENTS

ACKNOWLEDGEMENTS

We readily admit the foolhardiness of trying to thank people adequately because this project involved so many that we are bound to leave someone out, but we simply must acknowledge the following people and sources:

Michael Slosberg and Robert Denesha from United Builders Supply Co. Inc. for originating the concept of the newspaper series and funding it.

Andrew Burris and Nancy Young at *The Westerly Sun* for layout and graphics of the newspaper series and Gloria Russell for her feature articles as we went along.

Dwight C. Brown, Jr., Richard Comolli, and Isaac G. Smith Jr. for their invaluable resources, photographs, and lifelong dedication to preserving the granite industry.

Susan Sullivan Brocato for the finished work on the list of granite workers and her willingness to handle pre-publication sales.

Betty-Jo Cugini Greene for her marketing skills and service as liaison with *The Westerly Sun* for the series.

The Board of Trustees at the Orlando R. Smith Trust for their unwavering support of this book project.

The John and Irene Walker Estate, Maxson Automatic Machinery Co. and the Washington Trust Charitable Foundation for financial support.

The Westerly Public Library for sharing The Oral History Project and artifacts from its granite collection. Kathryn Taylor and Frank Illuzzi for their assistance.

The Story of Westerly Granite by Stephen W. Macomber, 1958; *Gettysburg: Stories of Men and Monuments* by Frederick W. Hawthorne, 1988, published by the Association of Licensed Battlefield Guides; *The Strength of the Stone*, 1985, produced by R.I. Feminist Theatre in cooperation with Westerly Library Granite Project; *Westerly and Vicinity*, circa 1915; *Extra Fine Grained Blue-White Granite*, 1922, *The Sullivan Granite Company; Memorial Types*, Smith Granite Company, *History of Washington and Kent Counties Rhode Island, 1889*; *The Keeper's Log*, January-March 1998; *Westerly City Directory* 1875, 1884, 1890, 1896, 1912, 1924/25, 1928/29, 1932/33, 1943, and 1954.

Articles from *The Narragansett Weekly* and *The Stonington Mirror*, nineteenth century local newspapers, compiled by Dwight C. Brown, Jr. *The Westerly Sun* articles shared by community members.

Street Atlas Plus by DeLorme Software for the use of quarry maps.

John Linton for his dramatic photographs and his willingness to take the pictures we needed at a moment's notice.

Members of the Westerly Historical Society for their publishing savvy.

Gail Bonner for her donation of Bonner Monument records and photographs, and Lido J. Mochetti for his father's collection of designs and other draftsman-related materials.

Brenda Linton for her years of helping to organize the Museum collection.

Joann Carboni, Carol Crandall, Edward Fazio, Anthony Smith, and Gertrude Smith for proofreading and catching those things we missed.

Our guest writers: Susan Sullivan Brocato, Lisa Guerard Cugini, Melanie Waters Degler, Betty-Jo Cugini Greene, James Hawkins, Ph.D., Peggy Kelly, Anthony M. Lementowicz, Jr., Anne Gervasini Liguori and Thomas E. Wright.

People who shared with us both current and historic photographs, granite memorabilia, anecdotes and research efforts: Brad Benson, Bruce Brawley, Susan Sullivan Brocato, Dwight C. Brown, Jr., Roberta Burkhardt, Harold Buzzi, Judith Carson, Linda Smith Chaffee, Dorothy Clarke, John B. Coduri, Joseph E. Coduri, Irene Sposato Gaccione, Kam Ghaffari, Mary Jo and Nelson Girard, Granite One

Hour Photo, Betty-Jo Cugini Greene, Susie Sposato Greene, Melanie Degler, Shelley Dziedzic, Lonnie Foberg, Dawn Marie Hancock, James Hawkins, Ph.D., Linda Holman, Kevin Kuharic (Oakland Cemetery, Atlanta, GA), John Macomber, Ellen L. Madison, Ph.D., Florence Saunders Madison, Madeline Malaghan, Barbara Mehringer, Henry Nardone, New London Fire Department, Susan Olsen (Woodlawn Cemetery, Bronx, NY), Betty Jean Gavitt Page, Phil Panciera, Alan Peck, Constance Verno Pryor, Hank Randall, Umile Ritacco, Marian Sposato Santaniello, Felice Sposato Scialabba, Roger Shawn, Jr., Anthony Smith, Gordon Smith, Jr., Isaac G. Smith, Jr., Richard Smith, Keith Snyder (National Park Service, Antietam), Frances Steverman, Jim Szyjkowski (National Park Service, Chickamauga), John Tedeschi, Joseph Terranova, the Rev. Trevor E. G. Thomas, Donna Turrisi, United Builders Supply Co. Inc., William D. Wallace, Kathleen Gavitt Walton, Brock and Mary Weatherup, Westerly Fire Department, Westerly Historical Society, Dorothea Winnicki, Thomas E. Wright, and many more. The majority of the photos are owned by the Babcock-Smith House Museum.

All the people we interviewed.

Members of the community for their enthusiastic reception of our work and sharing of stories, artifacts, and photographs.

All uncredited articles were written by Linda Smith Chaffee, John B. Coduri, and Ellen L. Madison, Ph.D. We assume responsibility for errors or lack of clarity.

And, trite as it may seem, our families and friends for their willingness to share us.

Linda Smith Chaffee, John B. Coduri, and Ellen L. Madison, Ph.D.

Stone Chips

Many of the Stone Chips in this book are transcriptions of interviews with men and women connected to the granite industry. The interviews, compiled by David Marshall, were conducted from 1983 to 1985 as part of the oral history component of the Westerly Public Library Granite Project. The following people with their birth year are quoted in this book:

Thomas Barber (1913)
Mrs. John (Selena) Burne (1900)
Patsy Capizzano (1911)
Peter DePerry (1916)
Arthur Ferraro (1917)
Thelma Hill Gardner (1917)
Nettie Coduri Salimeno Jones (1910)
John Keena (~1885)
Tony Morris (1918)
Ruth Mosena (1917)
Carl Myllymaki (1918)
Hannah Hill Robinson
Isaac G. Smith, Jr. (1922)
Frank Turco (1910)

On this Ground through the Years has been demonstrated the Skilled Craftsmanship of that GREAT COMPANY of MEN who wrought here the many noteworthy Memorials of WESTERLY GRANITE that stand forever through the Land

This tablet at the Babcock-Smith House Museum recognizes the contribution of the men of the Westerly granite industry.

FOREWORD

Although both the majestic and the humble products made from Westerly granite will be around for generations to come, the number of people who have an intimate knowledge of the granite industry are quickly diminishing and, with them, records and artifacts. This book is an attempt to share bits and pieces of the Westerly granite story so that the present generation can take pride in Westerly's granite heritage.

The effort started when Michael Slosberg approached a small group of trustees of the Babcock-Smith House Museum and representatives from *The Westerly Sun* with an idea to publish a full-page informational ad once a week in the newspaper for a year. Slosberg would fund the project if we would supply the content and if the newspaper staff would design the layout and graphics. He knew that the Museum has an amazing collection of records and artifacts, great volunteers, and a reputation for hard work.

We saw a larger mission which would involve guest contributors, the sharing of our own collection, the opportunity to educate, and a chance to gather information, photographs, ephemera, and artifacts from the community.

Five people with connections to the industry formed the nucleus of our team: Susan Sullivan Brocato (Sullivan Granite Company), Linda Smith Chaffee (Smith Granite Company), John B. Coduri (Joseph Coduri Granite Company), Betty-Jo Cugini Greene (Cugini masons), and Ellen L. Madison (Richard Opie). We could not have done this series without the invaluable contributions of Isaac G. Smith, Jr. and Dwight C. Brown, Jr. and their lifetime of work preserving and cataloguing the records of the Westerly granite industry.

Before the series had run for three months, we were besieged by people asking if and when a book would be published. They told us that they were saving all the articles, but wanted something permanent to share with their children and grandchildren. Although we were exhausted from researching and writing the newspaper series, we willingly accepted the challenge.

We have attempted to give a glimpse of various aspects of the granite industry and the people who worked with stone. We incorporated most of the information in the newspaper series, added previously unpublished material, and reorganized the content so that there is a more unified story. The book is not meant to be an exhaustive work. In many cases, the records no longer exist. In other cases, we have too much material to share. We have tried to be correct, but we realize that not all memories and not all written records are accurate. We invite you to visit us at the Granite Research Center at the Babcock-Smith House Museum if you wish further information or have information to share.

Linda Smith Chaffee, John B. Coduri, and Ellen L. Madison, Ph.D.

opposite: Coduri mausoleum, River Bend Cemetery, 1938

History

Combine the forces of heat, cold, pressure, water, moving ice, millions or billions of years, and you might end up with the granite which lies under Westerly. The native peoples used granite for tools and weapons. Early settlers moved surface rocks to use for steps and chimney foundations. By the early 1840's Orlando Smith had established a business on Mechanic Street in Pawcatuck, cutting boulders and small outcroppings for foundation stones, walls, curbstones and hitching posts. In 1846, he established the Smith Granite Company on Quarry Hill which was followed quickly by the New England Granite Works and later by Joseph Newall & Co.

Following the Civil War the demand for monuments plus the excellent quality of the granite and the influx of both skilled and unskilled workers, meant that Westerly became the foremost supplier of granite works of art. By 1900, 4,000 (57%) of the 7,000 residents of Westerly were involved in the granite industry. Small companies mushroomed and some stonecutters worked in their own backyard sheds. At times, skilled craftsmen might go from company to company wherever there was a demand for their talent.

By the early 1900s, the availability of electricity, coupled with the use of steam and compressed air, changed the way stone was quarried and products were manufactured. The Joseph Coduri Granite Company and the Sullivan Granite Company bought the Newall shed and quarries respectively and became major players. The heyday continued until several factors, such as union strikes, the Great Depression, the '38 Hurricane, and World War II dealt some severe blows to the industry. Granite was then used for more utilitarian purposes: buildings, runways, bridges, and industrial uses. After 1960, smaller companies, such as Buzzi Memorials, Bonner Monument Company and Comolli Granite Company continued the artistic tradition. Most recently, United Builders Supply Co. Inc. and Cherenzia Excavation have supplied architectural elements and crushed stone respectively.

1846 — 1880: THE BEGINNINGS

Very few men have the opportunity to shape a town, but in 1845 Orlando Smith, with the help of his mother, did just that when he discovered an outcropping of granite on top of Rhodes Hill on the old Babcock property. He knew that this outcropping (located just east of the present water tower off Tower Street) could supply him with raw material for his granite business. The $8,000 price was too much for the thirty-year old, but he shared his dream with his mother who, it is said, rode on horseback from Ledyard to Westerly to bring Orlando $2,000 for the down payment.

Shortly after Smith had begun quarrying on the hill, John Macomber purchased the Vose Farm and accompanying land (the present high school campus plus more) on the other side of the 1846 road to begin his quarrying operation. Later, Smith bought out Macomber and moved the road (lower portion of current Tower Street) to its present location so that the quarrying operations could be combined.

In 1865 a quarry on adjoining land was opened by George Ledward who later sold to J.G. Batterson who operated it as the Rhode Island Granite Works, a subsidiary of New England Granite Works based in Hartford, CT.

In the early years stonecutters focused on practical items such as walls, foundations, steps, hitching posts and curbstones which are still found throughout Westerly. As the nation matured, so did the granite industry which was in an excellent position to make the transition to works of art. Westerly's granite was ideal; its fine grain, uniform color, strength and easy workability were the characteristics needed for the finest monuments.

Sarah Smith, Orlando Smith's mother, is said to have ridden on horseback from Ledyard to Westerly with the $2000 down payment.

As the market for more elaborate monuments grew, the granite companies hired talented stonecutters from Scotland, Ireland, Italy, Finland, and the United States. These highly skilled stonecutters were needed to produce a more finely finished surface on the stone, cut letters, and carve moldings and decorative designs. As the trade developed, men began to specialize. Specific skills were needed by letter cutters; different skills were needed by carvers. A hierarchy developed -- apprentices, journeymen, letter cutters, carvers, statue cutters. The further up the hierarchy, the greater the prestige and the greater the hourly wage.

Everyone wanted to be a part of this boom. Small companies sprang up. Quarries opened and closed, leaving slabs of rock for hikers to find many years later in the middle of the woods. Men flocked to Westerly for employment. In 1880, with the raw material available, the craftsmen in place, and the product in demand, the industry was poised to become nationally famous.

Westerly, R. I. Aug 10th 1857

M State of R. I.

Bought of ORLANDO SMITH,

DEALER IN GRANITE,

790½ feet of 7 inch Granite Curb Stone, at 50 cents, | 395 | 25
To carting 790½ feet, at 5 cts. and 1 Corner Stone, 30 cts. | 39 | 83
To 1 Corner Stone, at $ 3.37 cts. | 3 | 37
| 438 | 45

Received Payment, Wm Butchiller
Correct, Wm Butchiller Surveyor. By Wm Butcher

Receipt to the State of Rhode Island for the purchase of curbstone from Orlando Smith dated August 10, 1857.

Early monuments include the Orlando Smith obelisk, a cenotaph, now located on the grounds of the Babcock-Smith House Museum. A cenotaph is a monument erected in honor of a person or group of people whose remains are elsewhere.

STONE CHIPS

On various business philosophies: "All the granite that they [Smith Granite Company] quarried, they cut. They didn't give you any granite. If you wanted any stone from the Smith Granite Company, you came to the Smith Granite Company and had it done. They had a fine product. Most everybody [else]… the Bradford quarry, the Crumb quarry, the Newall quarry, the Klondike and all of these which were the Sullivan quarries… quarried stone for anybody. They didn't cut stone. They just quarried it and sold you the rough stock. So a great deal of the Westerly granite from Bradford went to other granite centers. They say there was more Westerly granite cut in Quincy [MA] then there was in Westerly."

Isaac G. Smith, Jr.

1880 — 1900: THE HEYDAY

Three factors serendipitously coalesced during the last twenty years of the nineteenth century to create a demand for fine monuments. The exceptionally fine quality of Westerly granite and the response of its skilled work force would skyrocket the Westerly granite industry to dominance.

First, the trend away from stark churchyard cemeteries toward park-like cemeteries had been growing for nearly fifty years. Most cities featured a tranquil setting, such as River Bend Cemetery, where people could go for a Sunday afternoon picnic or stroll amidst dignified artistic monuments.

A second driving force was the desire to commemorate the heroes of the Civil War. National battlefields were established in Gettysburg, PA; Antietam, MD; Chickamauga, GA and Vicksburg, MS, and Westerly companies supplied exquisite monuments to them all.

The third factor was the value that society placed on elaborate monuments to commemorate the lives of famous men or of deceased loved ones. Ornate carving, statues, elaborate dies, and multiple bases were components of these Victorian monuments which can be seen in both cemeteries and public squares. The men who designed the monuments had an eye for proportion, pleasing design and detail, and the statue cutters carved delicate ornamentation in the hard, unforgiving granite.

The rich and famous, as well as municipal representatives, came to Westerly from as far away as California in a time when communication and transportation were difficult. They wanted their monuments to be the best and the best monuments came from the quarries and companies of Westerly. Frequently, the same design was reproduced for several clients, but occasionally a wealthy client paid a higher price to guarantee that the model would be destroyed after his monument was complete.

James Pollette was representative of the superb carvers working in Westerly. He carved this angel's delicate crown through which one can see the sky. McDowell monument in Laurel Hill Cemetery, Philadelphia, PA

Some of the statues were admired for their delicate and exquisite details even though they were very large. Other statues were impressive because of their massive size. For the combination of massive size and exquisite detail, the Washington Equestrian Monument is an outstanding example.

By 1900, 4,000 of the town's 7,000 residents (57%) were directly or indirectly involved in the granite industry and examples of their fine work can be found throughout the United States.

The elaborate Sanders monument in Calvary Catholic Cemetery, Evanston, IL honors a deceased loved one. It has three statues, multiple bases, and a die with engaged columns and ornate carving. Andrew Farrell, Joseph Fraser, Dennis Moore, and Angelo Perlotti did the carving on the monument's elaborate die. The Smith Granite Company produced this monument in 1893 for $8,113.

inset: One of three statues on the Sanders monument shows the talent of Westerly craftsmen to portray an emotion. James Pollette and Charles Rezzi were the statue cutters.

The Washington Equestrian Statue, one of many honoring civic heroes, combines massive size and delicate details.

Allegheny Commons Park, Pittsburg, PA

1880 – 1900: THE HEYDAY
COMPETITION AND COOPERATION

Joseph Newall & Co., the New England Granite Works, and the Smith Granite Company were the three dominant companies in the local granite industry and became natural competitors during the closing decades of the nineteenth century. Smaller companies, such as A.G. Crumb, Charles P. Chapman, and Nathan Dixon found their niche as well and each advertised for business. There was perhaps more cooperation among companies than we might ordinarily believe.

On August 14, 1894, the Freemason's Franklin Lodge No. 20 A.F. & A.M. adopted a resolution expressing hearty thanks to these six companies for the three beautiful granite pedestals they jointly presented to the Westerly Masonic Lodge. Each granite enterprise received an 18" x 24" framed copy of the adopted resolution.

Recently, John Coduri accidentally discovered one of these Masonic Resolutions behind a framed photo of his grandfather, who purchased the former Joseph Newall & Company in 1916 and established the Joseph Coduri Granite Company. The cardboard on the back of the photo frame had been damaged by moisture so Coduri decided to take it apart and reassemble the picture with new backing. He was shocked to find the Masonic resolution right behind his grandfather's photo. This is the only one of the original six resolutions known to have survived.

Companies often worked together. Smith Granite Company had the only stone lathe so other companies would send a stone to be turned. In turn, Smith might have Coduri & Marzoli carve their crosses or help them hoist a large monument into a railroad car and brace the stone for shipment.

Individuals on all levels, with the support of their employers, occasionally moved from company to company as their skills were needed. Because Sullivan Granite Company used an undercutting method in their quarrying operations, quarry workers could work there when the cold and snow might prohibit them from working in the open quarries at Smith Granite Company. Men often established their own small quarries or businesses, but a few years later could be found with a new company name and new partner or working for a different company.

Men mingled socially as well. On Saturday afternoons stonecutters from various companies gathered at the Martin House (Railroad and Canal Streets) in downtown Westerly where it was said that more granite was cut than in any stone shed in town as the men talked shop.

One Saturday a new carver came in and the other men eyed him closely. They asked him what he had been doing and he replied that he had been carving an eagle. He had finished the wings, the feathers, the head and was carving the claws away from the branch "when the darned thing up and flew away."

Of course, competition also existed and professional courtesy was displayed.

Isaac Smith said, "If my father was going to go see Frank Sullivan in Sullivan's Quarry, he'd call up and say, 'Frank, I want to come and see you.' Frank would say, 'Okay, come Tuesday.' And you didn't go until Frank says 'you come Tuesday' and Frank didn't come to the Smith Granite Company until these arrangements were made. You didn't just walk into somebody else's operation and start looking it over. You did it on invitation and quite often I'm sure they prepared for your visit."

The three pedestals (Doric, Ionic, and Corinthian) in the Westerly Masonic Hall on Elm Street represent the cooperation among six companies in 1894.

LABOR DAY PARADE

Unions, companies, and various craft groups of all sizes participated in a huge Labor Day parade in 1895. The headline in *Westerly Narragansett Weekly* for September 5, shouts "THE PARADE" and then goes on extensively describing the first ever Labor Day parade in Westerly. More than 1,000 men marched; more than 10,000 watched; 6,000 copies of the program were distributed along the route. It seems as though every industry was represented by a float; many individual companies within an industry also had floats. The idea for a parade had originated at a picnic of granite workers and carrying it to fruition must have been a Herculean task.

The parade was delayed in getting off on time because "the fine display of the Smith Granite works had been marred by the breaking of one of the statuary models, and the float had been sent back to the quarry for another. It soon returned" and the parade began. The whole first division was composed of granite workers: 165 members of the Westerly Branch of the Granite Cutters' National Union, all of whom wore "a new apron, . . . a light soft felt hat and a badge"; 23 tool sharpeners; and 20 tool and water boys, for example. Companies such as Joseph Newall & Co., Rhode Island Granite Works and the Dixon Granite Works had floats.

Ten yoke of oxen were attached to the Smith Granite Company float containing the statuary models, two of which were broken during the day. The Rhode Island Granite Works attracted a great deal of attention as every branch of the business was represented and all the men were actually at work on the float. Their names and occupations were all listed in the newspaper and most of the granite-related floats were described in detail, but they were not the favorites of the "small boys" along the route who followed the float of I.G. Barber, the candy man, who from start to finish liberally scattered candies to the crowd.

The Rhode Island Granite Works was a division of the New England Granite Works based in Hartford, CT. The Rhode Island Granite Works' sheds and quarry were on Ledward Avenue.

The Labor Day Parade in 1895 involved more than 1,000 marchers and 10,000 spectators. Pictured here is the Smith Granite Company float in front of the company store. The number of oxen was in honor of the day's festivities rather than necessary to pull the load.

1880 – 1900: THE HEYDAY
SMITH GRANITE COMPANY: FIRST GIANT ON QUARRY HILL

In about 1837, the Providence and Stonington Railroad was completed through Westerly, leading to rapid growth and a great building boom along both sides of the Pawcatuck River. It was this boom that attracted Orlando Smith (1814-1859), a stonemason from Ledyard, Connecticut, to come to Mechanic Street in Pawcatuck in 1839 to continue to build stone steps and foundations from the plentiful granite boulders. Later, he discovered a promising outcropping of high quality granite that was easy to quarry on the old Babcock farm on Rhodes Hill (now the top of Granite Street). In 1846, he purchased the Babcock farm from Oliver D. Wells.

Orlando Smith married Emeline Gallup of Ledyard. They wanted to move into the old Babcock house, but, after thirty years as a tenant farm, the house needed much work. Using granite from the property, her father, Isaac Gallup, rebuilt the foundation in the north wing (now the caretaker's apartment) and made other improvements.

Wedding photo of Orlando and Emeline Smith, 1845

Smith moved his masonry operation to the top of the hill adjacent to the granite outcropping and worked with his friend William A. Burdick. Smith's expertise was in building foundations and setting curbing, while Burdick's expertise was in architectural monuments. Gradually, the business began to concentrate more and more on formal monuments.

Orlando Smith died in 1859, at the age of only 45, leaving his wife with four small children, ages 2, 4, 6, and 8, to raise, a farm to manage, and a business to run. She needed help. Burdick was the natural choice to be the manager of the granite business, freeing Emeline from the day-to-day responsibilities. William A. Pendleton was appointed by the bank to oversee its interests.

Concerned about having a school for children of the nearby granite workers, Emeline Smith deeded a plot of land to the town of Westerly to be used for a school – Quarry Hill District #2. Presently the Rite-Aid Pharmacy is on the site of the old Quarry Hill School.

After the death in 1886 of Emeline Gallup Smith, the business was incorporated as the Smith Granite Company under the able leadership of Isaac G. Smith as president and Orlando R. Smith as treasurer. These were prosperous times for the Smith Granite Company which became a force both locally and nationally. A company store was established and operated for 39 years as a service and convenience to its employees. Monuments were shipped to 32 states across the country as well as used locally. The company produced 69 of the monuments at Gettysburg; 38 at Chickamauga; 8 at Antietam and 1 at Vicksburg. Many well-respected names from the Victorian Age began to appear in the order books such as Jay Gould, financier and railroad magnate, and George Babcock, inventor and manufacturer.

Since the visiting customers were often overnight guests at the Babcock-Smith House, the Smith home needed to reflect an air of prosperity and in 1884 the house underwent a Victorian renovation. The front hall was extended outward to where it is now and the lovely colonial doorway was moved forward. The stained-glass windows, currently part of the

The 1884 Victorian renovation of the Babcock-Smith House reflected the prosperity of the company. The elaborate outhouse is behind the house on the right side of photo. Orlando Raymond Smith, Jr. returned the house to its colonial appearance in 1928.

Carriage House at the Museum, were added on either side of the foyer. Further additions included a second-floor balcony and a porch that wrapped from the front around to the south side of the house.

The outhouse had plaster walls and mahogany woodwork and even had a stove for comfort during the winter months.

With high-society clients accustomed to the very best and with a product that defined excellence, the Smith Granite Company also found it desirable to upgrade its facilities in order to make a favorable impression on prospective customers. Isaac Smith convinced the company to erect a new cutting shed in 1885 so that the facilities looked up-to-date and reflected modern and efficient processes. Unfortunately, Isaac's health failed and he died in 1888. The loss of his contribution to the business was tremendous, probably never entirely overcome.

For three generations an Orlando Smith headed the Smith Granite Company. The first Orlando (1814-1859) discovered the outcropping of granite on Rhodes Hill and began the Westerly granite industry in 1846. The second Orlando, Orlando Raymond Smith (1851-1898), was just a child when his father died; he worked in the granite business from an early age and headed the company during its most prosperous days. The third Orlando, Orlando Raymond Smith, Jr. (1877-1932), left Brown University to work in the business office after his father's death.

After the death of Orlando Raymond Smith, it became apparent that the court would step in and freeze the assets of the Smith Granite Company. The finished stones for this mausoleum were shipped out of town on a Sunday night before the courts stepped in. The company could then receive payment and have sufficient cash to keep the business going a bit longer. This is the White Mausoleum in Mount Auburn Cemetery, Cambridge, MA.

Orlando R. Smith became president and continued to administer the business. During the late 1890's, he became alarmed at the serious drop in the sale of monuments and by his own failing health, which was unknown to those around him. He made an agreement with David Newall of the Joseph Newall Granite Company of Niantic to merge as the Smith and Newall Granite Company. Serious financial problems arose and, before they could be settled, Orlando R. Smith died in 1898. A drawn-out lawsuit followed and litigation ended in an award of heavy monetary damages to Newall, leaving Smith with very little operating capital. Consequently, the Smith operation was down for many months.

By 1922, Orlando R. Smith, Jr. (1877-1932) had become president and the rest of the third generation had all graduated from college and joined the business. The two older brothers, Orlando and Franklin Smith, ran the office; Isaac, Sr. gradually took over design and planning and general superintendence of granite cutting; Edward was in charge of all quarrying and heavy equipment. For the first time granite rough stock was offered and sold to the trade, whereas previously the company had cut and finished almost all the granite it produced.

In 1924, following the death of James G. Batterson, Jr., Smith Granite Company bought all assets of the adjoining New England Granite Works. This consolidation simplified some complex boundaries in several quarries, secured the two-mile private railroad over the "long bridge" to the New Haven main line, and meant that all granite production on the hill was being run by one company, but it involved a considerable financial outlay. The volume of business expanded through several years as planned, but then came the Great Depression. Twelve lean years followed. It became evident that people could live without the exceptional monuments that had earned the Smith Granite Company such a stellar reputation for the past 75 years. The 1938 hurricane delivered a particular destructive blow. The blacksmith shop blew down, windows blew out of the big shed on Granite Street, and the crane barn blew down. Most critical was the loss of electrical power. There was no power to run the pumps in the quarry. No air compressors. No cranes. Because water could not be pumped to the boiler, even steam cranes could not be used. All operations had to be curtailed, many employees laid off, and all belts tightened.

Before there could be any significant recovery from the effects of the depression and the hurricane, World War II was thrust upon the local industry. It was hard for a non-essential business to obtain steel, coal, power, tires and many other resources. To lighten the load, Isaac G. Smith, Sr. left the company in 1942 to work at Pratt and Whitney at East Hartford. Production of any kind of granite work fell to a very low level. Eventually the war was over, but, before a quick recovery could be made, the bank foreclosed on all the Smith assets on August 16, 1945. The company was reorganized as Smith Granite Works with Edward W. Smith as president. Eventually the machinery was sold, the derricks taken down, the buildings eliminated and the land sold for a shopping center and housing. In 1955, the once great granite company went out of business.

Advertisement of the Smith Granite Company circa 1920.

left: Marsh Vase manufactured in 1886 for $1800.

above: The office of the Smith Granite Company around 1915 was located near the company store. The building was once owned by New England Granite Works. When they no longer needed it, they sold it to Smith around 1880.

Smith Granite Company monuments are confirmed in the 32 shaded states

Number of monuments in each state:

CA-29	MA-399	OH-116
CT-315	MD-31	OR-4
DC-11	ME-40	PA-411
DE-16	MI-38	RI-598
FL-4	MN-7	TN-4
GA-5	MO-21	VA-19
IA-28	MS-1	VT-11
IL-98	NE-5	WI-41
IN-13	NH-14	WV-4
KS-1	NJ-122	WY-1
KY-8	NY-574	

STONE CHIPS

"Ed Smith considered everybody as part of his family because when the Depression came along … he didn't lay the gang off. What he did, he split the gang in half …. He had them working 3 days and then the other gang worked 3 days so one week you got 3 day's pay and the other week you got 2 day's pay, but at least you got enough money comin' in so you had food on the table. This is the way Ed Smith operated. Because he had good men he wanted to keep."

Arthur Ferraro

Smith Granite Company circa 1893 from Granite Street looking southeast. Buldings (l to r) SGC office (shear poles to the rear); stonecutting shed; polishing and turning shed (formerly Hoxie Buick); engineering and drafting building; statue cutting shed

Looking northeast from Granite Street. Buildings (l to r or north to south) company store at Granite and Tower Street (built in 1884 and still standing, but not visible) SGC company office (barely visible); stonecutting shed (built in 1885); polishing and turning shed (formerly Hoxie Buick); engineering and drafting building; statue cutting shed (the stone building in foreground)

BOSS BURDICK

If there was ever a man behind the granite industry in Westerly, surely it had to be William A. "Boss" Burdick (1822-1891). He came to Westerly in 1846 to work for, and board with, Orlando Smith at Smith's shop in Pawcatuck. In 1848, Smith made him foreman of the emerging Smith Granite Company and he continued his association with the company for 45 years.

Early in 1870, he built a house at the corner of Granite and Summer Street (59 Granite) which, many years later, became The Roger Williams Inn.

In 1874, under Burdick's management, 200 people were working on a $50,000 job of supplying paving blocks for Hope Reservoir in Providence and were also getting out and shipping stone for the engine house of the Providence Water Works, a job which came to about $40,000. He was also guiding the company toward becoming a leader in the monument business. Without Burdick's able leadership, it is doubtful that the Smith Granite Company could have survived the untimely death of its founder and achieved the status it did.

William A. Burdick, (1822-1891), business manager of the Smith Granite Company from 1859-1887

ESTABLISHED 1846.   INCORPORATED 1887.

ORLANDO R. SMITH, *President and Treasurer;* JOHN P. RANDALL, *Secretary.*

O. R. SMITH, H. H. S. CATHCART, J. E. SMITH, J. P. RANDALL,
W. S. MARTIN, *Directors*

The SMITH GRANITE CO.,
Monumental Designers and Sculptors,
All Kinds of Cemetery Work in their Original Westerly Granite.

WESTERLY, R. I.

One of the best known granite quarries in the United States is that conducted by the Smith Granite Co., at Westerly. Originally started in 1846 by Mr. Orlando Smith the business has grown year by year and now gives employment to over 400 men and covers several acres of land. The present company was organized in 1887 with a capital of $100,000. The officers are Mr. Orlando R. Smith, President and Treasurer, and John P. Randall, Secretary. The company manufacture every description of Monuments and Building Work, and of late years have given special attention to Granite Statuary; in this department they have few, if any equals, in the United States, as they employ artists and sculptors of recognized ability and produce statues which are portraits both in form and feature. Among their most noted work we would mention the Washington Equestrian Statue at Allegheny, Pa., made from a solid block of granite weighing 20 tons, the Soldier Monuments for many of the Ohio Regiments on the Chickamauga Battlefield, over 100 of the Gettysburg Monuments on the Gettysburg Battlefield, the Mausoleum for Ex-Senator Jas. G. Fair, of California, (costing over $60,000), the Mausoleum erected for Jay Gould at an expense of $50,000, and a very large number of Monuments and Cemetery work in all parts of the country. Portait work is made specially, and some very lifelike statues have been made by this company from photographs the expression being wonderfully reproduced. A large number of sheds are occupied which are heated by steam and contain every facility for the production of the best and most artistic results both in winter and summer. The facilities of this company are so extensive that the largest orders can be filled with dispatch. The company using pneumatic tools, steam turning lathes and steam planers and drills. They have quarries for blue, white, red, pink and gray granite. This company do more monumental work than any firm in the United States. The granite for a number of public buildings in various sections of the United States came from this well known quarry. The branch offices of the company are located as follows: 10 West 23d St., New York; 104 Pullman Building, Chicago; 3 Bromfield St., Boston; 948 No. 42d St., Philadelphia; 350 The Arcade, Cleveland; 5 Weybosset St., Providence, R. I., 604 Ellwanger & Barry Building, Rochester, N. Y.; 10 Arcade, Utica; 5 Sylvan Ave., New Haven, Grand Haven, Mich., and Norwich, N. Y. Estimates and designs for any contemplated work will be furnished promptly on application.

2

Westerly and Vicinity, an advertising booklet circa 1915.

The Number One quarry hole and Smith company buildings on the rim circa 1885. In the hole is the pump house. It was a continual effort to pump water out of the holes to allow quarrying.

1880 – 1900: THE HEYDAY

NEW ENGLAND GRANITE WORKS: A GIANT ON QUARRY HILL

New England Granite Works was a large company, founded in 1845, with its headquarters in Hartford and with quarries and cutting sheds in Westerly, RI and Concord, NH. The Westerly quarry had been opened in 1865 by George Ledward who later sold it to James Batterson. For a while it operated under the name Batterson & Ledward and later became known as the Rhode Island Granite Works, a division of the Hartford-based parent company. This company was unusual in that it excelled in both elaborate monumental work and major building projects.

New England Granite Works produced many outstanding monuments of Westerly granite including the massive Soldiers National Monument in the Gettysburg National Cemetery, the Antietam Soldier in Sharpsburg, MD and the Mallory Gates at the Elmgrove Cemetery in Mystic, CT. The company erected the statue of Alexander Hamilton in Central Park, New York City; the Thayer monument at West Point, NY; the Texas Revolutionary monument in Galveston, TX; and the Hallock monument in San Francisco, CA.

It also erected many impressive granite buildings including the Travelers Tower and Connecticut State Capitol, both in Hartford, and, in Westerly, the Town Hall and the former Industrial Trust Company. Because Batterson, a man with political connections, was a leading supplier of granite and other construction stone, President Abraham Lincoln appointed him building contractor for the Congressional Library building in Washington, DC. Batterson also constructed the Masonic Temple in New York City.

In 1874, the company reported a 1.5 million dollar payroll (in 1874 dollars) in Westerly for the previous five years.

New England Granite Works circa 1900

Following the death in 1924 of Batterson's son, James G. Batterson, Jr., all Westerly assets of the New England Granite Works were bought by the Smith Granite Company. All the granite cutting was moved to the Smith shed, most of the machinery was moved and all granite work on Quarry Hill was consolidated.

The epic-sized Antietam Soldier, being viewed for approval by the committee who ordered it, is displayed on the grounds of the New England Granite Works on Ledward Avenue.

J. G. BATTERSON, PRESIDENT

James G. Batterson, a business visionary, introduced the concept of profit-sharing in a January 4, 1886 letter to his Westerly superintendent, James Gourlay. He proposed that an individual's share of the profits would increase for each year of continuous service up to five years. A workman who was discharged during the year for good and sufficient cause, such as drunkenness, insubordination, or bad workmanship, or who left the employment of the company without the consent in writing of the superintendent, would not be entitled to participate in any dividend of profits for that year.

James Batterson (1823-1901) owner of New England Granite Works

"When the workmen are all interested in the results of their combined labor, there will be no room for those who are unwilling to earn, and fairly earn, the wages which they demand. When the industrious and skillful workman sees that his own earnings are being diminished by the slothful and unskilled workman at his side, he will rebel, and demand, as he will have the right to do, that a better man shall be put in the place of the laggard." Batterson was an industry leader with this plan a century ahead of its time.

A man of many talents and diverse interests, he was a forerunner in the development of insurance companies in the United States. While in England, he was so impressed with the record and success of the Railway Passenger Assurance Company that he resolved to gather a group of progressive men to launch a similar venture in the United States. Thus the Travelers Insurance Company was born and he remained in charge until his death in 1901.

As a champion for the arts, he joined forces with Elizabeth Colt to make the Wadsworth Athenaeum a free public art museum. On October 16, 1880, he was honored at the Athenaeum by former President Ulysses S Grant for his contributions to historic preservation. Batterson also traveled to Italy to find talented sculptors to work on his designs for bronze and stone sculptures for monuments.

During his several years in Egypt, he developed an interest in Egyptology and passed for such an authority in that field that he became honorary secretary of the Egyptian Exploration Fund.

In June of 1870, Batterson bought the Thomas Segar farm (known as the Vose farm) for $5,000 in order to put a spur from the Stonington Railroad to the Batterson and Ledward quarry thus eliminating the difficult and dangerous task of oxen-powered carts delivering the product to the railroad yard. By September 8, the railroad was finished and stone began shipping out to Hartford for the Hartford Bank Building. Batterson did not, however, have a suitable locomotive, so empty cars were hauled by horse power up hill from the Stonington Track to the quarry. When loaded, they came down the hill with only the aid of brakemen. Eight to ten loaded cars would take stone down to be shipped to Hartford for buildings or to New York City to be used as pavers. By October 6, 1870, New England Granite Works purchased a locomotive, making the spur fully operational. Pictured is a later locomotive.

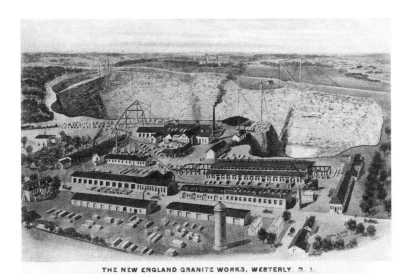

THE NEW ENGLAND GRANITE WORKS, WESTERLY, R. I.

Postcard with artist's rendition of the New England Granite Works on Quarry Hill. The water tower in the foreground in the wedge of land between Tower Street and Ledward Avenue is still in use.

Detail of the Charter Oak and supporting columns on the Connecticut State Capitol, Hartford, CT, typical of the building work done by New England Granite works. The bas relief is made from marble; the polished columns are of Westerly granite.

In 1892, the New England Granite Company constructed this impressive entrance to the Elmgrove Cemetery in Mystic, CT. Dedicated in memory of Charles Henry Mallory, it was given by his widow, Mrs. Eunice Mallory, and their children. The gateway spans 54 feet, is 32 feet high and measures 6 feet thick. It consists of three arches, each with double wrought iron gates. The main archway, which serves as a driveway, is 20 feet wide by 22 feet high. It is flanked by smaller arches, 6 feet wide and 10 feet high, for pedestrian use. Over the arches and just beneath the capstone is chiseled in relief the words "I am the Resurrection and the Life," and above the curve of the arch on either side are the Greek letters Alpha and Omega.

1880 – 1900: THE HEYDAY

JOSEPH NEWALL & CO.: THE BEDROCK OF FUTURE COMPANIES

Alternate spellings abound for this nearly-forgotten company which owned both a quarry and a manufacturing company. Most sources agree that the Joseph New All & Co., Westerly, RI, established in 1885, was a branch of the D.H. & J. Newall, in Dalbeattie, Scotland established by David, Homer and Joseph Newall in 1820. For many years, they had exported to the United States, but opened a quarry in 1883 in Niantic, RI, now Bradford, and started the manufacturing business run by David McG. Newall. This quarry produced blue-white Westerly granite, ideal for monument work.

On June 26, 1901, the Newalls purchased property just off Oak Street along the main railroad line and moved their cutting shed to Westerly. According to sources at the time, they had "improved machinery and appliances necessary for carrying on their business."

Their most easily recognizable local monument is the Loveland-Langworthy angel in River Bend Cemetery. They produced mausolea in Philadelphia for Peter A. B. Widener, William L. Elkins, Robert D. Carson and James P. McNicol; they cut monuments for Senator Thomas C. Platt of New York, and John Sherman of Ohio. Their work also included the Cornelius Harrigan monument which at that time was the largest cut from Westerly granite. The lower base is 15' 6" by 10' 6" and the die of the monument was cored out to receive two caskets.

Because of the Scottish connections, Newall employed many of the Scots in the area, Dinwoodies among them. Both father and son worked in the quarry and advanced in skill and responsibility. Born in 1859 in Dalbeattie, Scotland, John Dinwoodie came to Bradford in 1889 to work at Newall Quarry as a stonecutter and later became "boss quarry man" or superintendent. His son, John Dinwoodie, Jr. (1886) began as "water-boy" at Newall Quarry at age 10 and became "tool-boy" at age 14. It appears that they were in the news quite frequently.

On June 16, 1916, Joseph Coduri purchased the sheds, marked "Joseph Newall & Co.," on Oak Street for $15,000 from Mary Agnes Newall and David McG. Newall; the company became the Joseph Coduri Granite Company.

The Taunton Gazette of June 28, 1919 reported that the Crumb Quarry Company, Frank A Sullivan president, had purchased the quarry property of Joseph Newall & Co., including machinery and equipment. Later the Klondike Quarry (Gourlay family) became a part of the operation and these three Bradford quarries became the Sullivan Granite Company.

Newall's role seems to be one of building the granite industry and providing a rock-solid (pun intended) foundation for later important companies.

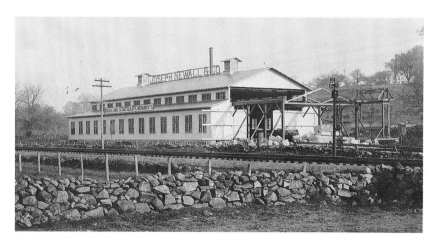

The Joseph Newall & Co. on 40 Oak Street before it was purchased by the Joseph Coduri Granite Company in 1916. The close proximity of the railroad track was instrumental in making the shipping of monuments easier.

Windows provided adequate light for the cutting operation for the more than twenty-five workers in the Joseph Newall & Co. shed in the early 1890's.

The Widener and Elkins mausolea in Laurel Hill Cemetery, Philadelphia, PA are excellent examples of the magnitude and quality of the work done by Joseph Newall and Company. The Elkins mausoleum was cut from Sullivan blue-white granite.

Loveland-Langworthy "Angel of Peace," carved by Angelo Zerbarini at the Newall sheds circa 1901.

SHOOTING AT NIANTIC

Narragansett Weekly. December 28, 1893 ~ : SHOOTING AT NIANTIC. Officers Gavitt and West, who went to Niantic yesterday to bring William Corris before Judge Whipple, returned to Westerly empty-handed. They found the victim of John Dinwoodie's shotgun was unable to be moved, so they placed him in the charge of two deputies until such a time as his physical condition would permit his appearance before Judge Whipple.

Dinwoodie is a boss in the employ of David McG. Newall, and the other day was obliged to discharge Corris, because of lack of work. The latter took heart and also took considerable liquor. These two set him in a frenzy, which was all directed against Dinwoodie. He was warned three times to keep away from the latter's house, after he had smashed the windows and threatened people with carving knives, and only then did Dinwoodie shoot. Corris will recover and then must appear on a charge of threatening to take Dinwoodie's life.

Narragansett Weekly. August 28, 1896 ~ : The little two year old child [David Dinwoodie] of John Dinwoodie, foreman at Newall's Quarry, who fell into a kettle of boiling soup on Sunday, is in critical condition, and is not expected to live. The child continues to have convulsions, and the flesh is in a terrible condition. The sympathy of the people at Niantic, where the family resides, is extended to both the child and parents. [The child lived.]

John Dinwoodie, Sr., superintendent of both Newall and Sullivan Quarries, shot a quarry employee in self- defense.

1880 — 1900: THE HEYDAY

SMALL QUARRIES AND COMPANIES

We all have seen them—those heaps of quarried stones signifying an abandoned quarry—and, for a fleeting moment, we may wonder what the history is. Ellen L. Madison decided to see what she could discover about just one—Brand's Oven Quarry, off South Woody Hill Road, which she had frequently explored as a child. Her Aunt Eloise shuddered as the children shimmied out on the poles which still extended over the hole in the 1950's. Still quite visible are the grout pile, a couple of holes, a shaped mound of earth which probably once supported the engine and tracks, the remnants of a huge chimney which was the forge, and a stone wall about ten feet high built to support a road. Ellen turned to others for help.

Dwight C. Brown, Jr. found a reference in the April 1908 issue of *Granite, Marble and Bronze*: "Niantic, R.I.—Boston capitalists have started the granite business, under the name of The Rhode Island Redstone Co. It is planned to operate a quarry, with building stone a specialty, at Brand's Oven in the Woody Hill section of Niantic, which is within the boundary of the town of Westerly. The required machinery has arrived."

Florence Madison, Ellen's 92 year old mother, said that the quarry was subsequently abandoned, and then reopened in the late 1930's under the aegis of George W. Bishop. Two quarrymen from Stonington, Maine, Joel and Arnold Carver, operated the quarry. Red granite was taken out to build Green Hall (1937) at URI and the base of the Providence County Courthouse (now The Supreme Court Complex on 250 Benefit Street) built in the early 30's.

Brad Benson, a volunteer researcher, scoured business directories from the 1930's but could find no reference to the men or their company.

Tom Dinwoodie, a neighbor, said that his grandfather, James Ernest "Ernie" Dinwoodie, had been the last engineer for the steam crane at this quarry, but had left when a strike occurred and never went back. Whether that was the end of the operation or not is still to be determined.

The 1895 map of Westerly shows fourteen other named quarries or companies, some well-known, but some as elusive as Brand's Oven. We know that they existed only by finding a fleeting reference to them or stumbling across them in the woods.

Sometimes we know a smidgeon of history, but the location is unknown. Madison's great-grandfather Richard Opie owned a quarry which family oral history said was off Chase Hill. In some legal papers, she found that the land was leased from Charles H. Burdick. On the 1895 Hopkinton map, Dwight Brown located a quarry belonging to Burdick, right along the river, thus giving one more clue to the location.

Richard Opie (1849-1925), born in Penryn, Cornwall, England, was a stonecutter and quarryman. In 1891, he, along with other Westerly firms such as Joseph Newall & Co., Dalbeattie, and New England Granite Works, were advertising in *Monumental News*, a Chicago publication.

In some cases, men who worked for a large established company would freelance out of a backyard shed. The names of small companies changed as men shifted partners and locations, making it difficult for us to know much with certainty except for the fact that, during its heyday, Westerly was full of small quarries and companies.

Business card of Richard Opie. Opie, with an office on 40 School Street, worked both as an independent contractor and as a partner. Even this small quarry operator/stonecutter did business under the name of Opie and Van Gunden (1891-1893) with an office in Philadelphia and also under the name Opie and Seccombe (1895) with an office in Sheldon, CT.

Typical of small operators, Robert Lemuel Means (1827-1903) had a small backyard quarry at 186 High Street.

Richard Opie's quarry in 1894, probably on the site of the Charles Burdick quarry off Chase Hill Road, Hopkinton, RI.

1880 – 1900: THE HEYDAY

LABOR UNREST (1871 – 1920'S AND 1930 – 1945)

by Anthony M. Lementowicz, Jr., Social Studies Department Head, Westerly High School

The men who labored in Westerly's granite quarries and work sheds benefited greatly from the high demand for the stone in the latter half of the nineteenth century. During the industry's heyday, both skilled and unskilled workers typically received a wage considerably higher than most workers in other industries. Despite the prosperity enjoyed by its workforce, the industry was not always spared from labor unrest. In fact, when workers did organize to protest, it usually had to do with a working condition that they considered more important rather than with any wage-related issue.

The famous "Striker's Case" of 1871 involved the stone cutters' protest of a breach in their agreement with the Rhode Island Granite Works. They walked off the job because the company had taken on too many apprentices without hiring the contractually-agreed-upon, additional journeymen to train them. The stone cutters were certain that, by withholding their invaluable skills and talents, orders would go unfilled, profits would be lost, and eventually management would be compelled to honor their original agreement.

Unfortunately, company profits were not the only casualties of the strike. Once the stone cutters walked out, the quarrymen were locked out, as the company had no need to continue extracting stone that would go unfinished. These unskilled workers had to find employment elsewhere.

Fortunately, the work stoppage did not last too long and it did not cripple the industry in Westerly. Instead, it led to the creation of the Westerly Granite Company, a cooperative purchased and operated by the striking stone cutters. Westerly granite was in such high demand during this time that both companies were able to thrive despite this significant disruption in business.

The 1890's saw at least two more strikes in the Westerly quarries. It was during these protests that labor truly tested its limits. The most aggressive attempt for concessions occurred in 1890 as workers demanded the shortening of the workday from ten to nine hours while retaining a ten hour wage. They held out for forty days, relying on their personal savings and a modest strike fund established by their union. In the end, the workers settled for a nine hour day with nine hours pay, believing that they had achieved their underlying goal of establishing a shorter work day.

Labor would never win a settlement greater than this, for it was during this period that Westerly began to experience changes in the industry that would lead to its decline during the first half of the coming century. The quarry owners were eventually forced to lower the price of granite as demand dropped off with the introduction of alternative building materials and as competition from other granite centers around the country increased. The workers experienced this downturn in real time as wages dropped steadily during the 1920's. Labor actions taken to block decreases in wages in the 1920's failed and may have further compromised an already weakened industry. Westerly granite workers would never be able to effectively bargain for their pay or conditions of employment as they once could.

Seal of the Granite Cutters International Association of America, part of the AF of L. The quarrymen's union in Westerly was part of the CIO.

Craig & Richards Granite Company had a shed east of High Street near Craig Field.

THE GRANITE DIFFICULTY

The solution of the local granite trouble seems as far away as it did a month ago. The seven men who arrived in town last week to work for the Smith Granite Company are still here, but their ranks have not been reinforced by men who reside here. One day last week, O.R. Smith received a threatening letter, which read as follows:

"Lando Smith--Sir--Settle this strike or we will blow your d--- steamboats hie and dry and your d--- night watchman rite to hell the first time we get a good chance. You can't have a committy skab yard hear. ...."

The prevailing sentiment among the granite workers is that the letter was written by some boy, who is endeavoring to have what he would call fun. To be on the safe side, however, Mr. Smith sent the following letter to the Town Council of Westerly:

Dr. A. H. Spicer, President of Westerly Town Council: Dear Sir--Having received this day, through the mail, a letter threatening violence to our quarry property and our river steamers, we hereby demand protection from the town of Westerly, and shall hold them responsible for any unlawful damage to our property from this date.

Narragansett Weekly, June 30, 1892

Following are excerpts from a letter sent on May 9, 1922 from Frank Sullivan to Ernest Dinwoodie, Bradford. RI. regarding his participation in a union strike.

Dear Sir:

No doubt you realize by this time that you went out on a foolish strike——a strike that it is impossible to win.

. . . If our former employees want their jobs back and if you and our other men signify your intentions of coming back within a reasonable time we will hold your jobs for you. Otherwise we will replace all men needed with new men and if they prove satisfactory we will guarantee them steady jobs so far as we have work for them to do.

You have worked for us several times, had good positions, and for one reason or another left our employ. In spite of this we gave you a position of trust and responsibility with us, you being in charge of a valuable piece of machinery. We believe that you owe more to this Company who put you in charge of this piece of machinery and more to yourself and family than you owe to any outside influence. We believe that you acted unwisely when you betrayed this trust. You have nothing to gain by sticking to a Union who has not one single advantage to offer any of its members and cannot assist or help you in any way.

... The position you held with us was a desirable one and naturally will not be left vacant long and we consider that you have already had enough time to give this matter careful thought and consideration.

Under these circumstances you can not expect to stay away indefinitely and still get your old job back, and if you are not back to work within the next few days do not blame this Company for the mistake you yourself have made.

Very truly yours,

SULLIVAN GRANITE COMPANY

Frank A. Sullivan, Pres.

Wm. R. Pellett and Son, Monumental Works, is an example of a small cutting shed.

When Linda Holman was cleaning out the home of her mother, Bertha Strong, she found something that no one at the Granite Research Center had ever seen. About 8 inches long, the silk ribbon has a beaded fringe and is printed with "Niantic Union Workers." It is probably a convention ribbon worn to identify members of the Niantic (Bradford) delegation. There is no date on the ribbon. Linda's grandfather, William Dow, was a granite worker.

Recently, Umile Ritacco presented to the Babcock-Smith House Museum three books from the Dixon Granite Works that were found in the attic of a house he owns on the corner of Tower and Joshua Streets. Two of the books appear to be records of Branch #18 of United Stone and Allied Product Workers of America dating from the 1930's. The third book, pictured with Mr. Ritacco, is a record book from the Dixon Granite Works.

STONE CHIPS

"I remember my father talking about … a stonecutters' strike here. They had a lot of scabs come in from different places. There used to be some wicked brawls and fights. When the strike got settled— some of the scabs were working—they didn't last too long. They used, you know the wrap around the stone when they pick the chain, regular fire hose. But it gets saturated with stone dust and water and is just like a block of cement. They used to throw those at those guys. They get hit on the side of the head. They end up in the hospital. They didn't last too long. Stonecutters were a rugged bunch."

Carl Myllymaki

WESTERLY-PAWCATUCK GRANITE ENTERPRISES (105)

This is a sampling of the granite companies listed in the local newpapers, city directories, company records and elsewhere between 1870 and the present day, showing how extensive the involvement of the community was in the granite industry.

Archie Brothers Granite

Joseph A. Barbone

Batterson-Canfield Company

Alex Bessett Granite

Charles G. Blake

Bonner Monument Company

Robert J. Bonner

Booth Brothers

Bottinelli Monumental Company

Buzzi Memorials

Calder & Carnie

Calder, Robert & Co.

John Catto

Catto Granite Company

Chapman Granite Works

Stanton Clarke Quarry

Joseph Coduri Granite Company

Coduri & Marzoli

John Collins Cormorant Hill Granite

Columbia Granite Company

Comolli Granite Company

Comorant Quarry

Cottrell Quarry (William)

Craig & Richards Granite

Alexander G. Crumb & Sons

John Currie & Son

Dalbeattie Granite Works

Dixon Granite Works

Duguid, Bisset & Webster Granite

Ewen & Company

Ewen & O'Neil

Andrew Farrell & Sons

Antonio E. Faverio

Faverio & Currie Co.

Fitzpatrick & King

Archie Fletcher Quarry

Fletcher & Palmer

Maurice W. Flynn

Fraquelli & Brusa

Henry R. Gavitt Quarry

Gourlay Granite Works

Hogg & Co.

George H. Hutchins

Hutchins-Crandall Granite Company

John W. Johnson

Kenyon & Company

Kimball & Combe Company

E. G. King & Sons

Hugh King

James Kirkpatrick

Kirkpatrick & Sheehan Granite

Eugene S. Larkin

Lazzari and Barton

L. McDonald Granite

Macomber Quarry

McGowan & McAvoy & Co.

McKernan & Newall

John Melville Granite

Andrew Morrison

Michael Morrone Granite

Murray

Murray & Bird

Alexander Murray & Company

National Union Granite Works

D. & I. Newall Granite

Joseph Newall & Company

New England Granite Works

New York & Stonington Granite Company

Norcross Bros.

Nathan F. Noyes

O'Neil & Company

Richard Opie

Frederick Pascoe

William P. Pellett & Son

Pierce & Co.

Redstone Quarry

Reinhalter Granite Works

Rhode Island Granite Works

Rhode Island Monument Company

The Rhode Island Redstone Co.

Alexander Robertson

Shawn Monument Company

Sawyer & Thompson

Smalley Pink & Red Westerly Company

Smith Granite Company

William G. Spargo

The Star Granite Co.

Stevenson & Co..

James Stewart Granite

Stewart & McDonald Granite

Stonington Granite Company

Sullivan Granite Company

Horace Swan Granite

Sweeney Granite Works

Thackaray & Company

J.M. Thompson Granite

Thompson & Palmer

Thompson & Platt

Robert Thompson Granite

Vars Granite Quarry

Veal & Rowe

S. P. Wells Co.

Westerly Blue Quarries

Westerly Blue & Light Granite Company

Westerly Granite Works

1900 – 1930's: A TIME OF CHANGE

One of the most significant changes in the manufacturing process within the granite industry occurred during the waning years of the nineteenth century and the early decades of the twentieth century—mechanization. Up until that time, quarrying, stonecutting and statue carving had relied solely upon the physical efforts of man and beast. The expansion of readily available electricity, coupled with the use of steam and compressed air power, brought about huge production advances and significantly better health conditions.

Taking advantage of these changes, there emerged new companies: Fraquelli & Brusa Co., Joseph Coduri Granite Company and the Sullivan Granite Company. Whereas the earlier major granite companies had operated both quarries and sheds, this appeared to be the time of specialization. Fraquelli & Brusa Co. and The Joseph Coduri Granite Company operated sheds in which fine monuments were produced, whereas Sullivan Granite Company consolidated and operated the Niantic (now Bradford) quarries and did no manufacturing.

SULLIVAN GRANITE COMPANY

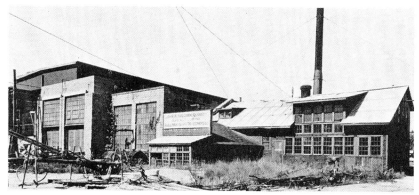

Plant No. 7 of the Sullivan Granite Company shows how fully mechanization was utiltized. This plant housed the machine shop, the boiler house, the air compressor house, and the saw building.

Constantine Brusa, born in 1888 in Lombardia, Italy, operated Fraquelli and Brusa, a monument business on Oak Street. Described in his obituary as "one of the town's most prominent Italo-American residents," he was one of the founders of the Bocce Club, president of Loggia Operiaia, and a member of the Westerly Lodge of Elks, the Westerly Italo-American Club and the Granite Manufacturers' Association.

All Contracts Taken Subject to Strikes, Accidents and other Contingencies Beyond Our Control
Telephone 2769

THE JOSEPH CODURI GRANITE CO.,
MANUFACTURERS OF
FINE MONUMENTS, VAULTS, STATUARY

NEW ENGLAND WHITE GRANITE
DEER ISLAND, ME., GRANITE
SOMES SOUND GRANITE
STONY CREEK GRANITE

WESTERLY, RHODE ISLAND

BLUE-WHITE WESTERLY
PINK WESTERLY
RED WESTERLY
GOLDEN PINK GRANITE

A 1935 gathering of area granite men. Second row (l-r) Joseph Coduri (#1), Constantine Brusa (#2), and Angelo Buzzi (#5).

1900 – 1930's: A TIME OF CHANGE
MECHANIZATION

The demand for more finished stone stimulated the development of machinery to perform the time-consuming, laborious task of removing great amounts of stone from what would become the finished product. Saws were eventually developed which could cut large blocks of granite into slabs of stone thereby lessening the waste involved in cutting stone to the needed size. Today's diamond saws have also increased production rates with less risk of damage to the stone.

The introduction of carbide steel tools also had a profound effect. During the nineteenth century, the industry relied on hardened steel which wore down rapidly in the drilling and shaping of granite. Blacksmith shops sharpened great quantities of tools each day. It was not unusual for a blacksmith to handle 800 drill bits (two a minute) a day. Carbide-tipped pneumatic chisels replaced arm-powered hammers significantly reducing the human muscle factor in the stone cutting process.

One of the greatest technical advancements in finishing stone was the introduction of sandblasting to carve inscriptions and ornaments. Before the use of sandblasting, all inscriptions were cut by hand. The sandblasting process has recently become computerized allowing even greater machine-created detail and ornamentation development.

Combined with harvesting and manufacturing advances, the introduction of electric compressors brought about the development of specialized vacuum air-handling systems that removed much of the silica dust associated with stone cutting, statue carving and sandblasting. Silica, a common, naturally-occurring crystal found in most rock beds, forms a dust during the quarrying, cutting and granite carving process. Intense exposure to the stone dust caused chronic silicosis which led to the early death of many of Westerly's finest granite workers.

Patsy Capizzano, sandblast stone cutter, preparing the stone

Large lathe at the Smith Granite Company

Richard Comolli using pneumatic chisel to carve figure of a bird

Diamond saw at Bonner Monument Company

STONE CHIPS

When pneumatic tools were introduced to the Smith Granite Company in the 1890's, most stone cutters welcomed them, but one did not. William J. Veal left to open his own shop where he chose to continue to cut by hand.

1900 – 1930's: A TIME OF CHANGE

JOSEPH CODURI GRANITE COMPANY

Joseph Coduri arrived in America at the age of six in March of 1889 from the small town of Colico in the Lake Como region of Italy. His father, John, was a farmer who eventually settled in Waterford, Connecticut, along with wife Barbara and sons Charles, Albino, Louis and Joseph.

From around 1897 until 1906, Joseph lived in Barre, Vermont, working in the granite quarries and learning the stonecutting trade. In 1907, after his marriage to Antoinette Marzoli, he (age 25) and his new brother-in-law, Joseph Marzoli (age 20), formed the Coduri & Marzoli Granite Company. The 1912 *Westerly City Directory* lists the Coduri & Marzoli Granite Company at 98 Granite Street. Records in the Westerly Town Hall document that in March of 1911 Coduri & Marzoli entered into a formal five-year lease of a granite cutting shed on the east side of Granite Street (98 Granite Street location referenced above), which was part of the already well-established Smith Granite Company. Frequently, Coduri & Marzoli received sub-contract work from Smith. Such was the case with the Robert A. Gray Civil War Memorial in Groton, CT. Coduri & Marzoli were the statue cutters for this Smith Company monument. Apparently Coduri & Marzoli also specialized in the carving of crosses. During just the three-year period from 1908 – 1910 they carved five Celtic crosses as subcontractors of the Smith Granite Company.

Sometime around 1916 Joseph Marzoli developed a form of tuberculosis/silicosis and he moved with his wife and two daughters to California. Later that year Joseph Coduri purchased the existing Joseph Newall & Co. granite cutting sheds on Oak Street in Westerly for $15,000 (about $300,000 today) and established the Joseph Coduri Granite Company. The Oak Street sheds were adjacent to the main Hartford & New Haven Railroad (now Amtrak) tracks. A special track spur was installed which ran right into the far-west end cutting shed making shipping of monuments to all parts of the country a very convenient process.

The ten-year period from the end of World War I until the start of the Great Depression in 1929 were prosperous years for the Joseph Coduri Granite Company during which time its sheds cut and finished the granite for some of the largest and most beautiful monuments and mausolea produced in the Westerly area. During these flourishing years, Joseph Coduri hosted an annual outing of the New York City Memorial Crafts Institute on Brightman's Pond off Shore Road in Westerly as a way to strengthen his business relationship with this organization's members. The contacts made resulted in numerous large monument and mausoleum contracts for clients within the greater New York City area.

Joseph Coduri standing next to Geddes monument in 1931

On Monday, March 5, 1934, a huge fire swept through the sheds of the Joseph Coduri Granite Company on Oak Street. Nearly $60,000 would be needed to rebuild the damaged buildings and $40,000 to replace the monumental stones and statues that were also destroyed. The three-alarm blaze required the services of more than 100 firefighters from both the Westerly and Pawcatuck departments. Unfortunately, the fire left the shed unusable. When disaster struck one company, another would help. During the construction of a new shed, the Smith Granite Company rented space to Coduri in its 1885 Granite Street cutting shed, thus enabling business to continue.

Much of the demand for elaborate monuments and expensive family mausolea faded as the Depression continued throughout the 1930's up to the years following the end of World War II. During this time, however, the company produced the Father Duffy monument in Times Square, the Second Division Memorial on the White House South Lawn in Washington, DC, the Roger Williams monument in Providence, and the Lee-Jackson monument in Baltimore. In 1940, Joseph Coduri died of silicosis and ownership of the company passed to his son Richard (1915-1980).

Three recognizable local works that were produced during this 20 year period are the World War Memorial at the intersection of Granite Street and Grove Avenue, and the Memorial Fountain Bowl and the Columbus monument, both in Wilcox Park.

Demand for large monuments had subsided even further by the 1950's and readily available local granite was lost with the closing of both the Smith (1945) and Sullivan (1955) quarries. The Coduri sheds ceased operations in September of 1958 and orders were then handled by the Bonner Monument Company until the Joseph Coduri Granite Company was officially dissolved in the early 1960's.

THE HAND

At the time of the 1934 fire, Ferruccio "Frank" Comolli, father of Richard Comolli, had nearly completed a statue that was part of a large Berwind family monument. Many monuments and statues cracked when exposed to the extreme heat of the fire and the application of the cool water needed to quell the blaze. One remnant of a damaged statue was the raised hand of the Berwind monument which was safely kept at the Westerly Fire Department on Union Street for 75 years until it was donated to the Granite Collection at the Babcock Smith House Museum.

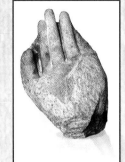

right: Damaged hand from the original Berwind monument

below: Berwind monument in Philadelphia was completely re-cut and carved after the 1934 fire.

The Dumbra mausoleum, one of Westerly's greatest creations, in Woodlawn Cemetery in The Bronx, New York was produced at the Joseph Coduri Granite Company.

The Pierson memorial in the Rosedale Cemetery in Montclair, NJ was cut by the Joseph Coduri Granite Company from Sullivan blue-white granite.

The Temple of Love monument, created for the Chapin family in 1926 by the Joseph Coduri Granite Company, is located in Springfield, MA.

The Andrus mausoleum was cut by the Joseph Coduri Granite Company and erected in Kensico Cemetery, Valhalla, NY with Westerly granite from the Sullivan Quarry. It consists of some of the largest pieces of granite ever quarried in Westerly. The mausoleum's general dimensions are 43' x 39' x 24'. The lower course is comprised of four large stones with a combined weight of 115 tons. The polished floor is in three pieces and there are sixteen columns and four ceiling stones.

Coduri shed. The picture was taken from Oak Street. The sign on the roof (reversed in the picture) faces the railroad so that it serves as an advertisement to passing railroad passengers.

Craneway of the Joseph Coduri Granite Company circa 1924. Note the main train line spur running right into the west cutting shed. Barely visible Joe Coduri, Jr. in the car; Albino Coduri, Tony Turco and John Nichols, standing

Workers at Joseph Coduri Granite Company 1924/25

1. Thomas Gourlay
2. Albino Coduri, Foreman
3. Joseph Gervasini
4. Antonio Croci
5. William Bell
6. Dominick Federico
7. Philip Gallagher
8. ?
9. Frank Morenzoni
10. ?
11. ?
12. Peter Villa

13. ?
14. ?
15. ?
16. James Servidio
17. James Bonner
18 ?
19. Joseph Rizza
20. Richard Coduri
21. Joseph Coduri, Jr.
22. Joseph Coduri, Owner
23. ?
24. Mario Selvidio

25. ?
26. Vittario Croci
27. ?
28. ?
29. Patrick Priore
30. Giuseppe Comolli
31. William J. Bell
32. Francesco Turco
33. ?
34. ?
35. ?
36. ?

37. Gaetano Bianchi
38. ?
39. Angelo Stella
40. Victor Rauschi
41. Pinardi
42. ?
43. ?
44. Peter Bottinelli
45. Dominick Turco
46. Mario Host
47. Angelo Panciera
48. ?

49. ?
50. ?
51. ?
52. ?
53. ?
54. Arthur Bernasconi
55. Thomas Ahern
56. Parnigoni

1900 – 1930'S: A TIME OF CHANGE

SULLIVAN GRANITE COMPANY : EXTRA FINE GRAINED BLUE-WHITE WESTERLY GRANITE

by Susan Sullivan Brocato, granddaughter of Frank A. Sullivan

Sullivan Granite Company was across the street from where I grew up and, as a young girl, I went with my father and grandfather to watch large stones being removed from the quarry holes. My sister and I were often told to stay away from the quarry unless we were with an adult because the holes were way more than 200 feet deep, but to a child the warning was an open invitation to go exploring and we did. I particularly loved collecting pollywogs for science class from one of the small holes.

Sullivan Granite Co. spanned three generations. John B. Sullivan, the founder and my great grandfather, started the business with a retail monument shop on Washington Street in Taunton, MA during the latter part of the 1800's.

In May 1907, my grandfather, Frank A. Sullivan, moved to Westerly and purchased the Crumb Quarry (1907) and the Newall Quarry (1919). The purchase of the Klondike Quarry (formerly Gourlay Granite Works) soon followed giving Sullivan Granite Co. about 700 acres of land. Using modern equipment, he quarried the best fine grained blue-white granite anywhere around.

When my grandfather first came to Bradford, men would take the train from Westerly to Bradford, walk a little over a mile to get to the quarry, and walk back after a long day of work.

top to bottom:
John B. Sullivan (1845 – 1911), Founder and First President

Frank A. Sullivan (1877 – 1961) President 1911 – 1952

John F. Sullivan (1912 – 2003) President 1952 – 1956

The stone was rough cut to approximate size, at the request of the customer. This process created a lot of waste stone which was discarded in order to produce a perfect piece of stone which was then shipped by rail to the stonecutters and artisans. They then turned this beautiful stone into elaborate monuments that can be found across the United States, Europe, the Hawaiian Islands and as far away as South Africa.

Sullivan Granite Company was probably the first quarry in the world to use the technique of tunneling. The veins of granite pitched down on an angle of about 45 degrees and, instead of cutting straight down, the men would undercut the granite, leaving an overburden (roof) and extract the stone this way. This not only saved some time, but money as well by not having to remove the overburden. It also provided a closed quarry for the men to work in and be out of the weather. The timbers for the massive derrick that hoisted the stone came by rail, all the way from Oregon.

Frank Sullivan had a special platform area built for the public to view the operation. It allowed everyone to see the huge hole, tunnel and depth of it all.

The company marketed one grade of extra fine grained blue-white Westerly granite and all the imperfect stone was put through the stone crusher which cost about $100,000. The crushed waste stone was used for road construction and the grout chunks were used for protective barriers along the shore. The stone crusher was most useful during World War II to make the runways at Charlestown Air Base as well as other road surfaces where needed.

In 1942, Sullivan Granite constructed a railroad spur to run from the New York, New Haven & Hartford Railroad depot in Bradford to the Sullivan quarry. This was done at considerable expense, but made the transportation of the stone much easier. Some property owners along this route were not happy and a lawsuit was filed and later settled in favor of one of the property owners.

During a labor strike, there was much unrest and a home of a Sullivan Granite foreman, who lived in Bradford, was bombed. Fortunately the family escaped injury; no one was arrested.

John F. Sullivan, my father, began working for Sullivan Granite in 1938 as a salesman in Boston until he was drafted in 1940. Upon his discharge in 1946, my father returned to the company and became the superintendent of Sullivan Granite Co. as well as starting Bed Rock Kennels.

In December 1949, my father, then Superintendent of Sullivan Granite, wrote a letter to each employee that it was deemed necessary to close the quarry operations down for the month of January, 1950, but the employees would return in February. Each employee received a letter thanking him for all his dedication and hard work. The employees were advised that monies that had been paid into the unemployment insurance fund would be available to be drawn upon during the first week of January. The company would continue to pay their health insurance so that they and members of their families would be covered. The company would also make payments to their Christmas Clubs during this time and, when they returned to work, they could repay the club funds to the company.

Sullivan Granite Company office 1941

THE JANUARY 1932 HEADLINE IN *THE WESTERLY SUN* READ "LARGEST STONE EVER SHIPPED BY RAIL FROM WESTERLY."

Sullivan Granite Company lifted a 65-ton stone, believed to be the largest ever shipped by rail in this country, from the deepest section of their quarry. In eight minutes a mammoth derrick hoisted the 119,000 lb. stone (400 lbs. shy of 60 tons after it was rough cut to size) onto a rail bed to be shipped to Barre, VT to be cut. A second rail car carried more stone to complete a monolith monument. The finished size of the monolith was 7'-3" at the bottom, 5' thick and 16'-6" high.

My grandfather retired as president in February 1952 after 45 years in the granite industry and my father became the president. The granite industry had already begun its decline. Sadly, Sullivan Granite was sold at public auction in November 1956. Bottinelli Monumental Company of Waterford, CT purchased the main quarry property, while Harold Slosberg of United Builders of Westerly and Rueben Grossman of Quincy, MA purchased tracts of land. In October 1971, James Romanella and Sons, Inc. purchased Sullivan Granite from Bottinelli. Today the quarry is owned by Richard Comolli of Westerly Granite Co. who purchased the quarry from Romanella in 1997. Fortunately, Mr. Comolli continues to harvest some of the beautiful blue-white stone that is on the property, and the pollywogs still swim in the small quarry hole.

Aerial view of the
Sullivan Granite
Company circa 1947

STONE CHIPS

At Sullivan's quarry in Bradford a three day's salary in 1934 was $13.00 Men worked for 3 days in winter and 5 or 6 in the summer about 7:30 – 4:00.

Ruth Mosena

"Mr. Sullivan asked John Dinwoodie (his head man at the time) to cut a very special stone for a very special friend. The first stone was cut, but was refused by Mr. Sullivan. It wasn't quite what he wanted. The second stone was then meticulously cut and also was not quite right. John Dinwoodie (my great grandfather) was really upset as the story goes. The third and final stone was cut. At last. It was perfect! Mr. Sullivan presented that third stone to John as a gift. It now is in River Bend Cemetery. It is magnificent."

Donna Turrisi 2010

left: Convention display featuring products of the Sullivan Granite Company

below: John B. Sullivan Quarry, Plant No. 7 circa 1941

One of the roof stones, quarried at the Sullivan Granite Company, for the massive Andrus mausoleum in Valhalla, NY. John F. Sullivan (future company president) is standing on the left.

MID TWENTIETH CENTURY:
BIG COMPANIES CLOSE AND SMALL ONES EMERGE

One might have hoped that the unparalleled success of Westerly's granite industry might have continued forever, but forces beyond anyone's control combined to whittle away its dominance.

Labor issues resulting in strikes or work actions in 1871, the 1890's and the 1920's may or may not have helped the workers, often handicapped management, and caused prices of finished products to rise. Competition came from other granite centers. The Great Depression effectively ended the demand for elaborate private memorials.

The 1938 hurricane wreaked havoc on company offices, sheds, and equipment, cutting off all electricity. All operations had to be curtailed and many employees laid off. The hurricane, however, did usher in a different kind of business. A.M. Gencarelli Co. moved tons of rocks from the Old Red Stone Quarry to the cottages in Watch Hill, and built jetties and walls to try to prevent similar disasters in future storms.

When World War II came, men who had used a pneumatic hammer were sought by Electric Boat to work as chippers on the hulls of submarines. World War II diverted men and materials, forcing many of the granite companies to close, downsize, or shift their operations. It was almost impossible for a nonessential business to obtain steel, coal, power, tires and other supplies. Sullivan Granite Company, however, converted to the war effort on September 11, 1942 starting to crush thirty years of accumulated scrap pieces of stone to be used for airfields, runways, and roads. A giant crushing plant, sometimes referred to as a "breaker," ran at least ten hours a day, crushing two tons of stone a minute, and continued for three years until the end of the war. The company worked around the clock loading and delivering crushed stone to such places as Charlestown Air Base, now Ninigret Park.

When the country emerged from the war in 1945, only a fraction of the local industry remained. Almost all of the two-state area granite companies ended their years of creating lasting memorials and institutional buildings. Fraquelli & Brusa ceased operation in the early 1950's; the Smith Granite Company quarries were sold in 1945 and its sheds were torn down in 1955 for the construction of the Granite Street Shopping Plaza; the Sullivan Granite Company closed in 1955; and the Joseph Coduri Granite Company ended its Oak Street production operation in 1958 after which its business became affiliated with the Bonner Monument Company in Hopkinton until 1963. The Crumb Quarry in Bradford was shut down in 1969 and the Westerly chapter of the Stonecutter's Union dissolved in 1981. The once great industry had been reduced to immense quarry holes filled with stagnant greenish water and sites littered with rusting wire ropes, chipstones and great pieces of waste.

Bonner Monument Company, Buzzi Memorials, and Comolli Granite Company were all that remained of this once thriving industry. For brief periods Bonner and Comolli were able to harvest small quantities of Westerly blue-white granite from some sections of the former Sullivan property in Bradford.

St. Pius X Church on Elm Street was constructed from granite donated by Angelo Gencarelli in 1955. The trim is Indiana limestone. The church is one of the last public buildings to be constructed of Westerly granite.

Richard Comolli is pictured using pneumatic tools to carve the Westerly-Pawcatuck War Memorial at the Bonner Monument Company in 1978. This and the Columbus monument in Wilcox Park are among the last significant local works produced.

Sullivan Granite Company's stone crushing plant played a part in the war effort, crushing two tons of stone a minute.

Damage to the Smith Granite Company from the September 23, 1938 hurricane. In this photo some wreckage had already been cleared and a section of one side had been braced. Some machines still stood after the storm, but the damage had long-lasting effects on the business.

MID TWENTIETH CENTURY

BONNER MONUMENT COMPANY: PRESERVING OUR LOCAL HERITAGE

"I learned from the best—Mr. Bonner" said Roger Shawn of Shawn Monument Company, Bradford, RI about Donald Bonner, owner of Bonner Monument Company and a recent legend in the granite business. In 1996, at 83, Bonner oversaw the installation of his last work, the URI Vietnam Memorial, and closed his company, but his legacy lives on.

Although Bonner had tried several different jobs following his graduation from URI, he returned to work at the monument business which had been founded in 1930. In 1947, he acquired the Main Street business from his father, Robert Bonner, and moved it to Route 3 in Ashaway in 1954, just after Hurricane Carol. The new location featured larger facilities, more modern granite-cutting equipment, and portable devices for lettering and cleaning in a cemetery.

In 1968, Bonner purchased the Newall Quarry in Bradford which had been unused since 1906; he renamed it the Blue Westerly Granite Quarry which ran until 1991.

A sales brochure mentions several of the monuments of which Bonner was most proud. One is the magnificently carved lion in Roger Williams Park, erected in memory of deceased members of Lions Clubs International. Others are a bust of Bernar (*sic*) MacFadden at Woodlawn Cemetery, replacement boundary markers for the Mason-Dixon Line, and a granite seal for St. John's University.

Locally, Bonner had a hand in the Westerly High School sign, the Westerly Korean War Memorial, the Westerly-Pawcatuck War Memorial, and the Stonington Fisherman's Memorial. His company cut all the granite for the Westerly Public Library 1992 addition and he worked tirelessly on the creation of a granite exhibit displayed from 1992-2010 at the library.

"Fancy work was our forte," he said. He had drawers of tissue

patterns labeled "lovebirds" and "leaves." Many of these patterns are now treasured by Roger Shawn in Bradford and the BSH Museum has many of his plaster models and rubber stencils.

In 1996, he closed his doors after methodically selling his equipment to places as varied as Quincy, MA and India.

Donald Bonner holding the cannon ball he created to replace the one stolen from the Battery B 1st RILA monument in Gettysburg

After the Civil War, units were allowed to choose the site in Gettysburg for their monument and most chose either the burial site or the place of a significant battle. Battery B, 1st Rhode Island Light Artillery, chose the place where the cannon, presently in the State House, jammed and men were slaughtered as a result.

Their monument is made of Westerly granite and stands 7 1/2 feet tall with a granite ball on top, replicating the cannon ball. Sometime before 1989 the cannon ball had been stolen, leaving only a spike. Bob Madison, then a member of Battery B, 1st RILA, a re-enactment group, measured the spike and calculated the diameter of the ball from an engraving in the history of the artillery written in 1894. Donald Bonner made a replacement of Westerly granite as a gift to the Battery who then installed it. The story is that Bonner made two in case one was ever stolen again.

left: Battery B, 1st Rhode Island Light Artillery Monument in Gettysburg

below: Westerly High School sign on the corner of Ward Avenue and Granite Street

Ellen Kenyon, secretary, with one of the Mason-Dixon Line markers

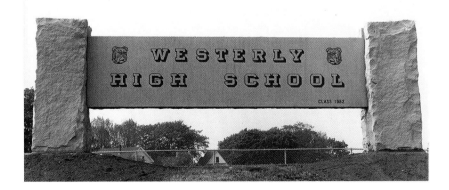

The Bonner Gang (circa 1960): (l to r) Richard Coduri, Tony Morris, Richard Comolli, Marcia Thompson, Ellen Kenyon, Andy Anderson, Patsy Capizzano, Angelo Vita, Charlie Rainey, Donald Bonner

Westerly Public Library Granite Exhibit 1992

Brown monument Block Island, RI

The Westerly-Pawcatuck War Memorial on the Westerly side of the Pawcatuck River Bridge was produced by the Bonner Monumment Company from blue Westerly granite.

FIREMAN'S STATUE

New London's Fireman's Memorial, first dedicated in 1898 to New London's volunteer firemen, was produced by the Smith Granite Company for $2,250. It has been situated in several locations. Following extensive rehabilitation in 1976, it was moved by the Bonner Monument Company from the New London County Courthouse area to its current location in front of the North Station, 240 Broad Street, New London, CT. The rehabilitation included fitting the granite statue with a new hat and nozzle, both of which had been heavily damaged by time and vandals. Richard Comolli, then the foreman at the Bonner Monument Company, sculpted the new hat and nozzle. It took four days just to remove the old hat and another four days to fit the new hat onto the statue using bronze dowels. The total cost in 1976 dollars for the rehabilitation and relocation was $6,000.

This statue of a fireman was carved from the same model as the New London Fireman's Memorial and shows details of the nozzle and helmet which Comolli replaced. This particular statue, a tribute to Providence firefighters, was produced in 1885 by the New England Granite Works and is located in the North Burial Ground in Providence, RI.

MID TWENTIETH CENTURY

BUZZI MEMORIALS: FINE CARVINGS ON PUBLIC BUILDINGS AND MEMORIALS

Angelo Peter Buzzi left his Italian family and his native Arzo, Switzerland near the border with Italy and came to America around 1923, eventually settling in the Westerly-Stonington area in 1933. Born on June 3, 1900, he watched and learned throughout his youth from his two older brothers who were already stonecutters. He began cutting and carving stone when he was only seven years old and perfected his trade at a special school in Zurich known for producing outstanding sculptors and stone carvers. Angelo was already an accomplished stonecutter by the time he arrived in the United States. Over a period of many years, his work earned him a reputation as one of the finest stone carvers in the Westerly-Stonington area.

Angelo's carving is present in the Library of Congress, the National Archives, the General Accounting Office, the Federal Courthouse and the John Erickson Memorial all in Washington, DC; Penn and Grand Central Rail Stations, the Museum of Natural History and the Equitable Trust Building in New York City; the Veterans Administration Building in Columbia, SC; the West Virginia Capitol Building; the Massachusetts War Memorial on Mount Greylock in the Berkshires; and the Federal Reserve Building in El Paso, TX. Closer to home his work includes the Roger Williams and World War I Memorials in Providence and the Moses relief statue on the Boston Court House.

In 1933, he established Buzzi Memorials on Route 1 in Stonington, CT and continued its operation along with his son, Harold, until Angelo's sudden death in 1963. In addition to his local business and his extensive regional municipality and government work, Angelo also frequently worked on individual monuments for the Bottinelli Granite Company in New London and the Joseph Coduri and Fraquelli & Brusa Companies in Westerly. Although gravestone carving is and was the Buzzi Memorial stock in trade, Angelo

Angelo Buzzi (1900-1963) carving one of the panels for the Providence, Rhode Island War Memorial which was erected in January of 1929

secretly preferred the memorial work for cities and towns. In a 1954 article in the *Mystic Valley River Journal,* he said, "Gravestone work is sad. All the while I work on one of them I can't help thinking that this is for someone who has lost a loved one. But when I work on the memorials to history, then I am happy."

During an interview in 1985, Harold told a story about an experience his father had when he was just a very young carver. "You're supposed to make it like the plaster model. You don't change anything. You don't have that license. He [Angelo Buzzi] was only 15 or 16 and making a statue in Switzerland and he broke the statue in the body somewhere. He was afraid, afraid the boss would fire him...so he smoothed off the dent that he made. Then he noticed that the model didn't correspond with his work. So what did he do, he fixed the model. He chipped that off in the body area and then blended it with his hand. When the sculptor came in to verify the finished product, he said 'It looks pretty good, but there's something different about it. I don't know what, something different. Can't put my finger on it.' After the gentleman leaves, the boss came over and took a look at the model and the finished piece. He said, 'I know what you did' and he kicked him right in the seat of the pants, quite hard. 'Don't ever do that.' He said, 'You should have said, "Look, it broke," and then you ask the sculptor how you correct it.'"

Harold is an accomplished designer and sandblaster, having learned his trade from Oscar Nurmi at the Bottinelli Monumental Company. At an age when most of us have been long retired, Harold, age 80, is still at his office and work shed on almost a daily basis. Since most of the major Westerly and Pawcatuck granite quarries have ceased operation, Harold receives most of his granite monument stones from the Rock of Ages Company in Barre, VT and from both India and China.

Harold Buzzi (b. 1930) preparing letters for sandblasting in his shed in Stonington, CT in 2010

The Buzzi Memorials Company on Route 1 in Stonington circa 1955

MID TWENTIETH CENTURY
COMOLLI GRANITE COMPANY: THE LEGACY LINGERS

Around 1910, Ferruccio "Frank" Comolli left his native Breno in northern Italy near the Swiss border and came to America. Only 16, he initially settled in Elberton, Georgia to work in the local granite industry with one of his brothers. Jennie Caccivio, his future wife, had immigrated the year before when she was only 8 years old and first lived in Milford, New Hampshire, another New England granite center. She met Frank when he relocated to Milford to be near his older sister and brother Martin. Little did Frank and Jennie know that their son Richard would continue the family interest in granite and become one of the finest carvers to work in the Westerly area.

After his discharge from the military, Richard "Dick" Comolli began his stonecutting training at the Columbia Granite Company operated by the Monti Family on Old Hopkinton Road. By this time, his parents and siblings had also moved to Westerly where his father worked for the Smith Granite Company. Dick remained at Columbia for about six years, learning and developing his stonecutting and carving skills. During those early years he studied and worked with well-respected local carvers such as Angelo Buzzi, Charlie Gattoni, and Peter Zanzi. He also studied monuments in local cemeteries to observe the techniques used by other carvers, in creating elaborate statues and monuments. Upon leaving Columbia, he went to the Bonner Monument Company where he continued to work for the next 15-20 years. While at Bonner, he carved the War Memorial on the Westerly side of the Pawcatuck River Bridge.

In 1984, the opportunity arose to purchase property on the corner of the Ashaway and Chase Hills Roads and the Comolli Granite Company was created. In 1998, Dick bought the Sullivan Quarry in Bradford and pumped the 80' deep Percy Bliven Hole dry. Richard Champlin used a 100 ton crane to pull out 10 or 12 pieces of Sullivan blue-white granite which were then sent to Barre to be sawed. When a car ran into the Westerly War Memorial at the foot of Granite Street in 2009, Dick was able to match the granite and

make the necessary repairs. The quarry hole refilled with water within two weeks, leaving no trace of what had been done, but Westerly granite and Westerly men had saved the day.

One of the more interesting demonstrations of the connections among local granite companies occurred when Dick, then working for the Bonner Monument Company, used Sullivan granite to carve cemetery tablets for members of the Smith Granite Company family.

For the past twenty-five years, Dick and his team of 5 – 7 workers have continued the legacy of the Westerly granite industry, producing many fine granite monuments.

Richard Comolli letter cutting in his shed in 2010

The amazingly realistic look to the drape of the dress is a testament to the talent of carver Richard Comolli. The arch was carved by Andy Anderson. The Serra monument in St. Sebastian Cemetery in Westerly, RI

Comolli Gang circa 2007: (l to r) Slim the Dog, Richard Comolli, Robert Greene, Barry Boeglin, Andrew Chiappone, Jesse Boeglin, Adam Comolli

STONE CHIPS

Richard Comolli bought the Larson Quarry off Chase Hill Road. It was said that Larson had three sons who were so strong that they loaded the trucks by hand.

The Comolli family monument carved by Richard D. Comolli

TODAY: A DIFFERENT SLANT

In 1962, Harold Slosberg bought 40 acres off Mountain Avenue and in 2006 our modern Orlando Smith, Robert Denesha, walked down an old quarry road and discovered thousands of tons of granite lying on the ground. These stones were the ones which could not be used for quality monuments and were discarded by the original quarrymen and piled into what is called the grout pile. United Builders Supply Co. Inc. now harvests these stones and has them processed into veneer stone. United Builders has found various uses for these stones. For example, it used several tons for a wall across from the Kellogg Mansion in Watch Hill, used pink granite veneer stones for a home in Weekapaug, and Westerly blue for pool steps and coping. As Denesha is fond of saying, "Westerly granite is back on the market after sixty years."

In truth, Westerly granite and the men who worked with granite have never disappeared, but have reinvented themselves. In 1989, Cherenzia Excavation, Inc. purchased eight to ten properties on Old Hopkinton Road and White Rock Road from various holders and began a large stone crushing operation.

Others are designing and lettering memorials even if the granite no longer comes out of the Westerly quarries. Computers and sandblasting have replaced chisels and drafting, and China and India have replaced Westerly as sources.

Harold Buzzi, nearly 80, knows the importance of design. He does the lettering layout by hand, saying that computers are fine for government markers, but not for monuments which require artistry in the spacing and presentation of the lettering. "Lettering makes the stone," he says, but adds that sadly for some people "as long as you spell it correctly, no one cares how it looks."

Roger Shawn, using some treasured tools from Bonner, also does hand lettering and then sandblasts to get the final results. Ron Nalbandian uses stones from Barre, Vermont and a computer program for stencil-cutting for the letters. Richard Comolli comes

from a noted family of granite workers and most days about noon, one can find him carving at his business. He and Robert Greene worked together for forty years (some of those for Bonner) and are probably the last of the active carvers in town.

In the tradition of past craftsmen like the Cugini brothers, fine masons continue to build walls, fireplaces, chimneys, kitchen counters and other structures which combine the useful and the aesthetic. Businesses, professionals, and non-profits are using granite signs to make a statement about their durability and desire to identify with Westerly.

United Builders Supply is harvesting granite from grout piles like this one.

Westerly granite is still being used.

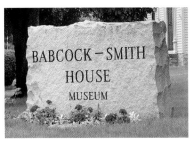

This sign was donated by Gail Bonner in memory of her father, Donald Bonner, of Bonner Monuments. It is made of red granite from Canada, a close approximation of Westerly red granite which is no longer available in pieces this size. The sign, erected May 2006, was cut by the Shawn Monument Company.

Skilled stone carving is still done today at the Comolli Granite Company.

Time Capsule, on display on the second floor of the Westerly Town Hall, is scheduled to be opened in 2050. The 1'x 1'x 3' capsule of pink, red and blue Westerly granite was made by the Comolli Granite Company to commemorate the new millenium.

Westerly Middle School students have recognized the importance of the granite industry in Westerly's history. Kayla Patten, Anika Kreckel, Paige Chighine, Adeline Hanssen, Amanda Boisclair, Alexandra Hayes and Alexis Hayes are pictured working on the mural (2004).

The mural of the sculptors' studio at the Smith Granite Company, featuring two sculptors in the foreground and plaster models on the shelf above, is under the direction of art teacher John Tedeschi.

TODAY: A DIFFERENT SLANT

DWIGHT C. BROWN, JR. (1928 –):
A DIFFERENT KIND OF QUARRYMAN

Some people quarry for granite and others quarry for information. Dwight C. Brown, Jr. fits into the second category. Over the last 25 years, "Brownie" and his wife Anna have spent hours finding bits and pieces of information, scanning old photographs, taking new ones to serve as documentation, and cataloging it all.

Dwight's interest was sparked as a boy when his uncle shared discoveries as they hiked through old fields and quarries. His interest flared when, as a worker at Bradford Dyeing Association, he had access to early records and found the research process to be like solving a mystery. One clue led to another, until the facts were uncovered and the mystery solved.

His first major project was to search the microfilm at the Westerly Public Library for information about the Pawcatuck River industries. All his notes were taken by hand. Excited when he got his first computer, an Atari 800, he discovered that he typed faster than the computer could accept the input. As the years passed, Dwight's search for history became more technology-dependent and the available technology improved.

Dwight C. Brown, Jr.

An invaluable project was the completion of the contact printing of the Burke Glass Negative collection for the Westerly Historical Society. It took twenty minutes to develop two negatives in the dark room. Every time that a copy of a particular image was wanted, the same procedure had to be followed. These prints, which Dwight has now scanned at very high resolution, take up a large portion of his terabyte external hard drive. Computer scanning, taking approximately 20 minutes, needs to be done only once. Dwight has catalogued both the digital and photographic images to be sure that the information is preserved.

Dwight, author of several books on various aspects of the history of Westerly, has completed many other local history projects, including cataloguing all the monuments in River Bend Cemetery and gleaning bits and pieces from *The Narragansett Weekly* and *Stonington Mirror* newspaper articles about the granite industry. He has documented innumerable names of granite workers from a variety of sources. He served as archivist for the Westerly Historical Society and willingly answered thousands of questions and supplied information and stunning photographs that we could not have found easily for this book. He is a Westerly treasure who has had a major role in preserving both verbal and visual images of the Westerly granite industry.

Dwight C. Brown, Jr., local historian, at his computer surrounded by his carefully cataloged discoveries

EUREKA! UNEXPECTED FIND..

Recollections of history of the granite used for President Coolidge & Mrs. Coolidge tombstones.

A number of years ago, a telephone call from New Bedford, MA., led to the retrieval of a granite item with a connection to Westerly, RI. The person identified himself as a person who owned a Granite Business in New Bedford which was in the process of closing down. He indicated that he found an item that might be of interest to Westerly. He went on to described a "sample" piece of granite enclosed in a box; the granite having an inscription on it which indicated that it was a piece of Westerly light pink Granite provided by the Smith Granite Co., of Westerly, R. I. He wanted to know if there was any interest — I replied in the affirmative and asked how I could get this item. He gave directions to the place of business in New Bedford and said I could have it if I wanted to drive up there for it — a time was set up to retrieve this article.

After picking up the article, and having read the inscription on it, which indicated just what he had told me, we brought the article home. Viewing this article when we arrived home, it was evident that this article had not been taken care of as there was a deposit of unknown nature, which had left the article in other than 'mint' condition. My wife asked me "what are you going to do with it?" I told her that someone would be interested in it sooner or later. And, then; leave it up to a woman's natural instinctive for investigation, my wife opened the velvet lined box, looked at it and then proceeded to remove the "sample" granite from the box! She was not done, for she turned it over; here it became obvious how important this article was! Ah! For the power of a woman . . . On the rear of the piece of granite was an inscription that indicated that this piece of granite was cut from the block of Westerly Granite that had been selected for the 'simple' headstone for Calvin Coolidge, formerly President of the United States of America.

To this day the writer does not think that the donor even knew what the reverse side of the so-called 'sample block' of granite had inscribed on it, probably never having been removed from its storage box.

Dwight C. Brown

The headstone of Calvin Coolidge, 30th President of the United States, in Plymouth, VT was cut from Westerly granite by a company in Quincy, MA.

Inscription on the exposed portion of the granite sample describes Westerly's light pink granite.

Inscription on "hidden" portion of the granite sample documents the link of Westerly granite to the Coolidge tombstone.

ISAAC G. SMITH, JR. (1922 –): A FEEL FOR GRANITE IN HIS HANDS AND IN HIS HEAD

Ask a question about the granite industry and you are likely to hear "Ask Ike. He knows." "Ike" is Isaac G. Smith, Jr., 88, the man who has done more than anyone else to preserve the history of Westerly granite from a hands-on perspective.

As a boy, he grew up in the industry, tagging along with his father; as an adolescent, he worked in the quarry doing one job or another. After serving in World War II, he became an apprentice and earned his status as a journeyman granite cutter. Although he worked at his trade for twelve years, designing and cutting monuments, it is what he did afterwards that is more important.

Isaac G. Smith, Jr.

Previous generations of his family had been actively involved with the Smith Granite Company, but Ike became the historian and preservationist. Using his "hunt and peck" typing system for at least twenty years, he computerized the information in twenty-two order books of the Smith Granite Company. There is a digital record of 3939 monuments with up to twenty-one fields in each entry. Now a researcher can enter a family name, a cemetery, the name of a monument, or a state and pull up all sorts of information about that person or monument.

His contributions vary from preparing granite chips for fifth graders, to designing the pillars that stand at the post office entrance to the park, to working tirelessly on the granite exhibit at the Westerly Public Library.

For the last eight years he has worked weekly with Brenda Linton, a retired history teacher, to organize thousands of photographs and documents. The Smith Granite Company, the New England Granite Works, and the Bonner Monument Company are well documented with these photos and ephemera in the Babcock-Smith House Museum. He has led illuminating tours of River Bend Cemetery, been the subject of a DVD, given interviews and lectures, and patiently answered questions from the Smithsonian Institute and hundreds of individuals seeking information.

Anyone who has seen Ike in action knows that he can look at a piece of granite and tell which specific quarry hole it came out of in Westerly. If the stone is not from Westerly, he can tell you whether it is from Barre, VT, Quincy, MA, Stony Creek, CT or elsewhere. He can walk through the cemetery and tell who did the lettering on a monument. His knowledge is more than encyclopedic and he has shared it willingly.

For both the granite newspaper series and this book, we have been asking Ike. He knew.

STONE CHIPS

"The Kellogg people that make Kellogg corn flakes had ordered a monument from the Smith Granite Company many many years ago. They wanted to match the original. Now that's pretty hard to do because Smith Granite Company hadn't quarried any blue in ten years. There was none around big enough to make this. We scouted all over for material. Donald [Bonner] found a boulder down by Dunn's Corners that the glacier had dumped there 10,000 years ago. It was just what we wanted. We had to break the boulder open to see if it was good inside. I would say before we cut the boulder it weighed for 12 or 15 ton. It was beautiful inside. We quarried that stone out of that boulder, brought it up to the shed, and sawed it."

Isaac G. Smith, Jr.

Ike at River Bend Cemetery explaining the fine points of cutting a monument

Ike cut this Celtic cross at the Holy Family Monastery, West Hartford, CT from red Westerly granite in 1956 while working for the Bonner Monument Company.

WESTERLY GRANITE STORY TIMELINE

@1830 Orlando Smith starts stone masonry business on Mechanic Street in Pawcatuck, CT

1845 Orlando Smith purchases the Babcock property on Rhodes Hill in Westerly to open quarry

@1847 John Macomber purchases the Vose Farm for his quarry which is later sold to the Smith Granite Company

1850's Irish immigration

1857 Alexander G. Crumb establishes first major quarry in Niantic (later Bradford)

1859 Orlando Smith dies at the age of 45. William "Boss" Burdick is appointed business manager of the Smith Granite Company by Emeline Smith, Orlando's widow

@1865 George Ledward starts a second quarry on adjoining Rhodes Hill land

1866 Master carver Columbus Zerbarini arrives in New York City

@1868 Ledward sells quarry to J.G. Batterson and it is operated as the Rhode Island Granite Works under the control of the New England Granite Works in Hartford, CT

1869 Stonecutters' union established in Westerly

1870 Railroad spur connects Batterson's operation on Quarry Hill to the Stonington Railroad

1870's Scottish immigration

1871 Stonecutters protest a perceived breach in their agreement with Rhode Island Granite Works

1874 Antietam Soldier unveiled in Westerly on Memorial Day

1875 Rhode Island Granite Works is incorporated as the New England Granite Works

1875 Many Westerly stonecutters go to Hartford to work on the Connecticut State Capitol Building

1880's Northern Italian immigration

1880 Joseph Newall & Co. establishes a quarry in Niantic (later Bradford) and a cutting shed on Oak Street in Westerly

1880 The Westerly granite industry begins to receive national recognition as producers of exceptionally fine monuments

1880-1900 More than one hundred Civil War monuments are created by Westerly companies for Gettysburg, Chickamauga, Antietam and Vicksburg battlefields

1880 Antietam Soldier produced by New England Granite Works

1884 Babcock-Smith House undergoes a Victorian restoration to reflect prosperity

@1885 Joseph Newall & Co. establishes in Westerly a branch of the Scottish Dalbeattie Granite Company

1887 Smith Granite Company incorporates

1889 Angelo and Columbus Zerbarini carve the Washington Equestrian Statue for the Allegany Commons Park in Pittsburgh, PA

1890 A forty-day strike to shorten the work day from ten hours to nine hours

1892 The Niantic Works managed under the name of Joseph Newall & Co.

1892 Railroad spur extended to Smith Granite Company

1894 The Westerly Masonic Lodge adopts a resolution expressing thanks to the Smith Granite Company, New England Granite Works, Joseph Newall & Co., A.G. Crumb & Sons, Charles P. Chapman and Nathan Dixon for the three beautiful granite pedestals presented to the Lodge

1895	Finnish immigration
1898	Orlando R. Smith dies at the age of 47 in the midst of merger negotiations. A subsequent lawsuit disposition leaves the company with limited operating capital
1900	Southern Italian immigration
1900-1930	Mechanization changes industry
1901	Newall moves cutting sheds from Niantic to Westerly off Oak Street
1907	Coduri & Marzoli Granite Company established
1907	Frank Sullivan purchases Crumb Quarry
1916	Joseph Coduri Granite Company is established and purchases the Joseph Newall & Co. sheds on Oak Street for $15,000
1919	Crumb Quarry, Frank A. Sullivan president, purchases quarry property of Joseph Newall & Co. and later the Klondike Quarry
1922	Extended strike plagues the industry
1924	Fraquelli & Brusa in existence by this time
@1925	Monti buys the long-closed Chapman Quarry
@1925	Smith Granite Company buys New England Granite quarries
1928	Smith Granite Company buys Smalley Quarries (Macomber, Dixon, later Sweeney, and Calder and Carney) between Route 3 and Old Hopkinton Road. Also buys Gourlay "Red Stone" (later operated by Batterson) as an inactive reserve
1930	Great Depression begins causing less demand for monuments
1930	Bonner Monument Company established
1933	Buzzi Memorials established
1936	Last order for paving stones taken by Smith Granite Company
1938	Hurricane causes great damage
1939	Neidel cross produced by Fraquelli & Brusa
1942-1945	World War II takes men and materials from granite companies; Sullivan Granite Company switches to war effort
1945	Bank forecloses on Smith Granite Company and it is reorganized as Smith Granite Works with Edward W. Smith as president
1949	Columbus statue in Wilcox Park produced by Joseph Coduri Granite Company
1950	Cherenzia Excavation, Inc. established
early 1950's	Fraquelli & Brusa closes
1955	All production and quarrying ends on Granite Hill and sheds torn down
1955	Sullivan Granite Company closes
1956	Sullivan Granite Company sells main quarry (about 95 acres) to Bottinelli Monumental Co. of New London, CT; five tracts of land to Harold Slosberg of United Builders Supply Co. Inc.; a dozen tracts to Reuben Grossman of Qunicy, MA
1958	Joseph Coduri Granite Company closes operations on Oak Street, but becomes affiliated with Bonner Monument Company until the early 1960's
1958	Westerly Historical Society publishes *The Story of Westerly* by Stephen Macomber

1960   Last of the large cutting sheds sold by Joseph Coduri Company to Angelo Gencarelli, Frank Gencarelli, and Salvatore Cherenzia. Bess Eaton Donuts used the railroad spur but not the sheds

1968   Bonner Monument Company purchases the Newall Quarry in Bradford

1971   James Romanella & Sons, Inc. purchases old Sullivan Quarry land from Bottinelli Monumental Co.

1976   The Blue Westerly Granite incorporated (Bonner)

1981   Westerly Chapter of Stone Cutter's Union dissolves

1984   Comolli Granite Company established

1985   The Westerly Public Library Granite Project includes seventeen oral histories, a production by the Rhode Island Feminist Theatre, and a publication, *The Strength of the Stone*. It led to a major exhibit at the Westerly Public Library.

1989   Cherenzia Excavation, Inc. purchases 8 – 10 properties on Old Hopkinton Road and White Rock Road from various holders and begins stone crushing operation

1992   Granite Exhibit opens at The Westerly Public Library

1995   Bonner Monument Company closes

1997   Westerly Granite Co, Inc. (Richard Comolli) purchases sixty-one acres from James Romanella and Sons, Inc. (old Sullivan Granite Company land)

2006   United Builders Supply Co. Inc. begins harvesting previously quarried granite

2010   A yearlong series of weekly full-page informational ads on the granite industry begins in *The Westerly Sun* as a collaboration of the Babcock-Smith House Museum, United Builders Supply Co. Inc. and Sun Publishing Co.

COMMUNITY

In many ways, granite was responsible for melding Westerly into one large community composed of men of different nationalities, religions, ages, and talents, but having love of family, a strong work ethic, and the granite industry in common. In the mid-1800's the Yankees were already here, but the Irish followed in the 1850's, the Scots in 1870, the Northern Italians in the 1880's, the Finns in 1895 and the Southern Italians in 1900.

No matter where they lived, granite families may have shopped in the company store and/or sent their children to neighborhood schools such as Quarry Hill School. They shared a love of music and the kids carried lunches to their fathers. People fell in love and suffered tragedies. They grew gardens, posed stiffly for family portraits, and worked together in the quarries and the sheds.

In the following chapters, the glimpses into the life of the granite community are representative of a shared experience.

THE GRANITE COMMUNITY

Granite workers tended to live in neighborhoods with people from their home country. In the mid-twenties, within walking distance of the quarries on the hill, "Oatmeal Alley" (Benefit Street between Cross and School) was the home of the Scots who generally settled from Granite Street to the other side of John Street and prided themselves on the education they gave their children. The Irish settled along Route 1 from the Babcock-Smith House to Quarry Hill School (at the intersection of East Avenue). A mixed neighborhood existed from there to Wells Street. John Street was settled from the top (Route 1) down with Italians and Scots. Many in these neighborhoods were Roman Catholics who walked from Wells Street all the way to the former Immaculate Conception Church on High Street.

Immigrant workers provided much of the work force in the granite industry.

Initially, most of the southern Italians (Calabrese) settled in the North End of Westerly, establishing social clubs such as the Calabrese Society on West Street and the Italo-American Club at the intersecton of Pond and Perkins Avenues. The northern Italians (Lombards) settled more on the south side of the railroad tracks with pockets in the Oak and Tower Streets and Narragansett and Ward Avenues area. The Bocce Club on Ledward Avenue became a favorite gathering spot.

Neighborhoods developed outside the immediate Quarry Hill area as well. The Finns tended to settle in the Chase Hill area where they would gather for saunas on some of the farms or go to the Finnish Hall in Potter Hill for music and dancing. The Scots settled in Niantic (now Bradford) and spent their free time in the winter curling on local ponds. Organizations such as the Caledonian Society and the Daughters of Scotia met regularly and the sound of bagpipes was not uncommon.

In the afternoon, eight hundred men poured out of the Smith and New England quarries and headed home to their neighborhoods and to their families who helped make Westerly what it is today.

Quarrying was an intergenerational experience and required a team effort. Some men rose to the position of foreman (Ledward, the man with the hat), responsible for the overall task. Older workers (the man on the left) who were beginning to feel the limitations of age did less physically demanding tasks. Men in their prime (the man sitting on the stone) were able to do the most challenging work both in terms of skill and physical prowess. Young men (the boy on the right) began working at an early age as go-for guys, but, as they learned by watching and doing, they were able to share in the work that required more skills. Within a few years they would be able to take up the full load. Circa 1904

STONE CHIPS

On stonecutters: "When they used to go for lunch, they always had aprons, always—they'd put the apron over their stone. The apron used to practically cover up their work. The only one who didn't give a damn was Mr. Comolli. He did beautiful work."

Arthur Ferraro

Narragansett Weekly. August 16, 1888 ~ The first ballgame of the season, between the Chapman Granites and the Smith Granites, was played Saturday afternoon, on the "Flatrock" grounds. It resulted in a splendid victory of the Smith Granites, the score at the end of the ninth inning being 9 to 4 in their favor.

TIN PAIL BRIGADE

The Narragansett Weekly on May 29, 1873 indicated that the quarrymen often carried their own lunch pails. "One of the most interesting of the daily sights of Westerly is the procession of quarrymen coming from the hill about six o'clock every evening [carrying their tin lunch pails]." The newspaper coined the term "Tin Pail Brigade" to honor these men

"One of my first chores, as I can remember, was to take my father's lunch to him on Saturdays, in his lunch pail, which had tea in the bottom. And on the top of it was always an English pasty. I would go up, and my father [William John Veal] would be cutting granite and he'd sit. He had a stove in his shed and he always had a fire in there, so he'd put his pail on the stove, and then we'd sit down and I always had the corner of his pasty . . . [which was] filled with meat and potato, folded in pastry."

Mrs. John Burne (Selena)

"All of the children [who] went to Quarry Hill School would have an hour and a half for lunch. They would go home and get their father's dinner pail and take it to him in the quarry or the stone shed so that he had a hot meal and then they would go home and have their lunch and go back to school."

Isaac G. Smith, Jr.

"The Italian men in those days had a great habit of eating eggs raw. They'd put a pinpoint in both ends and just drink the egg right out of that little pinpoint. That's what the granite cutters used to do. They'd take two or three eggs with them to work and you'd find all these egg shells around. They'd eat the eggs raw."

Nettie Coduri Salimeno Jones

The tin pail came in sections.

THE GRANITE COMMUNITY

A NEIGHBORHOOD: THE NORTH END

As told to Betty-Jo Cugini Greene in 2010 by Marian (Sposato) Santaniello, Felice (Sposato) Scialabba, Susie (Sposato) Greene, and Irene (Sposato) Gaccione over coffee at the family homestead on Pond Street

The sounds and smells of the old North End and the Pond Street area are fresh in the minds of many who still live there. At night people sat on the stoops sharing music, conversation and recipes - not just recipes for food but for tricks of the trade when it came to cutting that stone or building the perfect stone wall.

The older ones remember when men gathered at the corner of Pierce and Pond Streets to wait for someone who had a car to take them up the hill or else rode their bicycles to work. They carried lunches and tools in their overworked hands and trade secrets in their heads. Kids got up early to ride their bikes hoping to get a few pennies to buy candy or to find the peanuts that the men might leave on the wall.

The four remaining Sposato sisters, at the home they grew up in on Pond Street, told of their father Santo Sposato riding his bicycle to

From the North End neighborhood (l to r) Santo Sposato, unknown, James Cherenzia and Sam Cherenzia in the Smith Granite Company 6th hole, looking north circa 1920

Lillian Cugini Falcone in her backyard with clothesline in the background circa 1936

the Smith Quarry and in later years meeting Jimmy and Sam Cherenzia, or Angelo Gencarelli, to carpool. The men left for work about 6:45 and the women can still describe the whistle which called the men to work. After work, the family went "to the lot," a large parcel of land at the lower end of Pond Street, to work in the garden which fed them both summer and winter. The produce was boiled, canned and "put up." The sisters also remember the dust on the men's clothing and the shoes which had to be left outside each night.

Angelo Gencarelli from the North End is shown standing in the Smith Granite Company East Quarry, the 6th hole, where light pink granite was quarried. This piece of granite was used in the Trexler Memorial which had a finished weight of 32 tons. Angelo Gencarelli was the grandfather of Bangy (Angelo) Gencarelli, founder of Bess Eaton Donuts.

THE GRANITE COMMUNITY
QUARRY HILL SCHOOL

The neighborhoods near Quarry Hill grew as the granite business thrived and the children of both newly-arrived immigrants and established Yankees needed to be educated. Emeline Gallup Smith, executrix of the estate of Orlando Smith, had four school-aged children. During the Civil War, she became so concerned about not having a school nearby that she deeded to the town of Westerly a plot of land to be used for a school. The deed stipulated that the town would retain ownership of the land as long as there was a school there. Quarry Hill was designated as District #2. Initially the school had only one room, but two subsequent additions made it a three-room school. Children attended through grade six and then many went on to high school. During the early years they attended

high school at the Academy on Union Street. In 1870, Elm Street School (now St. Pius X School) opened as a high school with three floors. Julia Smith, Emeline's daughter and Orlando Raymond Smith's sister, was in the first graduating class from the high school.

After World War II, the town no longer needed the school and sold it to the American Legion for $1.00. Although this sale violated the terms of the deed, the postwar period was not a time to fight the American Legion. Later, the Legion sold the land to be developed for business. Because of the cloud on the deed, the land could not be sold until all the heirs of Orlando Smith had signed off. Presently the Rite-Aid Pharmacy is on the site of the old Quarry Hill School.

HIGH SCHOOL GRADUATES.

FROM THE FOUNDATION OF THE SCHOOL.

1874.

Evelyn S. Hall,
Alice J. Macomber,
Phebe W. Perry,
Julia E. Smith,

Eleanor C. Wolcott,
Theophilus R. Hyde, Jr.,
Frank A. Palmer,
Charles H. Pendleton.

1875.

M. Edwina Arnold,
Jennie A. Card,
Hattie E. Cottrell,
Henrietta L. Lewis,
Carrie Shumway,
Venie White,

Chas. H. J. Douglass,
William A. Stanton,
Howard Y. Stillman,
Arthur Perry,
Everett T. Tomlinson,
James L. Wells.

The first two graduating classes from the High School on Elm Street

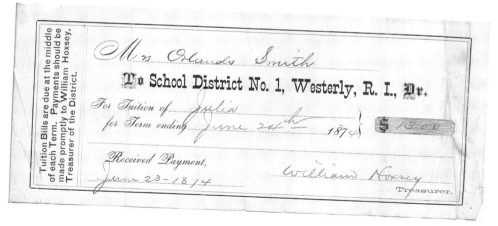

Receipt for $13.00 for the tuition of Julia Smith to pay for the last semester of her senior year in high school

Willie Ledward
Thos. Farrill
Thos. Gourlay
John Kenna
Phillip Dowd
Orlando Smith Jr.

Gene Dyer
Chas. Fraser
John Dovine
Jerry O'Connell
John Bray
Thos. Holliday

Frank Gilbert
Thos. McGraph
Michael Nestor
James Conway
Annie Keenan
Mary Cotter

Jessie Frasier
Emma Mullen
Mavy Mallen
Lizzie Wilcox
Katy ONeil
Katy Mullen

Etta Hughes
Katy Keenan
Ida Holmes
Lizzie Gourlay
Rosanna Holliday
Ella Burke

Lizzie Keena
Rosanna Farrel
Aggie Nestor
Katy Cameron
Lizzie Barrus

oldest man In Westerly
William D. Wells

The Teacher
Benjamin Franklin
Greenman

Students at Quarry Hill School circa 1885

THE GRANITE COMMUNITY

THE COMPANY STORE ON JULY 1, 1890

July 1, 1890 was a busy day at the Smith Granite Company store with more than 300 transactions recorded by Frank Barber, the storekeeper. J. O'Donnell bought yeast for 2 cents; Chas Ledward bought a cigar for 5 cents; Pat Holiday bought a bag of flour for 98 cents. Other orders were lengthy. William Holliday bought chops, sugar, tea, coffee, potatoes, currants, raisins, stove polish, a stove brush, gelatin, pickles, cheese, thread, 10 yards print fabric, matches, slippers, lemons, oatmeal, steaks, ham, cabbage, cookies, a hat, paper and envelope, sugar, crackers, vinegar, tapioca, cabbage and stamps, This order came to $13.32 which was debited to his account.

The store also served as a way to get cash. On that same day, Thomas Keenan got $6.00.

Even the owner took advantage of the convenience of the company store. Orlando Raymond Smith bought some candy, crackers and 6 yards of calico to take home to his wife Julia. He spent 98 cents.

Circa 1880: The original Smith Granite company store was housed in a small wooden building and records show that it was doing business in 1857. The Gourlay house on Tower Street is in the background.

Circa 1930: The store building was rented in 1919 to the Panciera brothers, Tony and Ernie, who operated the Granite Street Garage there. Later, Tony moved his share of the business to Railroad Avenue where he sold Packards. His brother Ernie moved circa 1945 to Main Street where he sold Studebakers.

1952: Pamela Waters Woods at her grandparents' home, which was the site of the former Recchia store. Across Granite Street is the Holliday and Joyce filling station, once the Smith Granite company store and later Hoxie Buick. It is now vacant.

Circa 1885: The second Smith Granite company store, built in 1884 and located at the corner of Granite and Tower Streets, operated for more than 30 years.

THE GRANITE COMMUNITY
THE IRISH: THE STRENGTH OF A FAMILY
by Peggy Kelly, fourth generation descendent of James Foley

Not every Irish family becomes as famous as the Kennedys, but the sense of family is just as strong. James Foley, his wife, Margaret (Whelan), three children and his sister Mary Foley immigrated to Westerly circa 1883 where James supported his family by working in Smith's Quarry as a quarryman and later as a stonecutter. Margaret died in 1891 leaving James with seven young children: Thomas 18, Delia 13, Laurence 12, Mary 9, James 7, David 5, and Patrick 1. The two girls devoted their lives to raising the boys and taking care of their father and, in turn, the boys, as they prospered, took care of the house and their sisters.

In 1896, James Foley bought a lot from the Smith Granite Company and established a small family farm at 158 Granite Street. The boys joined Pa working at the quarry and everyone worked hard to keep the family together, showing a solid work ethic, a strong faith, and a strong sense of patriotism and community.

Thomas served in the Spanish American War and later lost an arm in a construction accident. He lived in the family home and every morning he walked to the library to exchange books, a routine which he continued until he died of a heart attack in Dolan's store across from his home.

James Foley: immigrant from Ireland

Delia took care of the boys and also of Pa in his old age. A temporary move to New York where she worked as an expert seamstress enabled her to send money home to Mary.

Laurence, a quarry worker (probably a blacksmith), became International President of the Granite Cutters International Association with offices in Quincy, MA. He was an honest man admired by his peers and never forgot what his sisters did for the family. He built a rooming house, lost in the 38 hurricane, on Atlantic Avenue which Delia and Mary ran, and also added two rental apartments to the family house.

In Memoriam: Laurence Foley, International President of the Granite Cutters Association of America

Mary kept the home fires burning for any of the siblings who needed a place to live. Delia and Thomas both lived out their lives there and James, a good carpenter, moved into the family house with his own family of six children and helped Delia and Mary with the house.

In 1906, David went to San Francisco to help rebuild after the great earthquake. He became a master carpenter and later a NYC policeman and was promoted to Detective First Grade. Each year he returned to Westerly to help maintain the family home.

Patrick, a plumber, lived on Summer Street and also helped with the family home.

No Foley was ever turned away from the house on Granite Street. Eventually it became a summer retreat for great granddaughters Peggy and Elaine and a home for James' granddaughter Madeline who all treasured the sense of family that the house embodied.

Foley home at 158 Granite Street

Irish hand drill line near the top of a Smith Granite Company hole circa 1880

THE GRANITE COMMUNITY
THE SCOTS: BAGPIPES AND CURLING STONES

by Thomas E. Wright

The Scots came early to Westerly and were active in the shipbuilding and transportation industries. It was, however, the granite industry that drew most here in the nineteenth century from either Dalbeattie or Aberdeen to work in local quarries. By 1885, almost ten percent of the Westerly population claimed a Scottish birthplace. As late as 1910, the village of Bradford (known as Niantic) was described as "primarily Scottish families." In 1896, Dalbeattie Granite Works operated in Niantic with its office at 6 High Street. In town, the Scots settled primarily on Granite Street and on Benefit Street, known as "Oatmeal Alley" after the Scottish penchant for this food.

Organizations such as the Caledonian Society and the Daughters of Scotia met regularly to celebrate their Scottish ancestry. Every January Scots would celebrate the birthday of the Scottish poet Robert Burns with the traditional piping in of the haggis, a dish consisting of the heart, lungs, and liver of a sheep or calf, minced with suet and oatmeal, seasoned with salt, pepper, and onions and then boiled like a large sausage in the maw (stomach) of the animal. In Westerly, this event was held at the former Haversham Inn or at a local Scottish meeting place.

What would a Scottish event be without the distinctive sound of the bagpipes? In past years, two highland pipe bands could be seen in local parades commemorating Veterans Day and Memorial Day. The Westerly Pipe Band, the oldest known pipe band in Westerly, played in the 1920's primarily in band concerts in Wilcox Park and wore the Clan Leslie Tartan. The second band, the Westerly Kiltie Pipe Band, performed in parades in Southeastern New England. Today both the Mystic Highland Pipe Band and the Rhode Island Highlanders perform in the area.

The ancient game of curling was a favorite sport of local Scots. Curling is similar to shuffleboard on ice where the purpose is to get as many stones as close as possible to the penny which is placed in the center of the circle. Players use brooms to sweep away pieces of ice in the way so the stone can travel farther. The game was born in Scotland and, in the old days, men curled with 60 pound stones (once made of iron) and women used 32 pounders. Today everyone uses 44 pound stones made of granite. Stones that were not brought over from Scotland were made from local granite.

Scottish stonecutter Andrew Low carving a niche in a monument

STONE CHIPS

Narragansett Weekly. May 4, 1871 ~
Some twenty-five or thirty Scotchmen, a portion of them with families, arrived in Westerly Tuesday morning, and are to be employed at Batterson's Quarry.

Tom Wright (left, father of the author of this article) and Russ Neagle curling on Burden's Pond circa 1960

Local Scot piper band circa 1920

Donald Bonner, owner of The Bonner Monument Company

THE GRANITE COMMUNITY
THE FINNS: HARD WORK AND THEN A SAUNA

"Makkiluoma" became "Hill," but "Myllymaki" stayed "Myllymaki." ("Maki" in Finnish means "hill.") The Johnson, Lepikko, Rindell, Mattson, Unkurris and Rindell surnames all belonged to families who came from small towns in Finland to escape either the Russians or the poor economic conditions.

In oral histories recorded in 1984 and 1985, Carl Myllymaki and sisters Thelma Hill Gardner and Hannah Hill Robinson share memories of their fathers who were in the granite industry and of their family life. The sisters remember some things a little differently, as we all do, but all three agree that the Finns came together in the 20's and 30's on Saturday nights at the Finn Hall, just above the Potter Hill Mill, where the children slept until it was time to go home and the adults danced Finnish polkas and the Hambo, and listened to Finnish music and Amos Elson playing the accordion and violin.

The Millymakis also were among the Finns gathering on Friday nights at the sauna which Mr. Hill had built out in back of his farmhouse (now owned by Stephen Mack) on Chase Hill Road. Thelma relates that, after using the sauna, they would go "back in the woods and get black birch branches and beat [themselves]. My mother used to bake a lot of . . . coffee bread made with curdling cheese." In the summer, the Hills would take in Finnish boarders from New York City and "the boys would sleep out in the barn because there was a lot of hay out there." Summer festivals to celebrate Midsummer Day, the longest and therefore the lightest day in Finland, were held for large crowds in pastures at the Lepikko's or the Hill's.

When the Hills first came to Westerly, they lived on Tower Street where they took in a couple of Finnish boarders who worked in the quarries. Mrs. Hill worked as a tailor, creating the "fancy big sleeves" that were so popular in the 1890's for Watch Hill socialites and also made men's suits. After they moved to the farm on Chase Hill Road,

she would sell vegetables in Watch Hill or barter with Sophie Seidner of Seidner's Mayonnaise.

"My father from the stone cutting [at Redstone Quarry] was covered like a white snowman in dust and he did die of silicosis. He used to find the veins in the rocks so the rest could know where to drill," Thelma tells us.

Carl Myllymaki's father came to Westerly in 1907 and was called the "Iron Man" because of his great strength and the size of his hammer. "He could take a railroad tie (sic) and bend it. [As a young man] he looked like Charles Atlas."

Some of the Finns may have changed the spelling of their names, but they did not change their hard work ethic or their need to share good times.

Finlander Billy Luoma, a carpenter for the Smith Granite Company, is shown in the foreground packaging a granite roller for shipment to a paper manufacturer. Luoma had only one hand but did not let a handicap prevent him from working in the demanding granite industry. Also pictured is Louis Giorno.

Finlander Alex Palm (left), foreman, oversees a drilling operation in the Smith North Quarry. Angelo Gradilone operates the drill.

Quarrymen called this operation "drilling a core." It took long hours of drilling with this air drill before the 100 ton block of pink stone was cut away from the ledge and then cut into smaller pieces to be transported to the cutting sheds.

THE GRANITE COMMUNITY
THE ITALIANS: HARD-WORKING PROVIDERS
by Joseph Terranova, as told to Ellen L. Madison

"My father took his job to heart." Joe Terranova, 92, said. "When I was little, my father would come home, sit in the kitchen, and tell my mother all about some problem he had with drilling or blasting a rock at Smith Granite Company where he worked and I'd be listening. He and one of the Smiths, owners of the company, might spend a long time discussing a solution, and 99 percent of the time, they would be correct. There was mutual respect between the quarrymen and the Smiths."

Frank Terranova was one of the many Italians who, between 4:00 and 4:30, would cover Granite, then Tower, then Oak Streets on their way home from working on the hill. He, like so many other quarry workers, had come from Calabria early in the 1900's. In 1904 he put $10.00 down as a deposit and borrowed $2,000.00 from The Washington Trust to buy a house on Oak Street. Terranova says that most of these immigrants would never have been able to buy a house in Acri. One of the first things the family did was to plant a garden because Calabria, in southern Italy, had been a great agricultural area. They might

Retired quarryman Frank Terranova circa 1955

own some chickens or a pig, but most of the time they relied on the produce from their lush gardens. Tuesdays, Thursdays and Sundays were pasta days.

The sculptors and men who worked in the sheds tended to come from Lombardia, a section of northern Italy. At first, the two groups could not communicate with each other because of the different dialects, but gradually, a happy middle ground was found.

"The greatest day of my father's life was when he went to the post office and became a citizen, which would have been during WWI. Because the first generation had very little formal education, they pushed their children to learn. My father mortgaged his house so that I could go to college. I want to stress that they all believed that any honest work was honorable."

Terranova mused about the social distinctions in town. "Italians were not allowed to walk on Elm Street" which might be a slight exaggeration, "but when I was ten or twelve, Sam Nardone, a hard worker who had formed his own construction company, built a house on Elm Street, and every Italian in town walked ten feet above the ground."

It could be said that we all walk ten feet off the ground when we think of the contributions that these Italian immigrants made, be they quarrymen such as Frank Terranova with his skill in blasting or superb statue cutters such as the Zerbarini brothers.

Italian Louis Giorno at the Smith Granite Company with a large cylinder turned with the lathe and packaged for travel

Italian Angelo Gradilone and his son Louis at work with an air drill on hard pink granite from Smith's North Quarry

With the help of his family, John DeRocchi ran a store on John Street in addition to working as a statue cutter.

John DeRocchi from Arcisate, Lombardia, Italy, pictured here with his pregnant wife, was one of the highly skilled statue cutters who immigrated from Italy to work in the Westerly granite industry.

THE GRANITE COMMUNITY

THE SMITH FAMILY: LIFE CONTINUES IN SPITE OF LOSS

by Linda Smith Chaffee

Orlando Raymond Smith was only eight years old when his father died in 1859. When he turned 21 in 1872, he became the second generation of Smiths to manage the Smith Granite Company until his death in 1898.

When Orlando married his first wife, Sarah Chapman, he built a new house across the laneway (now the corner of Granite and Cross Streets) from his mother's home, the present Babcock-Smith House. Fifteen months after

Orlando Raymond Smith (1851 – 1898)

their marriage, they had a daughter Anna Raymond Smith. Sarah died a year after the birth and "Baby Annie" lived only to age one and a half.

Nine months after the death of the baby, Orlando married his first wife's older sister, Julia Chapman. For her he enlarged the house, adding a wing that included a new kitchen and an attached well-house. He also added south-facing bay windows on the existing first and second floors. Orlando and Julia were married seventeen years and had one son, Orlando Raymond, Jr., and four daughters.

At the age of 41, Orlando Raymond Smith was widowed for the second time. This time he had five children to raise and a thriving business to manage. A year later he married the niece of his former two wives. His new bride, Jennie Chapman Smith, was 20 years his junior. When she moved into the house on Granite Street, Orlando made the house special for her by adding a four-story tower, making an impressive Victorian home. A year later their first son Franklin was born; Isaac followed two years later and Edward two years after

that. Just a month after Edward's birth, Orlando Raymond Smith died. Twenty-seven-year-old Jennie was left with her three sons under four, a twenty-one-year-old stepson and four teenage stepdaughters aged 19, 18, 15, and 13.

Orlando R. Smith had experienced the heyday of the granite industry. During this successful period, he had also owned several steamboats that operated on the Pawcatuck River. He was a member of the Fat Man's Society—those were the days when "portly" was a complimentary adjective implying success as well as describing physique.

Twenty-one-year-old Orlando Raymond Smith, Jr., only six years younger than his step-mother, left Brown University and returned home to accept the challenges of the business and to assist in the raising of his siblings.

Sarah Chapman Smith (1849 – 1874), the first wife of Orlando Raymond Smith

Baby Annie (1873 – 1875), first child of Orlando Raymond Smith

Julia Chapman Smith (1842 – 1892), second wife of Orlando Raymond Smith and sister of his first wife

Jennie Chapman Smith (1871 – 1963), third wife of Orlando Raymond Smith and niece of his first two wives, who was left with eight children when he died

The home of Orlando Raymond Smith, 130 Granite Street, after his 1893 marriage to Jennie. Note the prominent new tower.

The home of Orlando Raymond Smith during his second marriage. Note the new wing on the north (left) side of the house. Pictured are Orlando Raymond Smith, Jr. beside the goat and with sister Sarah behind the gate. Sisters Julia and Emeline are sitting on the steps and baby Martha is in her mother Julia's arms. Behind the children are Orlando Raymond Smith and perhaps his sister Julia.

THE GRANITE COMMUNITY
CODURI AND MARZOLI:
FAMILIES UNITED BY STONE

by John B. Coduri

In smaller communities, such as Westerly and Pawcatuck, families are often brought together by a marriage. That was the case with two families with deep roots in the Westerly granite industry – Coduri and Marzoli.

Giovanni (John) Coduri, one of my paternal great grandfathers, arrived in America in 1882 from the small town of Colico in the Lake Como region of Italy. He was 35 years old at the time of his arrival. His wife, Barbara, and three sons, Carlo, Albino, and Giuseppe (my grandfather Joseph) did not initially come with him as was the case with many such immigrations. Later, a fourth son, Louis, was born in America. The family purchased a farm in Waterford, CT in 1906 which remained as a home for some family members until 1955. The three older sons all eventually became stonecutters and were drawn to the booming Westerly granite industry.

Carlo Marzoli, my other paternal great grandfather, immigrated from Arcisate, Italy on April 22, 1890 at the age of 29. He was a stonecutter and in 1898 he began his employment with the Smith Granite Company (worker #92). It was an easy walk to work from his home at 28 John Street. In 1902, his oldest child, Joseph, also became a stonecutter at Smith's (worker #103) at the age of only 15. His second-born, daughter Antoinette, my paternal grandmother, met her future husband, Joseph Coduri, at a carnival near the Westerly Old Town Hall. They were married on November 15, 1906.

Eager to work for themselves, brothers-in-law Joseph Coduri (age 25) and Joseph Marzoli (age 20) in 1907 formed their own stonecutting company, Coduri & Marzoli, and in March of 1911 they entered into a formal five-year lease of a granite cutting shed on the east side of Granite Street, which was part of the already well-established Smith Granite Company. At times, Coduri & Marzoli received sub-contract

work from Smith. Such was the case with the Robert A. Gray Civil War Memorial in Groton, CT. Coduri & Marzoli were the statue cutters for this 1916 Smith Company monument.

During the 100 years since the two families were initially brought together, they have remained closely connected, enjoying birthday celebrations, school graduations, weddings, special holidays and family reunions and have drawn strength from each other during times of family losses, many from a combination of tuberculosis and granite-worker silicosis.

Two families, like so many other granite industry families, joined by a chance social encounter, connected by the Westerly granite industry, solidified and tested over time, remaining "stone strong" long after the granite heydays have passed.

John Coduri family in 1922: (seated) Barbara and John, (l-r), Joseph, Louis, Charles and Albino

Carlo Marzoli family in 1914: (l-r), Joseph, Antoinette, Carlo, Esterina, Prassede, Ergia and Dante

Joseph Coduri married Antoinette Marzoli in a quiet wedding in New London, CT on November 14, 1906. The bride wore a gown of cream-colored silk. This wedding linked the two families and opened the door for a successful granite business.

THE GRANITE COMMUNITY
REPRESENTATIVE ARTISTS

There are some special sculptors, carvers, and statue cutters whose names are legendary in the granite industry. These men are representative of the many talented artists in Westerly.

Robert D. Barr (1858 – 1900) and Stanley Edwards, Sculptors

These two men are often linked because, not only did they work together, their families lived close to each other on Summer Street. They both had backyard studios where they worked for themselves when not working for one of the larger companies. Barr came to Westerly from New York City in 1884 and worked for the Smith Granite Company. After an active career of only about a dozen years, he became an invalid and died in 1900.

Tradition has it that the figures in the Richardson monument in River Bend Cemetery are Mrs. Bertha Barr, wife of the sculptor Robert Barr, and his son, Robert F. Barr, who died in 1937. The stature was cut by Columbus Zerbarini.

Robert Barr created this plaster model of the 14th Brooklyn (84th New York Volunteers). Angelo Zerbarini carved the monument now in Gettysburg.

Frederick Douglass monument, designed by Stanley Edwards, is located in Rochester, NY. The nine-foot base and die are from blue Westerly granite.

Stanley Edwards' most famous work is probably the statue of Frederick Douglass, the famous black leader, which is in Rochester, NY. Originally the statue was to have been carved from Westerly granite, but the customer changed the order to bronze. Of heroic size, the bronze figure is eight feet tall and rests on a nine-foot base of Westerly granite. Interestingly, the statue had to be approved by Douglass's widow and children, so Barr did most of the work in Washington, DC under their watchful eyes. Using an abandoned Methodist church as his studio, he studied Douglass's life for two years, and used both a death mask and photographs as a starting point for his sculpture. The finished statue captures the moment when, right after the *Emancipation Proclamation*, Douglass is saying "I stand before you tonight for the first time as an American citizen."

John Francis Brines (1860 – 1905), Sculptor

"Jack" Brines, a local boy, was sent at an early age to work on Quarry Hill where his father was a stonecutter. His widow wrote that his "thoughtful interest in the cutting of statues, and the carving or ornament . . . attracted the attention of the workingmen. He could use a pencil and at home was always drawing, or modeling clay; yes, designing as well as copying."

After serving an early apprenticeship, he was sent to Gettysburg to complete statues and was promoted to assistant sculptor for the New England Granite Works where he made models as well. From their headquarters in Hartford, he went to Albany where the carving for the State Capitol was in progress and worked on ornamenting the imposing Eastern approach and the magnificent Western staircase.

The carving on the Albany Capitol had been badly bungled and one day the state architect, who had been impressed by the fact that Brines had not only the stonecutter's skill but also the talent of an artist, asked him: "Could you make new designs, and superintend the cutting of all this work?" With both modesty and certainty, Brines replied, "Yes, I could, and I'd like the chance." For the next eight years, Brines did just that and hired many out-of-work carvers from Westerly who relocated to Albany to work for him. He also did some work on the side including a notable Celtic cross in the Rural Cemetery in Albany.

Finished in Albany, he accepted a commission for a statue of a beloved Dr. Sheldon, a pioneer in kindergarten work, to be paid for by schoolchildren. Brines decided to complete the work in Europe. "I shall never forget with what awe and satisfaction Mr. Brines laid his hand on the famous Torso by Michael Angelo (*sic*); the sculptor whom he most revered," his wife wrote. He completed the commission in Paris and also completed two bronzes which were given to the Westerly Public Library. Brines returned to New York where he established a studio and died at 45.

The Milner monument of a mother and son, although done at an early age, is a testament to Brines' skill. It is in River Bend Cemetery.

Brines' grave in River Bend Cemetery is marked by a small, but beautiful Celtic cross, executed by a fellow-artist from Albany, NY and made from granite from Quarry Hill.

Edward L. Pausch (1856 – 1931), Sculptor

Edward Pausch may have been the most talented of the sculptors who worked in Westerly. Here for just ten or eleven years, he lived on Spruce Street near Park Avenue and contributed greatly to the Smith Granite Company.

Born in Copenhagen, Pausch began studying sculpture as a teenager in a studio producing plaster models for the New England Granite Works in Hartford and helped in the modeling of the large equestrian statue of Gen. Israel Putnam in Putnam, CT.

By the time he arrived in Westerly in 1889, Pausch's artistry in clay and plaster was well-known. He designed many military monuments as well as many of the cemetery memorials, particularly ones including angels, which were executed at the Smith Granite Company. His major achievement was the equestrian statue of

General George Washington, erected in Allegheny City, PA in 1891. Only three other such statues of Washington exist and they are bronze. Pausch's was the first monument of this kind in modern times to be made entirely of stone and to contain such fine details.

Before he left Westerly soon after 1900, he went into business for himself in his own studio on Vose Street as well as working on Quarry Hill. Records indicate that he was in Buffalo, NY and took the death mask of President McKinley, who was assassinated there, and received a commission to design a memorial to McKinley now in Reading, PA. Pausch later donated a bust of McKinley which he had made at the same time to the Westerly Public Library.

When the demand for monumental art work lessened, Pausch was reduced to designing and modeling scroll work for theater interiors, but his soldiers and angels will forever testify to his talent.

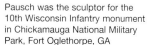

Pausch was the sculptor for the 10th Wisconsin Infantry monument in Chickamauga National Military Park, Fort Oglethorpe, GA

The Pomeroy Angel, carved by Columbus Zerbarini and located in Forest Hill Cemetery in Utica, NY, was the first of many statues cut from the model by Edward Pausch. The angel and cross are one piece of stone. In 1889 a reporter for a Providence paper called the plaster cast of the six foot angel "the finest piece of workmanship in clay ever produced in this place."

THE WASHINGTON EQUESTRIAN MONUMENT

On July 27, 1889, the Smith Granite Company received an order for a monument honoring General George Washington to be produced for $10,000. This monument was to have a granite horse and rider instead of the usual bronze, and this request would provide many challenges because of the statue's massive size, exquisite detail, and the weight of the granite. The order demanded the skills of an outstanding sculptor as well as superb statue cutters.

Edward Pausch designed and created the figure of Washington and the horse, first in clay and then in plaster. He created a design element of a column of leaves under the horse to help support the weight of the statue which the delicate legs of the horse could not do.

The stone, weighing about 42 tons, was taken from the quarry and, according to the record books, Angelo Zerbarini carved it and was paid $2,000. Local tradition says that his brother Columbus helped to carve. The reins, the stirrups, and even the spurs were cut from granite. In fact, all the detail in the statue is so fine that the Zerbarini brothers themselves were impressed. It is said that, when the committee came from Pittsburg to approve the statue, the brothers remarked tongue-in-cheek that, if they were given a few more weeks, the spurs would even turn.

The finished statue alone is nearly 10 feet high, one and a half times life-size, and the finished work with the base is 17 feet. Webs were left between the horse's legs and between its tail and its body to give the statue more structural integrity during shipment. The webs would be cut away when the monument was set. The pieces were boxed and taken down the hill to the railroad station with two oxen in front to steer and twenty oxen in back to keep from losing control. Angelo Zerbarini himself was sent to Pittsburg, PA to finish some fine points that were not safe to finish before the statue was shipped. The monument was dedicated on February 23, 1891, less than two years after the order had been placed.

The *Narragansett Weekly* said that the "statue will give to Westerly granite a prominence which it deserves and will help to spread abroad a greater knowledge of our thriving village."

Plaster model, designed and created by Edward Pausch, of the Washington Equestrian Monument

The webs between the horse's legs and between its tail and its body would be left in place to ensure its structural integrity during shipment. The statue, ready for shipment, is in the statue cutters' shed of the Smith Granite Company.

Finished monument in Allegheny Commons Park in Pittsburgh, PA. The webbing has been cut away but the column supporting the horse's weight remains.

Angelo and Columbus Zerbarini
(1852 – 1904: 1859 – 1921), Statue Cutters

Little did Angelo's father and uncle know in 1865 when they chose the thirteen-year-old to accompany them from Italy to New York that he and his brother Columbus would be among their new country's outstanding statue cutters. While attending night school to learn English in order to serve as the men's translator, Angelo found a job in a stonecutting concern where he vowed to learn to carve granite the way his father carved wood for furniture details.

Susequently, the rest of the family arrived and Columbus also set about to learn stone-carving. The brothers soon received job offers from the New England Granite Works which was working on embellishments to the Connecticut capitol. Here they worked for several years with other immigrant Italian carvers and, later, when Batterson, head of New England Granite Works, transferred them to the Westerly branch in 1881, they referred to themselves as the "Capitol Gang." Included in this close-knit group were Daniel Malnati, John Galli, Fotunato Zangrandi, Frank Baldi, Charles Lena and James Pollette. After buying houses for their families on Summer Street, the brothers left Batterson and went to the Smith Granite Company.

Here they often worked as a team on such monuments as The Great Equestrian. As the demand for great monuments diminished at the turn of the century, they turned to private memorials such as the Stephen Wilcox stone in River Bend Cemetery. About 1900, Angelo's health began to decline due to silicosis, forcing him to leave Smith Granite Company. He died at age 51.

From 1905 on, Columbus would complete a set of monuments to which others could only aspire. As a true craftsman, he was fanatic about his tools. Only Jeremiah Healy, the most exacting blacksmith of them all, could properly temper the scores of varying chisels, and only his favorite toolboy, Dick Mitchell, could carry them to him each day. He executed the Soldiers and Sailors Monument in Elizabeth, NJ, and many private memorials. In River Bend Cemetery, the Graf monument is an impressive figure and cross, and the

Each day Mrs. Loveland, who commissioned the ailing Angelo Zerbarini to carve this memorial, sent a cab to the statue cutter's home to take him to and from the Joseph Newall sheds where he worked on this statue. "The Angel of Peace," a beautiful tribute to its carver struggling to work with diminishing strength, faces the north entrance of River Bend Cemetery.

Charles B. Coon stone of a young woman in a flowing gown holding an hourglass is lovely.

Columbus Zebarini, highly respected, was elected as the first Italian-American on the Westerly Town Council in 1919.

Together the brothers left a legacy of art, skill, and devotion to craft which moves us still.

Columbus Zerbarini, 1859 – 1921

DeRocchi monument River Bend Cemetery. John DeRocchi, statue cutter, worked on his own monument; Columbus Zerbarini, believed to be the man in this photograph, finished the statue. The story is that DeRocchi's wife would not let him smoke in the house so, although they cut stone all day, friends John DeRocchi, and Mansuetto Comolli would gather to smoke, talk and cut this stone in a chicken coop on the corner of John Street Extension and Granite Street.

Carved by Columbus Zerbarini for his son Harry who died the same year as Angelo, this handsome piece of white granite with a beveled surface features an unrolled scroll upon which rests a skillfully tooled stalk of lilies which entwines about a rope and an anchor. The protruding stamen of the lily and the lifelike rope and anchor ring are a tribute to his extraordinary skills.

Columbus Zerbarini carved his own family's stone which is near the Babcock mound at River Bend. The young woman stands before an ivy-covered cross. At her side is perched an owl as a symbol that "death comes in the night."

Joseph Gervasini (1877 – 1949), Statue Cutter
by Anne Gervasini Liguori, granddaughter of Joseph Gervasini

Joseph Gervasini arrived at Ellis Island on April 14, 1901 at age 24. The ship manifest identified him as a sculptor who had begun his apprenticeship ten years earlier in the small Italian city of Varese, in the Lombardy region, between Milan and Como. By the time of his death 48 years later, he was one of the best known granite carvers in the eastern United States and his works were located throughout the country.

Shortly after arriving in Westerly, Gervasini married Caroline Favero and commenced raising a large family at his 48 Oak Street homestead abutting the Joseph Coduri Granite Company and participating in the civic, religious and social activities of Westerly. This home became a place where other Italian-Americans were welcomed when they sought assistance in assimilation or other help. He relaxed from the intensity of his work by listening to opera.

He was a founder and secretary of the local Sons of Italy lodge, a founder of the Westerly Bocce Club, a member of the Our Lady of Mount Carmel Society at the Church of the Immaculate Conception, a member of the local stonecutters union and a friend and supporter of John O. Pastore, the first Rhode Island governor and first United States Senator of Italian-American heritage. After his retirement, he served on the Columbus Monument Committee and watched his children follow their father's civic and religious traditions.

Joseph Coduri Granite Company carvers, (l to r) Joseph Gervasini, John Milby, and unknown, in a posed picture, putting the finishing touches on the angel statue for the Samuel Maynard monument destined for the Forest Hill Cemetery in Utica, NY. The granite was supplied by the Sullivan Granite Company.

Gervasini family circa 1940: (l-r) Eugene, Marion, Joseph, Jr., Caroline, Arthur, Caroline, Joseph, Albert, Olga

The McGuill monument, Springfield, MA. On March 19, 1931 *The Westerly Sun* reported that the Joseph Coduri Granite Company had shipped "one of the most beautiful monuments ever produced in Westerly." The blue-white Westerly granite monument for the McGuill family is 12 feet long and 7 feet high and includes "a bas relief carving of Christ in his mother's arms after being taken down from the Cross." The article praised this carving which Gervasini produced in four months as "an exceptional . . . artistic work, with figures being realistic and lifelike in every detail" and one of his "many fine pieces of work."

Monti angel carved by Gervasini in River Bend Cemetery. The sole remaining Westerly carver, Richard Comolli, describes Gervasini as having "the finest hand," saying that "if you run your hands along the angel wings on the rear of the piece, you experience the softness of feathers despite the medium actually being granite. This is a testament to both him and the quality of Westerly granite. Westerly granite is hard with only a small amount of mica, which in the hand of Mr. Gervasini allowed him to create the finest details." Unfortunately, the angel's arm has been broken.

Joseph Recchia (1855 – early 1950's), Carver

As told by Melanie Waters Degler, great granddaughter of Joseph Recchia

When Tizana Waters moved to Dunn's Corners with her new husband Andrew Waters in 1920 from her home in Westerly, she brought with her slips from her father's rose bushes which he dearly loved. Even though one of them, Dr. Van Fleet, lives on next to the farmhouse, her father, carver Joseph Recchia, wanted to make sure that his passion for roses lived on.

In 1904, he carved a rose out of granite and kept it safe under a glass case on the counter in the family store located at 85 Granite Street (now D'Angelo's) except for a period of time when the rose was displayed at the Westerly Public Library. The store was located below the family living quarters and Celina Recchia, Joseph's wife, and his daughters ran the store which catered to the quarry workers in the early 1900's. It sold dry goods, gloves for the workers, children's clothing, cigarettes, cigars and special tobaccos cut by Joseph himself who was an avid pipe smoker. Celina would ride the train to Providence to order goods for the store and used her dressmaking trade to make the work aprons used by the stonecutters and carvers at Smith Granite Company.

Recchia, born in 1855, had immigrated with his French wife in 1883 from northern Italy, and settled on Ledward Avenue in a large boarding house that was near the water tank across from the Smith Quarry and began working at Smith Granite Company as a carver. He molded his designs in plastaline modeling clay before beginning to carve them. Gene Waters, Joseph Recchia's grandson, now 98, can remember playing, along with his brother Hugo, with the modeling clay after Joseph was finished with it.

Between 1891 and 1908, Recchia carved at least 57 monuments which can be seen in many different cemeteries including River Bend. One might think, however, that the rose he carved was his favorite. When he died, the rose went to his daughter Tizana and was kept protected under glass on the table in the front sitting room of her home on Woody Hill Road. Melanie Degler, Recchia's great

granddaughter, remembers that, when she was a child, the rose sat on a shelf and the children were not allowed to touch or play with it. When Tizana's husband Andrew died in 1966, the rose was placed on their headstone at River Bend by Richard Comolli. Recchia's love for family, carving, and roses will live forever.

left: Joseph Recchia, smoking his beloved pipe, on the steps of the Recchia store/home opposite the Smith company store on Granite Street.

below: The rose, carved by Joseph Recchia in 1904, is now mounted on the headstone of his daughter Tizana Waters and her husband Andrew.

James W. Pollette (1848 – 1906), Statue Cutter

Little is known about James Pollette except for his exceptional skill and his prolific output. He worked for both New England Granite Works and Smith Granite Company with over 40 documented statues produced while he was working for Smith. He lived on 31 School Street.

James Pollette carved an exceptionally fine cherub for his own gravestone in River Bend Cemetery.

The 13th Massachusetts Volunteers monument in Gettysburg National Military Park was carved by Pollette from Westerly blue granite while he was working at the Smith Granite Company. The contract price was $1800 in 1885.

THE ANTIETAM SOLDIER: A GREAT CIVIL WAR MONUMENT

"Old Simon," as he is known in Sharpsburg, MD where he stands in the Antietam National Cemetery, or "The Antietam Soldier," as he is known in Westerly, is well-traveled and has an exciting history. We do not know who the model was for this Union army infantryman, but we do know that he is wearing a cavalryman's great coat rather than the infantryman's version. Called by some "the best-looking article of clothing of the War," the cape gives a much more dramatic flair than just the standing collar of the infantryman. The muzzle-loaded rifled musket that was used as a model for this statue and many of the Civil War statues produced in Westerly has survived and is owned by the Babcock-Smith House Museum.

Cut by James Pollette and Joseph Bedford who worked for the New England Granite Works, the colossal statue began life in Westerly. The monument, made up of 27 pieces, is 44 feet-7 inches tall, weighs 250 tons, and cost more than $32,000 in the 1870's. The soldier alone, made up of two pieces joined at the waist, is 21 1/2 feet tall and weighs about 30 tons.

James Pollette is on the ladder in front of the statue on the site of the Batterson Quarry on Ledward Avenue where it was erected for approval. Joseph Bedford, the other statue cutter, is not shown.

The pieces of the "Private Soldier" monument, as it is also known, were shipped to and assembled at the gateway of the Centennial Exposition in Philadelphia, PA in 1876. It was then disassembled and started its journey to Sharpsburg, but the top half of the soldier fell into the river at Washington, DC where it spent several months under water. When it was retrieved, it was transported on the C&O Canal and dragged by using huge, wooden rollers through Sharpsburg where it was erected on a small hill in the center of the cemetery. It was dedicated on September 17, 1880 and even today dominates the whole cemetery.

A plaster model of the Antietam soldier, one third as tall as the finished statue, is standing on the left in this picture of the statue cutter's shed of the New England Granite Works. Pollette, the statue cutter, is the third man from the right in the dark vest in front of the model of the woman. In the foreground is the plaster cast for another Civil War monument.

The colossal "Antietam Soldier" and its smaller model at the New England Granite Works

Believed to be Carl Conrads, sculptor, with the head of the Antietam Soldier.

The "Private Soldier" monument was exhibited at the entrance to the Centennial Exposition in Philadelphia, PA in 1876.

A crowd gathered with their umbrellas for the dedication of the "Private Soldier" monument on September 17, 1880 .
Note the size of the flags draping the statue compared to the people in the foreground.

The "Antietam Soldier," a Union infantryman, faces homeward to the North in Antietam National Battlefield, Sharpsburg, MD.

STONE CHIPS

Stonington Mirror. May 11, 1876. PAWCATUCK GLEANINGS – The Smith Granite Co. have commenced shipping stone for the new Rhode Island state prison. They don't intend to furnish it with any inmates, but the other granite yards in this vicinity expect to make up that deficiency.

Stonington Mirror. Jan. 31, 1877. WESTERLY WHISPERINGS . . . The New England Granite Works are now employing 250 to 275 hands, and are in a prosperous condition under the successful direction of Mr. James Gourlay, a gentleman eminently qualified for his responsible duties. Mr. Gourlay has been with this company for eight years, for the last four or five years as superintendent, and what he does not know about the granite industry evidently is not worth knowing. During the year 1877 the company shipped 200 monuments, and intend to increase that number the present year.

Stonington Mirror. Oct. 11, 1877. The granite pit at the Smith Granite Works, is now some 600 ft. across the mouth of the chasm, and is being extended southward. The granite in that direction improves in quality. This immense cavity represents a large amount of labor and wealth for Westerly, while the artistic work sent wide over the land has given us a well earned and extended renown.

Stonington Mirror. Oct. 2, 1880. BOROUGH BREVITIES . . . Work at the Anguilla quarry is soon to be resumed under the direction of lawyer Hull as Trustee. There are several monuments at this quarry in an unfinished state, which will be at once completed and the money received for them used in liquidating the debts due the workmen, etc. It will be remembered that quite recently a large granite tomb cut by Maxwell was totally lost by the burning of the schooner E.W. Babcock, of Westerly, on which it was being shipped to New York, and that loss caused a stoppage of the works at Anguilla. We hope the quarry will be able to resume again on a permanent basis.

Stonington Mirror. Nov. 28, 1878. WESTERLY WHISPERINGS . . . The Smith Granite Co. have work enough ahead to carry their labors into February next. During the past few days, twenty thousand "pavers" have been shipped by rail to Providence, while thirty thousand more are to be forwarded inside of the two coming weeks. At Batterson's more men have been discharged, but there are many hundred laborers still at work. Many of the first class workmen who have left the above quarry, have resumed work at the Smith Granite Co. We are informed that in the paver line enough cannot be obtained as ordered from city to city.

Stonington Mirror. April 24, 1879. WESTERLY WHISPERINGS . . . The Smith Granite Co., of Westerly, Burdick & Smith agents, have contracted with the heirs of Theodore D. Palmer to erect on their family lot in the cemetery a white granite monument of quite large proportions. We understand for design and finish it will probably surpass any monumental work yet placed there. The widespread reputation of that company for a high order of work ensures for them a goodly share of patronage.

WESTERLY GRANITE WORKERS

This list of nearly 2600 names of men and women who were part of Westerly's granite industry is as complete as we were able to make it and we acknowledge that names may still be missing. We took names from existing lists, city directories, granite company books, historical accounts, military records, issues of the *Narragansett Weekly* and *The Stonington Mirror* and the many people who gave us names. We urge you to contact us with any omissions.

Abbiarte, Frank
Abbiati, Alessandro
Abbiati, Constantine
Abbiati, Frank
Abbiati, Joseph
Abbiati, Louis
Abosso, Joseph
Ackerly, William
Ackley, William
Acolino, Alfonzo
Acolinco, Alfonso
Adan, John
Ademare, John
Ahearn, John E.
Ahearn, Michael
Ahearn, Patrick
Ahern, Alexander
Ahern, John
Ahern, John A.
Ahern, John E.
Ahern, John M.
Ahern, John P.
Ahern, Joseph
Ahern, Joseph H.
Ahern, Michael
Ahern, Patrick
Ahern, Thomas
Ahern, Thomas W.
Ahlstedt, Olaf
Ahuli, Alphonzo
Aiken, Alexander
Aiken, David
Aiken, George
Aiken, James
Aiken, John
Aiken, Robert

Aimetti, Mario
Aitken, Alexander
Aitken, David
Aitken, James
Aitken, John
Albemont, Samuel
Alexander, Samuel
Alfano, D.
Alfano, G.
Algier, Santo
Algeria, Antone
Algiera, Dominink
Algiere, Angelo
Algiere, Ernest
Algiere, John R.
Algiere, Santo
Allan, Alexander G.
Allen, Alexander
Allen, Allen
Allen, Edward
Allen, Herbert G.
Allen, William
Allen, William M.
Allesio, Neri
Alleson, Samuel
Allisin, Samuel A.
Allison, John
Allison, Samuel
Allyn, George
Aloni, John
Aloni, Patsey
Alonzo, Fred
Altimari, Giovanni
Amadora, Lugi
Ambriani, Natali
Ambrosini, G.

Ambrosini, Natale
Ambuami, M.
Anderson, Alfred
Anderson, Andrew (Andy)
Anderson, August
Anderson, Charles
Anderson, John C.
Anderson, Nestor
Anderson, Oscar
Anderson, William
Andrews, Alvin
Angelo, R.
Ansonio, Pasetta
Antonio, Geogia
Archangeli, Leo
Archie, Adam
Archie, David
Archie, James C.
Archie, Joseph
Archie, William
Argia, Francesco
Arsia, Francesco
Armenio, Annabale
Armstrong, Lednard
Arsenault, Larodia J.
Arsia, Francesco
Ashworth, Robert
Auld, Andrew
Auld, William McK.
Austen, Charles P.
Austen, William
Austin, Alexander
Austin, Charles
Austin, George
Austin, Matthew S.
Austin, William B.

Auston, Alexander
Autken, David
Autry, Curtis F.
Autrey, Samuel
Ayers, Francis D.
Babcock, Edward H.
Babcock, Edwin
Babcock, J. Alonzo
Babcock, J. Frank
Babone, Sal
Baggs, Milton
Bagley, Edward
Baird, David
Baird, Harry A.
Bailey, George
Bailey, Samuel
Baker, Oliver
Baldi, Eugene
Baldi, Frank
Baldi, James
Ballato,John
Balloni, Peter
Banaman, Robert
Bantella, S.
Baratti, A.P.
Barber, Angus
Barber, Erastns W.
Barber, Frank.
Barber, G.H.
Barber, Horace G.
Barber, Horace Q.
Barber, James M.
Barber, Thomas
Barbone, Albert
Barbone, Joseph
Barbone, Salvatore
Barker, Ludlow O.
Barnei, Peter
Barnes, Burt
Barnes, Clement
Barnes, Robert
Barnicoat, Fred
Barnicoat, Harry S.
Barnicoat, Henry
Barnicus, Frederick
Barnsfield, Maurice E.
Barr, Robert
Barratta, A. D.
Barrus, James Alexander
Barzicut, James
Batterson, H. R.
Batterson, James B.
Batterson, James G.

Batterson, James G., Jr.
Battislio, Molenari
Battolino, Antonio
Baum, Alexander
Beanchi, Carlo
Beanchi, Charles
Beanchi, John
Beanchi, Levi
Beanchi, Riccardo
Beason, William
Beattie, Albert
Beattie, Alexander
Beattie, Archie
Beattie, Francis
Beattie, Frank
Beattie, William
Beck, Walter E.
Beckwith, Frank
Beckwith, Orrin
Beebe, Richard
Beddones, Joseph
Bedford, Joseph .
Bell, Alexander
Bell, James
Bell, James, Jr.
Bell, Peter
Bell, Thomas
Bell, William (Billy)
Bell, William J.
Bell, William J., Jr.
Bellucci, L.
Bennett, Charles E.
Bennett, Thomas
Bennett, Thomas C.
Bennett, Thomas J.
Bentlt, John
Benvenuto, Natel
Benzie, James
Benzie, James S.
Beradinelli, Peter S.
Berelle, Frank
Berg, Klasse Edward
Bergonzi, Luigi
Berkley, Michael
Berkley, Thomas
Bermoiscuni, Ambragio
Bernasconi, Ambrogio
Bernasconi, Abrose
Bernasconi, Arthur
Bernasconi, Augusto
Bernasconi, Frank
Bernasconi, Jacoe
Bernasconi, Joseph

Bessett, Alex
Bewzie, James
Bezzie, Gerome
Bianchi, Ambrose
Bianchi, G.
Bianchi, Charles
Bianchi, Frank
Bianchi, Gaetano
Bianchi, John
Bianchi, Joseph
Bianchi, Louis
Bianchi, Riccardo
Bigelow, Charles
Bigini, Charles
Bigini, Charles 2nd
Bigini, Frank
Bigini, Henry
Bishop, George W.
Bishop, James
Bishop, Thomas
Bishop, William
Bisset, Alexander
Bisset, Alexander, Jr.
Bisset, Alexander, Sr.
Biswurm, John V.
Bizzi, Brondino
Black, James
Black, John
Black, Theodore E.
Blake, Alexander M.
Blake, Charles
Blake, Frank
Blake, George
Blake, James
Blake, Norman
Blake, William
Bliven, Charles
Bliven, Frank
Bliven, Frank, Sr.
Bliven, George H.
Bliven, George W.
Bliven, Joseph F.
Bliven, Mark E.
Bliven, Percy E.
Bliven, Samuel
Blynn, Michael
Boeglin, Barry
Boeglin, Jesse
Bogan, John
Boletti, Frank
Bonar, James
Bonar, Robert
Bonar, William

Bonner, Donald R.
Bonner, James
Bonner, James, Jr.
Bonner, Robert
Bonner, William
Bontella, S.
Bonvenuto, John
Bonvenuto, Natale
Booth, Ezekiel
Booth, Frank. G.
Booth, George
Booth, James W.
Booth, John S.
Booth, Morton
Booth, W. A.
Borden, George
Bossi, Cardoa
Bossi, Slavadiri
Bothwell, James
Bottenelli, David
Bottenelli, Ededio
Bottenelli, Frank
Bottenelli, Joseph
Bottinelli, Agednio
Bottinelli, Ambrosio
Bottinelli, Ausano
Bottinelli, B. E
Bottinelli, Bartista
Bottinelli, Batista
Bottinelli, David
Bottinelli, Joseph
Bottinelli, Leno
Bottinelli, Luigi
Bottinelli, Natali
Bottinelli, Paul
Bottinelli, Peter
Bouton, D. L.
Bowden, Michael
Bowen, Forest
Bozella, James
Brackley, Michael
Brackley, Richard
Branca, Louis
Branian, Michael
Bransfield, Cornelius
Bransfield, John
Bransfield, Maurice
Bransfield, Maurice, Jr.
Bransfield, Peter
Bransfield, Patrick
Bransfield, William
Bransfield, W. P.
Bray, John H.

Bray, Michael
Bray, Owen P.
Brennan, Michael
Brewer, Edward A.
Briady, Thomas
Bridge, Amos D.
Briggs, Arthur E.
Briggs, Charles A.
Briggs, Frank
Briggs, Isaac S.
Brightman, Charles
Brightman, Frank T.
Brico, Herman
Brines, John
Brines, John Francis
Brines, John, Jr.
Brines, John, Sr.
Brines, Richard
Brines, William
Brissin, John
Broadfoot, James T.
Broadfoot, John
Broadfoot, Thomas
Broadie, Peter
Broady, Thomas
Broccolo, Joseph
Broccolo, Tony
Brodie, Peter
Briody, John E.
Broggie, Angelo
Broggini, Frank
Broggini, Henry
Boggini, James
Broggini, John
Broggini, Joseph
Broggini, Louis
Brooks, Henry
Brooks, Henry F.
Brown, Amos P.
Brown, Avery
Brown, Daniel
Brown, David
Brown, Dorothy
Brown, Edward C.
Brown, Everett
Brown, Grover C.
Brown, James
Brown, John
Brown, Joseph
Brown, P.
Brown, Thomas
Brown, W.
Brown, William

Brucker, Frank
Budington, John
Bruner, Joseph
Bruner, P.
Brunie, William
Bruno, Carmine
Bruno, Charles
Brusa, Angelo
Brusa, Constantine
Brusi, Angelo
Btanchi, Frank
Buchanan, James
Buchanan, Robert G.
Buck, Charles A.
Bucklin, Harry
Buddington, John W.
Budlong, Joseph
Bunaldi, Charles
Bunovista, M.
Buonavitte, Michael
Burdick, Albert
Burdick, Alfred
Burdick, Bernice
Burdick, Charles
Burdick, Clyde
Burdick, Courtland
Burdick, Edward N.
Burdick, Elisha
Burdick, Fred
Burdick, Hillyer H.
Burdick, J. Benjamin
Burdick, James B.
Burdick, John M.
Burdick, Joseph C.
Burdick, Lenardo
Burdick, Matthew S.
Burdick, Ray
Burdick, Saxten
Burdick, Seky
Burdick, Walter C.
Burdick, William (Boss) A.
Burdick, Willie R.
Burdick, Zack C.
Burk, George
Burk, Michael
Burke, Edward
Burke, James
Burke, John
Burke, Michael
Burke, Patrick
Burke, William E.
Burney, Thomas
Burney, William

Burnie, Thomas
Burnie, William.
Burns, Jim
Burns, John
Burns, Joseph
Burns, Patrick J.
Burns, Philip
Burtley, John
Burton, Everett
Butler, James
Butler, John
Butler, Richard
Buzzi, Angelo Peter
Buzzi, Harold
Buzacott, Charles
Buzzicut, James
Byron, J. J.
Byrne, Patrick
Caddy, Peter
Cadori, Charles
Caduri, Battista
Caielli, John
Caladeia, A.
Calder, John
Calder, Robert
Calder, Thomas
Calderara, Guiseppi
Calhoun, Frank
Calimen, Valdina
Calla, James
Callahan, Charles
Cameron, James
Cameron, John
Campbell, Calvin
Campbell, Hugh
Campo, Valentino
Canales, Cecilio
Canbana, James
Cantein, John Sr.
Cantelin, John Jr.
Canto, Peo
Capalbo, Frank
Capalbo, John
Capalbo, Pasquale
Capalbo, Salvario
Capizzano, Damiano
Capizzano, Domenic
Capizanno, P.
Capizzano, Patsy
Capizzano, Santo
Capizzano, Leo
Capizzano, Leonard
Capron, Alphonso

Caravatti, Joseph
Carboni, Lepio
Carchal, Michael
Card, Frank
Card, Jeremiah E.
Card, Jerry E.
Cardine, B.
Cardini, A.
Cardini, Joseph
Cardino, Martino
Cardy, Henry
Carey, Daniel
Carey, John
Cargill, John
Carilli, G.
Carlbig, C.
Carlbing, C.J.
Carley, James
Carley, John
Carlson, Carl
Carlson, Emanual
Carmichael, Albert B.
Carneron, John
Carney, Henry
Carney, John
Carney, Vincent S.
Carney, William
Carnie, Henry
Carnie, John
Carnie, Peter
Caro, Antone
Carollo, Salvatore
Carpit, Nicholas
Carrazani, Charles
Carr, James
Carr, John
Carr, William
Carrani, Giovanni
Carricio, Peter
Carrick, John
Carson, Gordon
Carson, Jack
Carson, John
Carson, Robert
Carson, Thomas
Carson, William
Carter, William
Caruen, Samuel
Carver, Arnold
Carver, Joel
Carvinoli, Salvatori
Casani, Amileari
Casani, Giovanni

Casarico, Mario
Casarico, Peter
Casey, D.
Casey, Daniel J.
Casey, James
Casey, Martin
Casey, Maurice
Casey, Morris
Casey, Patrick
Casey, William
Cassani, Amilcare
Cassani, John
Casy, Martin
Casy, William
Castignello, James
Cathcart, H.H.S.
Cato, Thomas
Catto, Antonio
Catto, C.
Catto, Charles
Catto, Frank
Catto, Jacob
Catto, James
Catto, John
Catto, Peter
Catto, Thomas
Cautelin, John, Jr.
Cautelin, John, Sr.
Cavanaugh, James
Caven, Samuel
Cavin, J.
Cealb,
Cello, Frank
Cellucci, L.
Ceranzio, Salvatore
Cerenzi, Vincenzo
Chadwick, Edwin
Chamatare, Joseph
Champian, Frederick
Champion, Fred L.
Champlin, A. Lincoln
Champlin, Arthur T.
Champlin, George H.
Champlin, Henry
Champlin, Stephen
Champlin, William
Chapman, Charles D.
Chapman, Charles P.
Chapman, F.
Chapman, George P.
Chapman, Orsemus S.
Chapman, Otis P.
Chapman, Sydney

Charles, Austin
Chase, T. H.
Chase, T. Hyde
Cherenza, Salvatore
Cherenza, Vincent
Cherenzia, James
Cherenzia. Sam
Chester, Charles
Chiappone, Andrew
Chiaradio, James
Chiaradio, "Jimmy the Horse"
Chiaradio, Vinchinzo
Chiardi, Giuseppe
Chiardino, Giuseppe
Chiardino, James
Chimento, Frank
Chingella, Frank
Chistin, M.
Chistest, Olaf
Christie, James
Church, Floyd
Church, Henry
Cilio, James
Clancy, Charles A.
Clancy, James
Clancy, John
Clancy, Joseph
Clancy, Michael J.
Clancy,Timothy
Clancy, Thomas
Clancy, William P.
Clarica, Pasqua
Claritzin, Pasquale
Clark, Charles
Clark, Donald
Clark, George H.
Clark, Samuel
Clark, William E.
Clarke, James H.
Clarke, Joshua
Clarke, Stanton
Clarke, Weeden
Clarke, Will R.
Clemens, Peter
Clemens, Thomas
Clemens, William
Cobb, Wallace H.
Cobby, William
Coccoran, Patrick
Cocks, J.
Cock(s), James
Codding, A. C.

Coduri, Albino
Coduri, Charles
Coduri, Joseph
Coduri, Joseph, Jr.
Coduri, Richard
Cofone, Peter
Cofoni, Joseph
Cohens, Leonardo
Cohoni,
Colambo, George
Colargni, Edgio
Colavigge, Egedio
Cole, John
Cole, William
Coleman, James H.
Coletti, Daniel
Collins, George
Collins, J. E.
Collins, James
Collins, John E.
Collins, John H.
Collins, Joseph H.
Collins, Michael
Collins, Robert E.
Collins, William
Collins, William 2nd
Colter, James
Colvin, John
Colvin, Peter
Colwell, Robert
Combe, A. H.
Combs, Alfred H.
Comi, Charles
Come, Peter
Commi, Ada
Commi, Antonio
Commi, Charles
Commi, James
Commi, John
Commi, Leonida
Commi, Peter
Commiskey, John
Commiskey, Michael H.
Comolli, Adam
Comolli, Charles
Comolli, Ferruccio (Frank)
Comolli, George
Comolli, Giuseppe
Comolli, Joseph
Comolli, Mansuetto
Comolli, Natale
Comolli, Radolfo
Comolli, Richard

Comolli, William
Condon, James
Congdon, Edward
Congdon, S. A.
Connell, James
Connell, John
Connell, Michael Jr.
Connell, Patrick
Connell, Robert
Connell, William
Connelly, John
Conners, James
Conners, Timothy
Connor, Andrew
Connor, Patrick
Connors, James
Connors, John
Connors, Michael
Connors, Timothy
Conrads, Carl
Conroy, John
Constantine, A.
Constantine, Ambroseni
Conti, John P.
Conway, James
Conway, John
Conway, Michael J.
Conway, Patrick
Conway, R.
Conway, William
Cook, Albert
Cook, Frank
Cook, Frank B.
Cook, Henry H.
Coon, Abiel
Coon, Aldrich
Coon, Charles H.
Coon, Charles S.
Coon, Samuel
Coon, William H.
Cooper, Alberto (Bertie)
Cooper, Bertie
Cooper, Charles
Copeland, Richard
Copeland, Thomas
Cordner, William
Coreno, Mike
Cormack, Alexander
Cormack, Donald
Cornell, Jesse
Corona, John
Corris, William
Costi, Mattie

Cotter, David
Cotter, Edward
Cotter, James W.
Cotter, John
Cottrell, Everett D.
Cottrell, George W.
Cottrell, Gordon A.
Cottrell, Gordon P.
Cottrell, W. Liance
Cottrell, Will
Cottrell, William
Couch, George H.
Couch, James
Courage, James
Cowie, George
Cox, James B.
Craddick, Bernard
Craddick, Jeremiah D.
Crafts, John
Craig, Alexander G.
Craig, Charles G.
Craig, David
Craig, James
Craig, James A.
Craig, James C.
Craig, James, Jr.
Craig, James, Sr.
Craig, William
Craig, William, Jr.
Craig, William, Sr.
Craig, William T., Sr.
Crame, James
Crandall, Alva D.
Crandall, Ed
Crandall, Everett
Crandall, Phebe J.
Cranshaw, Nicholas
Craven, Samuel
Crittenden, C. H.
Croci, Antonio
Croci, J.
Croci, Vittario
Crocci, Tony
Crocci, Victor
Crockett, Eben
Crockett, William
Crockwell, John
Cronin, P.
Cronin, Timothy
Crowley, Daniel
Crowley, James
Crowley, John
Crowley, Joseph

Crowley, Martin
Crowley, Thomas 2nd
Crowley, William
Cruickshank, Stuart
Cruickshank, Stuart Jr.
Cruickshank, William
Crumb, Alexander G.
Crumb, David
Crumb, Edward A,
Crumb, Erskine
Crumb, Franklin
Cuch, James
Cugini, Brent
Cugini, Donato (Dan)
Cugini, Gerardo (Jerry)
Culley, William
Cully, W.
Culver, Nathan
Cummisky, Michael H.
Cunningham, John
Cunningham, William
Curran, James
Curran, Michael
Curran, Richard
Currie, John
Currie, Richard
Currie, Walter S.
Curry, John
Curtin, Michael
Curtin, Minnie
Daday, Thomas
Daddone, Ralph
Dady, Thomas
Daiey, Felix
Dailey, Daniel
Dailey, William M
Dalbeattie,
Daley, Timothy
Dalton, Peter
Daly, James
Darius, James A.
Datson, Abraham
Datson, Abraham P.
Datson, Henry
Datson, James
Datson, John
Datson, Joseph
Datson, Patrick
Datson, Richard
Datson, W.
Datson, William
Daugherty, John
Davey, John

Davey, R. John
Davey, Robert
Davis, Charles
Davis, Samuel
Davis, William A.
Davy, John
Davy, Robert
Day, Patrick F.
Day, Robert P.
Day, William
Deacon, George
Dealey, David
Dean, Jeremiah
DeBartelo, James
DeBartilo, John
Debimish, John
DeFanti, Alex
DeFanti, Antonio
DeFanti, John
DeFanti, Leno
DeFanti, Lino
Delaney, John
Delfour, Theadore
Deluga, James
Denesha, Robert
DePalma, P.
DePeduzzi, P.
DePerry, Peter
DePlacido, Nicola
DeRocchi, Antone
DeRocchi, John
DeRocco, John
Devany, John
DeVillori, B.
Dey, John
DiBattista, Samuel
Dickens,
Dickens, Samuel
Dickson, Herman
Dickson, John
Diey, William
Dinwoodie, James "Ernie" Ernest
Dinwoodie, John
Dinwoodie, John Jr.
Dixon, Nathan
Dixon, Walter P.
Dodge, Jeremiah S."Jerry"
Dodds, John
Doherty, Patrick
Dolan, Edward
Dolan, George
Dolan, John

Dolan, John, Jr.
Dolan, Richard
Dolan, Thomas
Dolan, William
Doley, Nicholas
Dollery, Edward
Dollery, Philip
Dolliny, Edward
Dommioni, C
Donahue, Daniel
Donahue, David
Donahue, Jack
Donahue, James
Donahue, John
Donahue, Michael
Donahue, Patrick
Donahue, Timothy
Donason, Patrick
Doney, Joseph H.
Doney, Robert
Dongherty, John
Donnell, E. E.
Donnell, E. O.
Donohue, Daniel
Donohue, David
Donohue, John
Donohue, Michael
Donohue, Patric
Donovan, Michael
Donovan, Patrick
Donovan, Thomas
Doocey, Patrick H.
Dooley, James
Dooly, Nicholas
Doria, David
Dornan, John
Dotolo,
Doud, Thomas
Dougherty, Andrew
Dougherty, James
Dougherty, John
Dougherty, John H.
Doughtery, Partick
Douglas, A.
Douglas, Andrew
Dour, Benjamin
Doust, John
Dow, John
Dow, William
Dowd, C. M.
Dowd, Charles
Dowd, James
Dower, Alfred

Dower, Benjamin
Dower, James B.
Dower, John
Dower, Nick
Dower, Nicholas
Dower, R. J.
Dower, Richard
Dowie, Robert
Dowling, John
Down, Frederick J., Jr.
Doyle, Felix
Doyle, James
Drew, William
Driscol, Grace
Driscoll, D.
Driscoll, Dennis
Driscoll, Eugene
Driscoll, John
Driscoll, Michael F.
Driscoll, Patrick
Druscoll, D.
Ducey, Patrick
Duff, James
Duffy, Paul
Dufour, George
Dufour, Leo
Dufour, Leon
Dufour, Theodore
Duquid, Forbes B.
Duguid, John
Duguid, William
Duguid, William, Jr.
Dumerall, William
Duncan, James
Dunn, George
Dunn, John
Dunstan, Ray
Dunstan, Roy
Dunston, John
Dunston, Wesley
Durando, Michele
Dyer, J. B.
Ecclestone, C.
Ecclestone, Charles
Edgecomb, Frederick
Edmund, Andrew
Edmond, Arthur
Edmunds, John
Edwards, Charles
Edwards, Herbert
Edwards, Hubert
Edwards, John H.
Edwards, Stanley

Egan, Edward
Eitel, Warren
Eldridge, Charles F.
Elson, Amos
Elson, Jacob
Elson, Nicholas
English, James
Eronen, Kalle
Evans, John
Evans, William
Ewen, Charles
Ewen, Charles, Jr.
Ewen, John
Falciola, N.
Falck, Magnus Y.
Falco, Frank
Falcone, Arthur
Falcone, Frank
Falcone, James
Falcone, Peter
Fare, John
Farley, Michael
Farquelli, Arthur
Farrell, Andrew
Farrell, Frank
Farrell, John
Farrell, Thomas
Favro, Antione
Faverio, Antonio
Faverio, John B.
Fay, Charles
Fay, Charles H.
Fay, William
Fayerweather, Charles H.
Federeco, Dominac
Federico, Domenic
Federico, Dommico
Federico, Dominick
Feeley, Patrick
Fehmer, Albert
Feleceto, Frank
Felicetti, Francisco
Felichie, Natale
Feragolo, Carmine
Ferando, Luigi
Ferante, James
Ferguson, Daniel
Ferguson, Findlay
Ferguson, F. S.
Ferguson, John
Ferguson, William
Ferrano, Charles
Ferraro, Arthur

Ferraro, Fred
Ferraro, Joseph
Ferraro, Michael
Ferraro, Peter
Ferraro, Salvatore
Ferrigno, Nicola
Field, Henry
Fiddes, Alexander
Fiddes, James
Filpa, John
Finizio, Anunzio
Finizio, Nunzio
Finnegan, Charles W.
Finnegan, John P.
Finnegan, Patrick
Finnegan, Thomas
Fiore, Joseph
Fiore, Pasquale
Firtani, Giovanni
Fitzgerald, James
Fitzgerald, John
Ftizgerald, Michael
Fitzgerald, Walter
Fitzpatrick, John
Fitzpatrick, Mathew
Fitzsimmons, Michael
Flack, Magnus Y.
Flanigan, Thomas W.
Fletcher, Andrew
Fletcher, Archer, Jr.
Fletcher, Archer
Florence, John
Flynn, Maurice
Flynn, Michael
Fogerty, John
Foley, James
Foley, John
Foley, Laurence
Foley, Thomas
Foley, William
Fontana, Charles
Fontana, Earnest
Fontana, Nathan
Fontana, R.
Foran, Patrick
Force, Oscar
Forest, Oscar
Forley, John
Forss, Oliver
Foss, Oscar
Fox, Jack
Fox, John
Foy, Joseph

Foy, Michael
Fraizer, Alexander M/M
Fraizer, Horace M.
Frances, Henry
Franchi, R.
Francis, Absalom
Francis, Harry
Francis, Henry
Francis, Henry, Jr.
Francis, James H.
Francis, John
Francis, Thomas
Francis, William C.
Francis, William T.
Fraquelli, Arthur
Fraquelli, John
Fraser, Alexander
Fraser, Charles
Fraser, Donald
Fraser, Joseph
Frazer, Charles
Frazer, Joseph
Frazier, Charles
Frazier, Joseph
Frazier, Walter L.
Frazier, William R.
French, William R.
Fritz, Daniel
Fuge, William H.
Fuller, Edward
Fuller, Elisha W.
Fydis, James
Gaccione, Michael
Galandi, Angelo
Gall, Alexander
Gallagher, James
Gallagher, John
Gallagher, Philip
Gallagher, Phillip, Jr.
Galli, Ferruceio
Galli, John
Galli, Lodorico.
Galli, Mario
Gallow, William
Gallup, George
Gallup, Henry H.
Galuccio, Gesaro
Gambelli, G.
Gandini, Angelo
Garafolo, Patsey
Gardiner, Aveldo
Gardiner, J. Edwin
Gardiner, Rio

Garino, Charles
Garino, Tony
Garity, J.
Gattoni, Charles
Gaul, Alexander
Gavitt, Capt. Sylvester
Gavitt, Edwin P.
Gavitt, Franklin B.
Gavitt, Henry R.
Gavitt, John
Gavitt, John Jr.
Gavitt, John Sr.
Gavitt, Joseph
Gavitt, Munson W.
Gavitt, Oliver P.
Gavitt, Royal
Gavitt, Will C.
Gavitt, William W.
Gay, Edward
Geaison, Daniel
Geary, Dennis
Geary, Henry
Geary, John
Geary, John Jr.
Geary, P.
Geary, Patrick
Geary, Timothy
Geary, William
Gencarelle, Biasi
Gencarelli, Angelo
Gencarelli, Biagio
Gencarelli, Carmine
Gencarelli, George
Gentile, James
Gerola, M.
Gerry, John A.
Gerry, William J.
Gervan, John
Gervasini, Joseph
Gervasini, Victor
Gervasini, Vittorio
Gervial, Sam
Gervin, John
Ghaffari, Kam
Ghistedt, Olaf
Gianni, Carsar
Giannoni, Giovanni
Giannoni, John
Giardano, Walter
Gibson, James
Gilbert, Eugene
Gilbert, James J.
Gilbramon, Ferdinand

Gilchrist, Alex
Gilchrist, Alexander
Gilchrist, J.
Gilchrist, John
Gilchrist,"Slink" Michael Timothy
Gilligan, John
Gillvanson, Frederick
Gilpin, R.
Gingerella, Charles
Gingerelli, Angelo
Gingerelli, George
Gindic, Ledo
Giorno, Louis
Girala, Massimo
Glavin, John T.
Gomena, Frank
Gomena, John
Gomena, Joseph
Gomenia, Frank
Gomenia, Joseph
Gordon, Micky
Gorman, Frank
Gottstein, John
Gould, John
Gould, J. R.
Gourlay, Isaac
Gourlay, Jack
Gourlay, James
Gourlay, Joseph
Gourlay, Thomas
Gourley, James
Gradic, Edward
Gradilone, Angelo
Gradilone, James
Gradilone, Louis
Grant, George
Grant, James
Grant, John
Grant, Joseph
Grant, William
Grassigh, Charles
Gray, James
Grayson, Thomas
Green, Bryon D.
Greene, Byron D.
Greene, Charles W.
Greene, Robert
Greenman, Charles
Greenway, D.
Greenway, John
Greenway, Richard J.
Gregg, Alexander

Greig, Alexander
Greto, Vincent
Grey, Murray
Griffin, Frederick
Griffin, John
Griffini, J.
Griffini, John
Grignola, John
Grinola, John
Grinoli, A.
Gritta, James
Grogini, Louis
Gropelli, James
Guiliano, Louis
Gulley, William
Gully, John
Guzzani, Louis
Hadden, David
Hadden, Robert J.
Haka, August
Haley, Cornelius
Haley, Dennis
Haley, Jeremiah
Haley, Patrick
Halliday, John
Halvosa, Charles
Halvosa, Thomas
Hamilton, A.
Hamilton, Constanie
Hamilton, James
Hamilton, J. G. B.
Hamilton, James G. C.
Hanefy, Michael E.
Hanna, Turo
Hannah, Isaac
Hannah, John
Harman, Charles
Harper, Alexander
Harper, David
Harper, W.
Harrigan, Michael
Harrington,
Harris, Allen
Harrison, Hugh
Hartly, L.
Harty, Laughlin
Harty, William
Harvey, Patrick
Haven, Walter
Havens, Walter
Hawk, William
Hawke, Joseph
Hawke, Martin

Hawke, William
Hawkins, Michael
Hawkins, Samuel
Hayes, Fred
Hayes, Henry
Hayes, William
Healey, Cornelius
Healey, Dennis
Healey, Michael
Healey, Patrick
Healy, Jeremiah
Heaphy, William
Hefferman, William
Helme, David
Henderson, S.
Hendrickson, Michael
Henrickson, John
Hepburn, William
Herlihy, James
Herlihy, Michael
Hermanson, David
Hern, Michael A.
Herrin, H.
Herrin, John
Herrin, Michael
Heughan, E.
Higgs, Charles
Higgins, James
Higgins, Patrick
Higgins, Timothy
Higgins, William
Hillard, Ed
Hillard, Edward
Himes, John
Hodge, Thomas
Hogan, James
Hogg, James
Holden, Jacob
Holihan, James
Holland, Jacob
Holland, John
Holland, William H.
Holliday, John
Holliday, Patrick
Holliday, Thomas
Holliday, William
Holmes, Thomas
Holt, Joseph
Hooper, Edward
Hooper, Martin
Horgan, James
Hosken, A.
Host, Frank

Host, Mario
Howard, Thomas
Howard, William
Howe, George
Hoxie, A. E.
Hoxie, Caleb. B.
Hoxie, Ralph
Hoxsie, Chapman
Hoxsie, Perry
Hoxsie, Ralph
Huckings, R.M.
Hughes, Henry
Hughes, John
Hughes, Michael
Hughes, Walter
Hughes, William
Hunt, Frederick
Hunt, George J.
Hunter, Alfred
Hunter, George
Hutchings (Hutchins), George T.
Hutchins, George H.
Illo, Joe
Irving, George
Irwin, Alexander
Irwin, Robert G.
Irwin, Thomas
Ivers, James
Ivers, Michael L.
Ivers, Timothy
Ivers, William
Jacobs, Andrew
Jacobson, Frank
Jacobson, J.R.
Jacobson, Richard
Jalger, Charles
James, Edwin F.
James, Frank
James Fraser
James, James
James, Martin
James, Thomas
Jarvis, John
Jeffrey, James P.
Jeffrey, Peter
Jenkins, Alfred
Jenkins, John
Jenkins, Simeon
Jenkins, W. H.
Jennings, Thomas
Jerrah, Israel
Jerrah, Joseph

Jerrah, Moses
Johns, F. E.
Johns, John Bryant
John, Jones
Johnson, Barney
Johnson, Charles
Johnson, John
Johnson, John, Jr.
Johnson, Knute
Johnson, O.
Johnson, Oscar
Johnson, Robert
Johnson, Samuel M.
Johnston, Charles
Johnston, Robert
Johnstone, James
Jolly, James
Jolly, Thomas
Jones, Antoinette Coduri Salimeno
Jones, John
Jordan, Alexander
Jordan, Andrew
Jordan, Frank
Jordan, James
Jordon, William J., Jr.
Josefson, Leonard
Joyce, John
Joyce, John Jr.
Jusula, John
Kane, Patrick
Keast, Edwin
Keast, Thomas
Keast, William
Keating, H. X.
Keefe, William
Keefe, William, Jr.
Keegan, Dennis
Keegan, James
Keegan, John
Keegan, Michael
Keena, Andrew
Keena, Billy
Keena, John
Keena, William
Keenan, John
Keenan, Thomas
Keleher, Captain
Keleher, Daniel
Keleher, Edmond
Keleher, Edmund
Kelgour, Peter
Kelleher, Daniel

Kelleher, Edmund
Kelleher, Edward
Kelleher, James
Keller, Andrew
Keller, Arlene
Kelley, James
Kelley, John
Kelley, Peter
Kelliher, Daniel
Kelliher, Edward
Kelliher, Mike
Kemp, George
Kemp, George U.
Kennedy, Christopher
Kennedy, J. J.
Kennedy, James
Kennedy, John
Kennedy, William
Kenneth, Alexander
Kenneth, William D.
Kenney,
Kenyon, Ambrose
Kenyon, Ellen
Kenyon, Frank
Kenyon, Gardiner B.
Kenyon, Jerry T.
Kenyon, Perry B.
Kenyon, Ray B.
Kerr, Fred
Kescini, Nicolas
Kesell, Michael
Kessell, Nicholas
Kessell, W. H.
Kilgore, Peter
Kilgour, Peter
KilKrise
Kim, George
King, Edward
King, Edwin C.
King, Hugh
King, James T.
King, Peter
King, Peter
King, William
Kingsley, Arthur .
Kingsley, Manford O.
Kinne, D.
Kirby, William
Kirkpatrick, James
Kitchen, George
Kitchen, John
Kopp, Geirge
Koski, Oscar

Knight, James M.
LaBrech, Roderick
Lahey, Michael
Lang, James
Lang. M.
Laing, James C.
Laing, Stanley
Lanphear, Elmer
Lanphear, Ephrain
Lanphear, Jonathan
Lanphere, Everett
Lanphere, Thomas H.
Lanzzetti, Rocco
Laonido. Areangele
Larkin, Eugene S.
Larkin, Samuel E.
Larkum, Clarence
Larson, Harry
LaThrop, Jason P.
Laucetta, Rocco
Laudone, James
Lavena, Henry
Lavier, Stadler
Lawless, William
Lawrence, Albert
Lawrence, Alexander
Lawrence, Alexander, Jr.
Lawrence, John T.
Lawry, John
Lawson, Alexander
Lawton, Peter
Leary, John
Leary, Timothy F.
Ledward, Arthur J.
Ledward, Capt. Charles H.
Ledward, Charles
Ledward, George
Ledward, Henry
Ledward, James
Ledward, John
Ledward, Joseph
Ledward, William
Ledwich, John
Ledwidge, John
Lee, Russell
Legate. W .S.
Legate, Walter S.
Legnberg, A.
Lehnberg, Andrew
Leiper, Arthur
Leiper, Arthur, Jr.
Leiper, George G.
Leiper, John

Leiper, Leslie
Lemar, Alfred
Lena, Charles
Lena, Patrick
Lens, Arnold B.
Lens, Arthur B.
Lenz, Arthur B.
Leonida, A.
Lepikko, Alf
Leslie, John
Levesque, John
Lew, John
Lewis, Henry
Lewis, James
Lewis, John
Lewis, Samuel
Lewis, William
Lewis, Whitman T.
Liary, John
Libby, S. L., Esq.
Liguori, Antonio
Liguori, Joseph
Liguori, Pasquale
Lionetta, Pasquale
Lisa, Edward
Little, George
Longli, Guiseppe
Lonida, Areangeli
LoPriore, Peter
Lorte, Rosario
Low, Andrew
Lowe, Andrew
Lowery, John
Lowry, David
Lucietti, Secondo
Luigi, Olgioti
Luizi, Bossi
Luoma, William
Luzzi, Louis
Lyme, James
Lynch, Charles
Lynch, Dennis
Lynch, Francis
Lynch, James
Lynch, John H.
Lynch, Michael
Lynch, Owen
Lynch, Patrick
Lynch, Thomas
Lynch, William
MacAnichee, Gordon
MacCall, Gordon
MacCall, John

Maccki, Zechariah
Macckie, L.
MacDonald, John
Machesi, L.
MacIntyre, Patrick
Mack, Daniel
Mackenzie, John
Mackey, Thomas
MacKnight, James
MacMahon, F.
Macomber, John R.
Macomber, Joseph H.
Maggs, George
Maggs, Milton
Magni, Carlo
Mahan, Patrick
Maine, Crawford
Maine, Daniel B.
Makilaci, Carl
Malion, Frank
Mallagan, George
Mallagan, Owen
Mallon, Francis
Mallon, Frank
Mallon, John
Mallon, Patrick
Mallon, Thomas
Mallon, William
Malnati, Daniel
Malnati, Mario
Malnatti, Daniel
Malnatti, John
Malnatti, Marious
Malon, Patrick
Malone, Daniel
Manfred, Frank
Manfredi, Frank
Manfredi, Pasquale
Manfreds, Angelo
Mann, Thomas
Marazzi, Vinenzo
Marchie, L.
Marchoni, Carlo
Margan, William
Mariani, Francis
Mariani, Francisco
Marizzi, Nat
Marizzi, Natal
Marki, Zachary
Markoff, M.
Marr, Alexander
Marr, Archie
Marr, David

Marr, James.
Marr, John A.
Marr, Robert
Marr, William
Mars, James
Marsuello, L.
Martin, Alexander
Martin, Florin
Martin, Frank
Martin, Frederick L.
Martin, William S.
Martinoli, Peter
Marzoli, Carlo
Marzoli, Guiseppe
Marzoli, Joseph
Marzoli, Joseph Jr.
Marzzarelli, Angelo
Masuello, L.
Matthews, Edgar
Matson, Antti W.
Matson, Patrick
Matthews, William
Mauheri, Luigi
Maxwell,John
Maxwell, Thom
Maxwell, William
McAlister, Ronald
McAlvey, Charles
McArthur, Florence
McAvoy, John W.
McAvoy, Mortimer
McAvoy, Mourt
McAvoy, William H.
McAvoy, William H., Jr.
McCall, Alexander
McCall, Alexander, Jr.
McCall, Gorden
McCall, James
McCall, John
McCaroll, Frank
McCarthy, Florence J.
McCarthy, James
McCarthy, John
McCarthy, Thomas
McCarty, James
McCarty, John
McClafferty, James
McClennan, Findley
McColl, James
McComb, James
McCloy, William
McCormack, M.
McCormick, Michael

McCruchen, Daniel
McCruchen, John
McDonald, Alex
McDonald, Donald
McDonald, Laughlin
McDonald, Michael
McDonald, William
McDougal, William
McFarland, Alexander
McGann, Frank
McGann, John
McGaughey, William
McGaure, Frank
McGee, James
McGlynn, Patrick
McGowan, James
McGowan, John
McGrath, Charles
McGrath, Patrick
McGrath, Thomas J.
McGrath, Timothy
McGrath, William P.
McGuire, Ed
McIntosh, Donald
McIntyre, James
McIntyer, James
McKenna, Francis
McKenna, Frank
McKenna, James
McKenna, John
McKeena, J.P.
McKeller, Duncan
McKenan, Edward
McKenzie, George
McKenzie, James
McKenzie, James Jr.
McKenzie, James, Sr.
McKenzie, John
McKenzie, William
McKernan, Edward
McKiernan, Edward
McKnight, James
McLaren, David
McLaughin, Alexander
McLean, J.
McLeavy, Charles
McLellan, A. M.
McLellan, Alexander
McMahan, James
McMahan, Patrick
McMahon, Francis J.
McMahon, James
McMahon, John

McMalion, John
McManus, James
McNabb, Peter
McNalay,
McNaley, Frank
McNalley, John
McNally, Patrick
McNamara, P.
McNamara, Patrick
McNelly,Frank
McPhail, Alexander
McPherson, Evan
McQueen, Daniel
McQuirk, James
McSweeney, William
McTurk, Robert
McTurk, Thomas
McTurk, William
McVeigh, Charles
McVeigh, Michael
McVeigh, Patrick
McVey, Charles
McVey, Patrick
Meallon, John
Means, Robert Lemuel
Mearns, Robert
Mearns, Robert, Jr.
Mearns, Robert, Sr.
Meda, Ettori
Medlin, John
Megann, John
Meggs, George
Mellon, Hart
Mellow, John
Mellow, W. John
Melloy, Charles
Melville, Charles
Melvillie, William
Mellville, John
Melvin, John
Merandi, James
Merchant, Archibald
Meriden,
Michie, Gordon
Middleton, David
Milby, John
Milne, Alexander
Milne, William
Miller, Hart
Miller, James
Miller, Robert J.
Miller, William
Mills, John

Milner, William
Mindini, Joseph
Miner, Robert
Miner, W. H.
Mitchell, Alexander
Mitchell, David
Mitchell, Davis
Mitchell, Dick
Mitchell, George
Mitchell, James
Mitchell, John
Mitchell, Richard
Mitchell, William N.
Mitchell, William N., Jr.
Mitcnie, Gordon
Mochetti, Lido R.
Molinari, G.
Molinari, John
Molinase, Baptist
Monaghan, William
Monahan, Philip
Mondina, Joseph
Monehan, John
Money, Charles
Money, Clarence E.
Montague, John
Montalto, Salvatore
Monti, Americo
Monti, Clement
Monti, Columbus
Monti, Edward
Monti, Elia
Monti, Harry
Monti, John
Monti, Stephen
Mooney,
Moore, Dennis
Moore, James
Moore, John
Moran, Frank
Moran, John
Moran, Thomas
Moranda, James
Morano, Louie
Morenzoni, Edward
Morenzoni, Frank
Morgan, George
Morgan, John
Morgan, W. A.
Morgan, William
Moriarty, Henry
Moriarty, Timothy
Morso, Charles

Morrarity, Henry E.
Morris, A.
Morris, Anthony (Tony)
Morrison, Andrew
Morrison, Hugh
Morrison, James
Morrison, John
Morrison, Patrick H.
Morrison, Richard
Morrone, Frank
Morrone, Michael
Morrone, Sylvester
Mortimer, Alexander
Mosena, Frank
Mosena, George
Mosena, Joseph
Mosier, W. H.
Mosso, Charles
Mosso, Frank
Mowny, Alanzo
Mowso, Frank
Moyle, James
Moyle, Richard
Mudge, Caleb
Mudge, William
Mukkin, James
Mulcahey, John
Mulcahy, Thomas
Muldmo, George
Mullen, James
Mullen, John B.
Mullen, Nick
Mullen, Thomas
Mullens, James
Mullins, John
Mundella, Rocco
Muraity, Henry E.
Murano. Sylvester
Muroon, Louis
Murphey, Cornelius
Murphey, John
Murphey, Michael
Murphy, C. J.
Murphy, Conrad
Murphy, Cornelius
Murphy, Dennis
Murphy, John
Murphy, John 2nd
Murphy, Joseph
Murphy, Michael
Murphy, Philip J.
Murphy, Timothy
Murray, Alexander

Murray, Anthony
Murray, Daniel
Murray, James
Murray, John
Murray, Patrick
Murray, Robert E.
Murry, Alexander
Murry, Daniel
Myllymaki, Carl
Myllymaki, K.
Nacastro, James
Nagle, David
Nagle, John S.
Nagle, Patrick
Nairn, John
Nalbandian, Ron
Nasi, William J.
Neagle, John
Neal, James
Nedler, Herbert
Needham, William N.
Negretti, John
Nelson, Alexander
Nelson, Axel
Nelville, Michael
Nester, Patrick
Nestor, Patrick
Neville, Michael
Neville, Patrick
Newall, A.
Newall, David McG.
Newall, John
Newall, Joseph
Newall, Mary Agnes
Newall, Robert
Newton, George S.
Nichols, John D.
Nichols, Simon P.
Nichols, William H.
Nichols, W. J.
Nigh, Albert
Nisler,George H.
Nocake, Peter
Noka, John
Norman, Albert
Norman James
Norman, George
Norman, Ira
Norman, J. Ira
Norman, James
Norman, William
Normandy, Joseph
Noyes, Nathan F.

Nster, Patrick
O'Brien, John
O'Briens, John
O'Conell, Louis
O'Connell, D.
O'Connell, Daniel
O'Connell, Dennis
O'Connell, James
O'Connell, Jeremiah
O'Connell, Jerome R.
O'Connell, John
O'Connell, Michael.
O'Connell, Michael, Jr.
O'Connell, Patrick
O'Connell, Thomas
O'Connell, William
O'Conners, Timothy
O'Connor, John
O'Connor, John, Jr.
O'Connor, Michael
O'Connor, Patrick
O'Connors, John
O'Connors, Timothy
O'Donnell, Edward
O'Donnell, John
Ogston, William
O'Hearn, Patrick
O'Herrin, Michael
O'Keefe, John
O'Keefe, William
O'Kelly, S. J.
O'Leary, Timothy
Olgeati, Antoni
Olgeati, Louis
Olgeatti, John
Olgiti, Louis
Oliver, Charles
Oliver, John
Oliver, William
Olliver, Charles
Olliver, John
Olliver, William
Olliver, William, Jr.
Olsen, William
O'Neal, Daniel
O'Neal, John
O'Neil, Eugene
O'Neil, Garrett
O'Neil, John
O'Neil, Patrick
O'Neil, Thomas
O'Neil, Timothy
O'Neill, Richard

Opie, Benjamin
Opie, George
Opie, Harry
Opie, James
Opie, John
Opie, Philip
Opie, Phillip
Opie, Richard
Opie, William
Oppi, Philip
Oppie, William
Oppy, Charles
Oppy, William
Osborne, Marmaduke
Osburn, M. H.
O' Sullivan, Cornelius
O' Sullivan, James
O' Sullivan, Morris
O'Tool, James
O'Toole, Joseph J.
Owens, Joseph
Owens, Thomas
Pachey, Albert
Page, Guy B.
Pagelli, Giovani
Paladino, David
Palle, Augustine
Palm, Alex
Palm, Axal
Palm, Axel
Palm, Alix
Palmer, Albert J.
Palmer, Dennison
Palmer, Grafton
Palmer, Ira H.
Palmiotti, Antonio A.
Panciera, Angelo
Panciera, Antone
Panciera, Bartolo
Panciera, Botolo
Panciera, John
Panciera, Louis
Panciera, Michael
Paramino, John F.
Parduzzi, Battisa
Parker, Edwin
Parker, Frederick
Parker, Frederick, Jr.
Parker, John Jr.
Parker, John Sr.
Parker, John T.
Parniconi, Leonardo
Parnigoni, Angelo

Parnigoni, G.
Parnigoni, Giovanni
Parnigoni, Jerome
Parnigoni, L.
Parnigoni, Leonardo
Parnigoni, Lenardo
Parrile, Bruno
Parsitti, Angelo
Parson, William
Pascoe, Andrew
Pascoe, Edwin
Pascoe, Frederick
Pascoe, George
Pascoe, Joseph
Paseti, Giovanni
Pasetti, C.
Pasetti, Cassiano
Pasetti, Columbus
Pasetti,, Ed
Pasetti, Guiseppi
Pasetti, Joseph
Passetti, Antoni
Passetti, Frank
Paterson, Peter
Patramano, Alphonzo
Patterson, Alexander
Patterson, John
Patton, Charles
Patton, Malcolm
Patton, Samuel
Patton Thomas
Patton, William
Paulena, John
Pauleria. Angelo
Pausch, Edward L.
Pavolo, Matti
Payne, J.
Payne, John
Peach, Albert
Pearce, Fred
Pearce, Ray
Pearce, William
Peckham, Arthur
Peckham, Charles
Peckham, Franklin
Peckham, Stephen R.
Peckham, William
Peduzzi, John
Peduzzi, P. D.
Pellett, Herbert Leroy
Pellett, William Palmer
Pellette, William
Pellegrini, D.

Pellegrini, Dominico
Pellegrino, D.
Pellegrino, Domenico
Penardi, Antoni
Pendleton, Albert
Pendleton, Charles L.
Pendleton, Jeremiah M.
Pendleton, William
Pengally, Agnas A., Miss
Pengelley, William
Penhall, John P.
Percy, Joseph
Percy, Nathan
Perlatti, Angelo
Perlatti, Antoni
Perlatti, J. D.
Perlatti, John G.
Perlattio, Angelio
Perletti, D.
Perlotti, Angelo
Perri, James
Perrine, Lewis
Perrone, Natale
Perry, Arthur
Peterson, Fred
Peterson, G.
Peterson, Martin
Peterson, Peter
Petre, Tizian
Phillips, Andrew
Phillips, F. W.
Phillips, Henry L.
Phillips, John
Phillips, Philip J.
Piatti, Vincenzo
Picchetti, Carlo
Piccolo, Acchele
Piccolo, Achille
Pickering, Thomas
Pierce, Adrian R.
Pierce, Adrid
Pierce, Frederick
Pierce, Roy
Pierce, Rufus
Pierce, Rufus William
Pierce, William
Pinardi,
Pinardi, Antonio
Pinardi, Charles A.
Pinardi, Enrico
Pinardi, Santino
Pinardi, Severino Rocco
Pine, James

Pingelly, William
Pignatare, Louis
Pignatare, Peter
Pinnitell, Antonio
Pirardi,Enrico
Pirie, James
Pitkaner, David
Pizzano, Charles H.
Placido, Fasso
Poberts, David
Polette, James M.
Poletti, Frank
Pollett, William
Pollette, James W.
Pollizzotto, John
Pollock Thomas
Ponaconi, Leonard
Porro, Frank
Pote, William
Potter, J. Henry
Potter, Henry
Potter, Lucius
Potter, Walter L.
Pozzi, Edward
Prace, Fred
Pratt, George
Prescott, William
Prestini, C.
Preston, Roger
Priore, Pasquale
Priore, Patrick
Pristeni, Cleudio
Priurella, Joseph
Prieulla, Joseph
Pucci, Annunziato
Pucci, Alexander
Pucci, Charles
Pucci, Frank F.
Pucci, Natale
Pucci, Patsy
Purtill, William
Qualey, William
Quinlan, Cornelius
Rae, George
Rafferty, Patrick
Rainey, Charlie
Raleigh, James
Raleigh, Master John
Raleigh, Andrew
Randall, Charles D.
Randall, John P.
Randol, Tony
Rathbun, Clifford R.

Rausch, Vic
Rauschi, Victor
Rawling, Charles
Ray, George
Read, Harry G.
Read, John
Reagan, David
Reardon, Daniel
Reardon, William W.
Recchia, Frank
Recchia, James
Recchia, Joseph
Recchia, Louse
Reid, Andrew
Reid, W. H.
Reinhalter, Joseph B.
Reinhalter, Peter
Reith, James
Rendel, Sulo
Rendel, Toney
Rendell, Sula
Rendell, Tony
Resetti, S.
Restelli, Gasper
Revase, Luigi
Rex, John
Rex, Samuel T.
Rex, William
Reynolds, Peter
Reynolds, William R.
Rezzi, Charles
Rhodes, Rodney
Rhodes, William
Ricci, Rocky
Ricci, Tony
Ricchi, L.
Rich, Dan
Richard, William
Richards, James
Richards, John
Richards, Nicholas
Richards, Samuel
Richards, William
Riche, David Jr.,
Richmond, L. D.
Richmond, Lorenzo
Richmond, William A.
Riddell, Alexander
Riddell, James
Riddle, Joseph
Riley, David
Riley, John
Riley, Thomas

Rindell, Antoni
Rindell, Solo
Riley, A.
Riley, Cornelius Aloysius
Riley, Cornelius Franklin
Riley, John
Riley, Michael
Riley, Timothy
Ritzzi, Charles
Rizutto, Francesco
Rizza, Joseph
Rizzi, Antoni
Rizzi, Charles
Rizzi, Joseph
Roach, Daniel
Roach, David
Roach, Edward
Roach, Frank
Roach, James
Roach, John
Roach, Patrick
Roach, Robert
Roach, Thomas
Roache, William
Roan, John
Roan, Robert
Roan, S. R.
Roan, Samuel
Roberts, Alexander B.
Roberts, Daniel
Robertson, Alexander
Robertson, David
Robertson, John
Robertson, Robert
Robiani, Antone
Robinson, Alexander
Robinson, Capt. Frank
Robinson, Orrin
Robinson, William
Roce, D. W.
Roch, David
Roche, David Jr,
Roche, David W.
Roche, Edward
Roche, James D.
Roche, James E.
Roche, John
Roche, Patrick
Rochi, John
Rodgers, Charles
Roediger, Richard
Roffo, Donato
Roisi, Antone

Roisi, J.
Rogers, Cady
Rogers, James
Romanelle, Al
Romanski, David
Ronaldi, Charles
Rose, A. V.
Rosetti, Angelo
Rosini, Antone
Rossi, Antone
Rossi, Augustus
Rossi, Charles
Rossi, Chris
Rossi, E.
Rossi, James
Rossi, Nicola
Rossi, Victor
Rossi, William
Rostelle,
Rosyter, Andrew
Rosyter, Charles
Roth, Frederic G.R.
Rothwell, William
Rowan, Joseph
Rowe, George
Rowe, John
Rowe, Samuel
Rowe, William
Rowland, Charles
Rowling, Charles
Rowling, R.
Royle, Joseph D.
Ruga, Cosmo
Ruschet, Victor
Rusconni, D.
Rush, Isaac
Rusich, Victor
Rusick, V.
Russell, Lee
Ryan, John
Sala, Matt
Salatone, Boutelle
Samson, George
Sampson, Oscar
Sandberg, Kenneth
Sanborn, George W.
Sander, Alexander
Sanders, Samuel
Sangster, William
Santora, Albert
Santora, Thomas
Santoro, Alberti
Santoro, Alberto

Santoro, Cataldo
Sarah, Nungatier
Sargent, Frank F.
Saunders, Allen
Saunders, Samuel
Savage, Patrick
Savage, William H.
Sawyer, A. J.
Sawyer, Adam
Sawyer, Adam, Jr.
Sawyer, Edwin
Sawyer, J. A.
Sawyer, Jack
Sawyer, John
Sawyer, John, Jr.
Sawyer, John, Sr.
Sawyer, Robert
Sawyers, Jack
Sawyers, John
Sawyers, Robert
Scaglione, Louis
Scaglione, Nunziato
Scatina, Carlo
Schackner, Joseph J.
Scharphler, John B.
Scmidt, Ernest M. C.
Scorgie, Alexander E.
Scott, Peter
Scott, Robert
Scott, William
Scott, W. J.
Segar, Charles E.
Selo, Francisco
Selvidio, Mario
Selvidio, Maxio
Serra, Charles
Serra, Joseph
Serra, Pasquale
Serra, Patrick H.
Servidio, James
Shae, Michael
Shae, Timothy
Shanks, Alexander
Shannon, W.
Shawn, Roger
Shay, Michael
Shea, Cornelius
Shea, Daniel
Shea, F.
Shea, Jeremiah
Shea, John
Shea, Martin J.
Shea, Michael

Shea, Patric
Shea, Timothy
Shea, William
Sheedy, Cornelius
Sheedy, John
Sheehan, Daniel
Sheehan, Timothy P.
Shehan, Dan
Shennan, William
Sherd, James
Sherman, Herbert
Sherman, John T.
Sherman, William
Sherry, Owen
Shery, John
Shev, John
Shortman, Frederich
Shortman, Frederick
Shugreri, Thomas
Shugrue, Daniel
Simmon, James
Simmonds, William
Simmons, James H.
Simmons, John H.
Simmons, William J.
Simone, Michael
Simonelli, Sylvia
Sinclair, William
Sisco, John
Sisson, Joshua
Skinner, William, Sr.
Slack, Charles H.
Sloan, James
Sloan, William
Slocum, Charles
Slocum, Peleg I.
Slocum, Russell L.
Slocum, Samuel
Slosberg, Michael
Slyne, David
Smalley, Henry C.
Smith, Arthur
Smith, Charles E.
Smith, Curtis M.
Smith, Dan
Smith, Duncan
Smith, Edward
Smith, Edward W.
Smith, Farquhar
Smith, Frank
Smith, Franklin C.
Smith, G.
Smith, George

Smith, Harry
Smith, Henry
Smith, Isaac
Smith, Isaac G.
Smith, Isaac G, Jr.
Smith, Isaac G. Sr.
Smith, James
Smith, John
Smith, Joseph.
Smith, Michael
Smith, Orlando
Smith, Orlando R.
Smith, Orlando R. Jr.
Smith, Peter
Smith, W.
Smith, William
Smith, William, Jr.
Smith, William, Sr.
Snasdell, John
Snow, A.
Sommers, Andrew
Spaigo, Edward
Spargo, Albert
Spargo, George
Spargo, Hugh
Spargo, William
Spargo, William Jr.
Spargo, William Sr.
Spellman, John
Spellman, Michael
Spellman, Thomas
Spencer, G.T.
Spitzana, Raphael
Splan, John
Splancie, Tad
Sposato, Angelo
Sposato, Antonio
Sposato, Carmine
Sposato, James A.
Sposato, Santo
Sposato, Salvatore
Sposato, V.
Spozzoni, Frank
Sprague, William
Stadler, Lavier
Stadler, Xavier
Stadler, Zavier
Stahle, Henry
Stahle, Henry A.
Stannard, Eli
Staplin, Henry
Steadman, C.
Steadman, Carroll V.

Steadman, Harry
Steadman, Lewis
Steadman, Louis
Steadman, Samuel K.
Stedman, Carroll V.
Stedman, R. Merton
Stella, A.
Stella, Angelo
Stenhouse, Edward
Stenhouse, George
Stenhouse, John
Stenhouse, Robert H.
Stephens, Richard
Stevens, Richard
Stevenson, William
Stewart, James
Stewart, Robert W.
Stiles, Charles H.
Still, James
Stillman, O.
Story, W.G.
Strachan, George
Strachan, James A.
Strachan, Robert
Straddler, H.
Strony, Steve
Suber, Anson
Suber, John
Sughrua, John
Sughrue,Daniel
Sughrue, Thomas
Sugrue, John
Sullivan, Bartholomew
Sullivan, Cornelius
Sullivan, Daniel
Sullivan, Florence
Sullivan, Frank A.
Sullivan Henry
Sullivan, James
Sullivan, John
Sullivan, John B.
Sullivan, John B., Jr.
Sullivan, John F.
Sullivan, John H.
Sullivan, John L.
Sullivan, John P.
Sullivan, Matthew
Sullivan, Maurice
Sullivan, Michael
Sullivan, Morris
Sullivan, Patrick
Sullivan, Patrick, Jr.
Sullivan, Timothy

Sullivan, Thomas M.
Surber, Anson
Surber, Fred
Surber, Frederick A.
Surber, John
Susena, Rinalda
Susenna, R.
Swan, Horace
Swanson, Edward
Swanson, Gustave
Sweeney, George
Sweeney, James
Sweeney, John W
Sweeney, Martin
Sweeney, Robert
Sweeny, Martin
Symes, James
Symonds, George
Symonds, James
Symonds, William
Symons, Henry J.
Symons, William
Tasca, S.
Tarrell, Frank
Tavernesto, Joseph
Tayla, Robert
Taylor, Henry
Taylor, James
Taylor, Joseph
Taylor, William
Tedeschi, Massino
Tefft, Peleg S.
Teft, Joseph
Telford, Joseph
Templeton, Joseph
Tennant, Benjamin
Terranova, Frank
Terranova, George
Terranova, Louis
Terranova, Pat
Terranova, Peter
Tetlow, Lewis
Thackery, James W.
Thackery, George W.
Thom, Alexander
Thom, John
Thom, Maxwell
Thomas, W. J.
Thompson, Adam
Thompson, Alexander
Thompson, Burden
Thompson, Frank
Thompson, John

Thompson, Joseph
Thompson, George
Thompson, Gordon
Thompson, H. Robert
Thompson, Henry
Thompson, Marcia
Thompson, Robert
Thompson, W. E.
Thornton, Richard
Thurber, Calvin
Tiff, Sylvester
Tifft, Joseph
Tillinghast, Everett
Tillinghast, Frank
Timbury, William
Timney, John
Tingley, F. F.
Tizianna, Caesar
Toesca, Maurice
Tognazzi, Louis
Tolfa, Victor
Tonelli,J.
Toole, Joseph O.
Toon, George
Torani, John
Torsea, Maurice
Tough, James
Toule, James
Toye, Rufus
Tranina, Wellington
Trant, John
Trant, John, Jr.
Travena, Henry
Travena, W.
Travenna, William
Trebisacci, Antonio
Treble, James
Trevena, John
Trevino, Wellington
Tuckerman, Newman
Tuckerman, N. P.
Turano, Francisco
Turano, Frank
Turano, George
Turano, John
Turano, Sam
Turano, Santo
Turco, Antonio
Turco, Dominick
Turco, Francesco
Turco, Frank
Turner, James
Turner, John

Turnover, Patrick
Tuscano, Charles
Tuscano, Frank
Tuscano, Louis
Tuscano, Sam
Tyler, Timothy
Underwood, William
Unkuri, Mat
Unkuri, Matti V.
Ure, John
Utter, A. J.
Van Amringe, W. B.
Vaner, Frank
Vars, William
Vaughn, Owen
Vazili, Nicholas
Veal, William John
Vebster, George
Vega, Alonzo
Vega, F. A.
Vega, J.
Vega, Joseph
Verzillo, F.
Verzillo, Frank
Verzillo, G. N.
Verzillo, Gaetano
Verzillo, Gaton
Verzillo, N
Verzillo, Nicholas
Villa, Constan
Villa, Peter
Visgilio, Nicholas
Vita, Angelo
Volpi, G
Vose, Charles
Vose, Horace
Vost, Oscar
Vuono, Annunzito
Vuono, John
Wagner, Erie
Waite, William
Walcot, Oliver
Walker, James
Walker, John
Walker, Robert
Walker, William
Wall, Richard R.
Walter, Joseph
Walters, James
Walters, Joseph
Walworth, James W.
Warmington, Elijah
Warmington, Thomas

Warmmington, Edward
Warmmington, John
Warren, F. L.
Watrous, Elias
Watson, Cyrus
Watts, Fred
Waugelin, Erik
Way, Albert
Way, John
Weaple, Patrick
Weaple, Thomas
Weaples, Thomas
Webster, Alexander
Webster, George
Webster, George, Jr.
Webster, John
Webster. William
Wedge, John
Weeple, Patrick
Weeple, Thomas
Weeks, George
Welch, Edwin R.
Welch, Martin
Welch, Thomas
Wells, Solomon P.
West, Edward
West, George W.
West, John
Westerland, John
Whalahen, Daniel
Whalahen, James
Whalen, John J.
Whaple, Patrick
Wheeler, Walter E.
White, Thomas
Whitmore, Fred B.
Whyte, Thomas
Wickland, Matthew
Wickland, Matthias
Wilcox, Albert
Wilcox, Albert R.
Wilcox, Charles D.
Wilcox, Joseph D.
Wiley, Henry
Wilkes, Jesse
William, G.
William, S.
Williams, A. F.
Williams, Albert
Williams, Frank
Williams, John
Williams, Thomas E.
Williams, William

Williams, Wills
Williams, William S.
Williamson, George
Williamson, Matt
Wills, Alfred
Wills, Henry
Wills, William
Wilson, George
Winn, Thomas
Winn, Thomas H.
Winn, Thomas, Jr.
Winslow, John
Winsor, L. O.
Wolcott, Oliver
Wood, Alexander
Woodward, Henry
Wright, John
Wright, Phineas
Wright, William
Wyness, Alexander
Yates, William
Yeats, William
York, Sauders
York, William
Young, Alexander
Young, R. A.
Zangrandi, Fortunato
Zanzi, Louis
Zanzi, Peter
Zerbarini, Angelo
Zerbarini, Columbus
Zerbarini, Columbus, Jr.
Zebrena, Columbus

One of the four large lower course stones (about 26 tons apiece) for the Andrus mausoleum in Valhalla, NY upon arrival at the cutting shed at the Joseph Coduri Granite Company in Westerly. Each of the stones required an individual freight car for transportation from the Sullivan Quarry in Bradford. Each of the four stones was longer than 38 feet, wider than 5 feet and nearly 2 feet thick.

PRODUCTION

The geologic qualities of granite make it uniquely desirable for basic practical uses
such as steps and foundations, for buildings which often combine the practical and
the aesthetic, and for fine monuments which showcase the artistry of skilled
craftsmen. Granite for these different uses most often came from different quarries
and required different skills for producing the final product. Treasured for their
aesthetic qualities, monuments, the most highly specialized product, required
specialists such as designers, salesmen, quarrymen, many craftsmen of various
skills involved in the manufacturing process, transporters, and setters. Real hazards
were a part of the lives of many of these men. Although granite was chosen
because of its relative imperviousness to degradation, our responsibility is to
maintain these treasures as best we can to reflect their original splendor.

THE RAW MATERIAL

The Geology

by Dr. James W. Hawkins, Geological Research Division, Scripps Institution of Oceanography, University of California. He is the great grandson of Frank Joseph Williams, teamster and later stonecutter for Smith Granite Company.

Rocks from the granite quarries of Westerly are well-traveled and are part of what geologists call the Avalon Terrane. They formed about 275 million years ago near present-day Morocco on the coast of Northwestern Africa. At that time, the Atlantic Ocean as we know it did not exist. About 220 million years ago the present Atlantic Ocean basin began to open when a part of Morocco split off and slowly moved west. Geologists call this large block the Avalon Terrane. Eventually it collided with ancient North America. Today, rocks of the Avalon Terrane make up much of the deep rocks of Rhode Island and southeastern Connecticut and extend north into the Maritime Provinces of Canada.

The three primary minerals in Westerly granite are: quartz (about 27%); plagioclase feldspar, or white feldspar (about 32%); and potassium feldspar, called microcline (about 35%). Microcline is usually pink, owing to a minor amount of iron, and is pink in Westerly red, but is white in Westerly blue. In addition there are minor amounts of mica in both types.

The granite is formed of relatively small crystals; most are a few millimeters in size. The small grain size indicates that the parent magma cooled relatively fast and, from that, we know that it was emplaced rather near the surface, although still down a few miles deep. The parent magmas probably came from at least 10 to 15 miles deep in the earth's mantle. The original melt, or magma, would have been at about 1200 degrees Fahrenheit. It cooled relatively quickly when it encountered older "cold" rocks near the surface and this gave rise to the uniform fine-grained texture.

The Westerly granites consist of a "blue granite" and a "red granite." The main difference between the "red" and "blue" granites is that the iron is more oxidized in the red granite. The "blue" typically has slighter smaller grain size. Westerly granite is prized for sculptures, monuments and other highly visible works of art because of the relatively fine grain size, the uniform color, and the fact that massive blocks can be quarried.

Granite of lesser quality was used for pieces not in the focal point of the monument, such as the base. Truly inferior pieces were used for foundations, curbing, and paving stones. In any case, granite is strong and can support a pressure of 22,000 pounds per square inch. It is less affected by acid rain and atmospheric pollution than other rocks.

In addition to being important for statues, Westerly granite has been very important for geologic studies. Early studies made on rock chemistry were based on hundreds of analyses of Westerly blue granite so that its composition was known with great accuracy. For example, it was agreed that the SiO_2 (silica) content was 72.22%. The other elements were known with similar accuracy.

The U.S. Geological Survey collected several hundred pounds of Westerly blue from the Smith Quarry which were crushed to a fine powder and named G-1. Small amounts were made available to geochemists to use as a granite standard. G-1 was totally used up so a second granite standard was made from another large block from Sullivan Quarry and named G-2 which had identical chemistry to G-1.

STONE CHIPS

"I have used G-2 in hundreds of rock analyses I have made. Also I have used samples of the granite in my classes. Over the more than 40 years I have been teaching geology, more than a hundred of my students have studied Westerly granite."

Dr. James W. Hawkins

Types of Westerly Granite

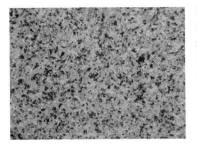

Blue (including blue-white and white)
Description: fine grain, grayish in color
Sources: holes # 1, 2, 3, and 5 on Quarry Hill and the Bradford quarries
Characteristics: easily "tooled" (hand cut)
Uses: statuary and fine carving

Light Pink
Description: very fine grain, white with pinkish tinge
Sources: hole #6 on Quarry Hill
Characteristic: very hard; difficult to cut by hand; better suited to machine finishing
Uses: monuments

Dark Pink
Description: fine grain with pronounced pink tinge
Sources: North quarries—lower (deeper) beds
Characteristic: very hard; well-suited to a polished finish
Uses: monuments

Red
Description: medium grain with decided reddish color
Sources: North quarries—upper beds; Brand's Oven
Characteristic: polishes well; machines well; cuts well by hand; breaks evenly
Uses: monuments and buildings

The Quarries

Most of the quarry holes that provided work for so many Westerly men have been reclaimed by nature, barely visible even to the experienced quarrying eye except for the piles of waste stone discarded during the granite quarrying process. On Quarry Hill alone there were six quarry holes behind and northeast of the current Granite Street Shopping Center. Five were operated by the Smith Granite Company and one belonged to the New England Granite Works, operated as Rhode Island Granite Works (formerly Batterson/Ledward Granite Company) until it was purchased by the Smith Granite Company in 1927. Hole #6 produced pink granite, the other five holes produced Westerly white and blue.

North of the railroad on Carr's Hill (now High Street) were quarries run by Macomber, Dixon (later Sweeney), Calder & Carney; all three were eventually combined to become the Smalley Quarry. This area also contained the Frazier Quarry (later Smith North Quarry) and the Gourlay "Redstone" Quarry, later operated by Batterson and eventually sold to the Smith Granite Company in 1928. Between Old Hopkinton Road and Route 3 there were seven more—Macomber, Smalley, Hunter, Chapman (after 1925—Columbia/Monti), New England and Smith (2). These "north" quarries primarily consisted of red and dark pink granite.

In Bradford (formerly Niantic) the Sullivan Granite Company eventually assumed ownership of the Newall, Crumb, Klondike and Gourlay quarries which provided "Extra Fine Grained Blue-White Westerly Granite."

There were a few very small quarries on the east side of Burden's Pond; Brand's Oven quarry and Fletcher quarry were located west of South Woody Hill Road; the Morrone quarry was south of Oak Street and west of Tower Street in the area at the end of Oaklawn Terrace; the Gavitt-Fitzgerald quarry could be found behind the former Tower Street School off Thompson Avenue. There were also many backyard quarries operated by individuals.

Across the border in Pawcatuck the Murray quarry was situated between what is now West Vine and West Arch Streets adjacent to the new Saint Michael's Cemetery. It supplied red granite for the Westerly Armory and the wall around the William D. Hoxsie estate on Elm Street – now the St. Pius X Church. The Anguilla quarry was operated north of Pequot Trail across from the intersection with Sergio Franchi Drive. It was part of the former Courtland York Farm and supplied extra dark blue granite, desirable for polished monuments.

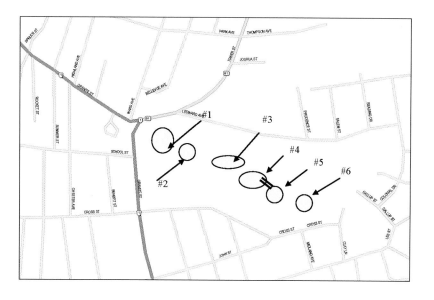

Securing chain around stone in preparation for lift

Quarry Hill

Type: white, and blue from holes 1-5; light pink from hole #6
Characteristic: suitable for monuments, statues

Hole #1
Years worked: ~1846-1936
Depth of hole: 160 feet
Smith Granite Company

Hole #2
Years worked: ~1910-1935
Depth of hole: 100 feet
Smith Granite Company

Hole #3
Years worked: ~ 1855-1927
Depth of hole: 160 feet
Ledward; New England Granite
Works (~1868); Smith Granite
Company (~1927)

Hole #4
Years worked: ~1880-1900
Depth of hole: 160 feet
Connected to Hole #5 by
underground tunnel, which carried
steam lines, power, and pump hoses
Smith Granite Company

Hole #5
Years worked: ~1910-1918
Depth of hole: 150 feet
Lost during a heavy rainstorm. Once
it filled with water, it was never
reclaimed for quarrying.
Smith Granite Company

Hole #6 - East Quarry or "Creamery"
Years worked: ~1914-1955
Depth of hole: 125 feet
Smith Granite Company

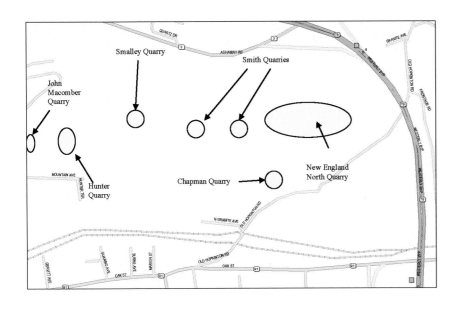

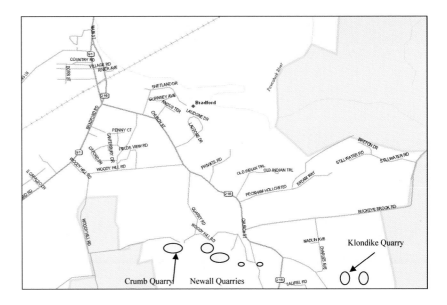

North Quarries (All North Quarry Holes)
Type: dark pink from the lower beds, red from the upper beds
Uses: good for buildings and monumental work

John Macomber Quarry
Years worked: ~1860-1900
Depth of hole: cut into the side of hill

Hunter Quarry
Years worked: ~1900-1930
Cut into side of hill

Smalley Quarry
Years worked: ~1910-?
Purchased by Smith Granite
Company (~1928); later Harold
Slosberg
Depth of hole: ~ 45 feet

Smith Granite Company
North Quarries
Originally owned by Frazier
Years worked: ~1880-1955
Depth of holes: ~150 feet

Chapman Quarry
Years worked: ~1880-1950
Cut into side of hill
Purchased by Monti (1925)

New England Quarry
Largest of the north quarries
Years worked: ~1870-1915
Started by Gourlay; later purchased
by New England Granite Company;
later still purchased by Smith Granite
Company (~ 1928)

Bradford Quarries (All Bradford Quarries)
Type: very fine grain; blue (grayish)
Uses: good for monumental carving and statue cutting

Newall Quarry (1883); later Sullivan
(1919); later Bonner (1968)
Years worked: ~ 1890's -1991
Cut into side of hill

Crumb Quarry (1852); later
Barnicoat; later Sullivan (1907);
Bottinelli (1956); Romanella (1971);
Comolli (1997)
Years worked: ~1890's – 1980's
Depth of hole: over 120 feet

Klondike Quarry
Developed by Gourlay; purchased by
Sullivan (1919)
Depth of hole ~ 100 feet
Very large area

GRANITE FOR EVERYDAY LIVING

Although the practical uses of granite, such as foundations, steps, hitching posts, gate posts and walls, do not get the attention that the monumental work does, they were the reason the industry was started and continually provided a reliable source of income. Cutting paving blocks took a special skill and providing them to major cities was a significant part of the granite business.

Industrial or heavy work involved everything from building jetties from chunks of waste stone, to providing rollers for the paper or chocolate industries, to crushing stone for airstrips and roads.

Building work, whether public, commercial or private, often represented a combination of the practical and aesthetic. Stonework, some executed by talented local masons, is evident on homes in Westerly from foundations to fireplaces, and porches to posts. New England Granite Works, the local leader in the production of granite for buildings, used red Westerly granite in such impressive buildings as the Travelers Insurance Building with its skyscraper tower in Hartford. After Smith Granite Company bought out the New England Granite Works, they, too, did some building work.

Green Hall, University of Rhode Island, Kingston, RI was built from red granite from the Brand's Oven quarry. Pictured here is the Boots Entrance, named after Mary "Boots" Herley Nardone, wife of Henry Nardone who chaired the $6.25 million restoration project, completed in 2003.

The Travelers Tower, a landmark in Hartford, CT, was built by the New England Granite Works with a 1912 addition by the Smith Granite Company. It was the seventh tallest building in the world, the first commercial building outside of New York City to rise higher than 500 feet, and the tallest building in New England for many years.

Kenyon Grist Mill

Kenyon Grist Mill in Usquepaugh, RI uses Westerly granite grinding stones that were purchased in 1886. There are two stones—the runner stone on top which turns and the bedstone which remains stationary underneath. The operators of the mill claim that the huge stones produce the exceptional texture not found in steel-ground flours and preserve the natural nutrition of the grains.

Even though Westerly granite is known for its hardness, it is sometimes necessary to sharpen the grooves in the grindstones when they are worn down. Years ago the stones had to be transported to the granite sheds. Ike Smith and fellow apprentice boy Tony Morris did this work in the late 1940's. Later, Paul E.T. Drumm, Sr., a talented machinist and grandfather of the current owner of Kenyon Grist Mill, made a tool to resurface the stone faces. The tool fits onto a jack-hammer, and two people are needed for the job which can now be done by mill employees.

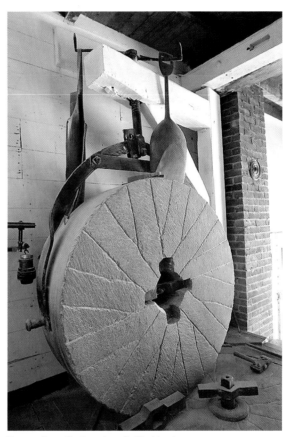

Runner stone, the top stone, is lifted to show grooves.

Millstones at Kenyon Grist Mill—the 5000-pound runner stone on top turns and the bedstone remains stationary underneath.

Granite was used for industrial purposes as well. The production of large and small rollers required granite lathes. Small rollers were made for soap machines and chocolate pulverizers. Larger rollers, such as the one pictured, made for paper-making machinery, were 30" in diameter and 21' long with a 12 3/4" hole clear through. It was quite a trick to stand one of these on end in a pit, line it up with the boring machine, bore halfway and then turn it end over end and drill the other half until boring holes met.

Today, Cherenzia Excavation, Inc. continues to crush stone on Old Hopkinton Road, the site of the North quarries, for building and landscape uses. Earlier the Sullivan Granite Company had produced crushed stone for runways in support of the World War II war effort.

PAVING CUTTERS

Because paving cutters had no shed to work in, their work was limited to good weather in spring, summer and fall. They cut pieces of granite not suitable for monumental work, because of flaws or insufficient size, into paving stones.

Their work stations were located between the quarry holes along the railroad spur to be accessible to the locomotive crane which would pick up granite from the quarry dumps and drop pieces at each work station. The paving cutter was skilled at quickly cutting the scrap into blocks of uniform size. First he would analyze the stone to determine which way it would split most easily. Then he would cut the stone along the more difficult plane into the appropriate length. Next, placing the stone between his feet, he made a notch with a chisel for the bull wedge, inserted the wedge, lifted his heavy maul waist high and swung it to

cleave the granite to the appropriate size. Paving cutters were paid by the piece. When the pieces were finished, they were piled neatly on the ground and marked with the color of the day and counted to determine the worker's pay. Speed, strength and skill in reading the granite were necessary to earn a living as a paving cutter.

Then a locomotive crane fitted with large tubs would come to each station. The paving cutter would load the stones into the tub by hand. The filled tubs were set aside until a barge was ready to be loaded. The tubs were then loaded onto a wagon in the early days or onto a truck in the later days and were taken to the foot of School Street to be loaded onto a barge. There a derrick would lift the tubs and dump the paving stones onto the barge. That derrick was a crude lifting device. The boom was moved by two men with ropes—one on each side of the boom. By pulling or releasing the ropes, they could swivel the boom from the wagon to the barge. It took many truck loads to fill the barge.

A locomotive crane used to deliver uncut granite to paving cutters and collect the finished paving blocks at the New England Granite Works circa 1910. The crane operator, just barely visible on the machine, was Ed Pasetti. Others in the photo include (front) Thomas Santoro, Jim Cherenzia, Jim Conway, (first name unknown) Barrus, George Rae, unknown and William Healey; (rear) Ernest Young, (first name unknown) Thompson, Thomas Lynch, John Rowe, Unknown, William Opie, unknown and Thomas Ahern.

CUGINI STONE MASONS

by Lisa Guerard Cugini and Betty-Jo Cugini Greene

Brothers Dan and Jerry Cugini were unparalleled stonemasons/stone-cutters. Born in San Danoto, Italy, a small town outside Rome, they started learning their trade at a very young age. Their family owned and operated a quarry and stone masonry construction business. This allowed them to learn the fine skills and techniques of Old World stone masonry construction.

Coming to the United States in 1903, the brothers practiced their craft in "Boomtown" New York City. At the turn of the century the emphasis was placed on quality which still stands today as a testament to the artisans whose level of skill goes unmatched.

Dan and Jerry were masters of cut-to-fit stone work. They excelled at the most challenging style, cutting granite to an Ashlar pattern. The Ashlar pattern was mainly seen on cathedrals, churches, and municipal buildings with their Gothic, Roman, Jack (flat), and segmental arches and fancy cut molding accent trim. This was the epitome of stone masonry, the style that required the highest level of thought and skill. Ashlar is stone cut true on all joint faces to permit very thin mortar joints; it has an interlocking pattern design and is desirable for building. Understandably, Dan and Jerry were always selected as the lead layout men, often working for months before anyone else was brought on site.

Masonry stonework was graded by how well the stone was cut to fit, regardless of the type of stone used. The criteria consisted of four levels: fine, good, fair, and rough. Their work stands today as the standard for others to emulate.

The excellence of their work can be attributed to the artisans from whom they learned their skills. The passing of their skill, vision, insight, and technique is one of the many traits that made Dan and Jerry's generation great.

Many of the houses in Westerly have walls, foundations or fireplaces that were built by "the Cugini brothers" and are not always made of just granite but also hand-cut field-stone and marble.

Beautiful ashlar on the Monti house on Tank Road. Ashlar is the use of a prepared or dressed stone with straight edges in an interlocking pattern. Every stone had to be cut and shaped to size from just a rough piece of granite.

The Cugini home on Spruce Street has unmatched stone work, inside and out, designed and built by Jerry and Dan Cugini along with friends and family who also had a love of quality granite and craftsmanship.

above left: Walls with hand pointed surface at the Elms Retirement Residence at 22 Elm Street

above right: The porch on the house at 16 Benefit Street demonstrates two types of granite used for color contrast and open work used as a contrast to the solid granite.

The house was once owned by John Cameron, a setter for the Smith Granite Company.

left: Weekapaug Bridge. Bridges made from granite could be simple structures composed of three pieces of granite, one spanning two others, or more sophisticated with pieces cut to fit as shown in this picture. The Weekapaug Bridge consists of three ashlar piers of Westerly granite pre-cut off site.—two abutment piers (one of which is pictured) and one mid-span pier.

SHELTER HARBOR'S STONEHENGE

Dr. F.J. Swanson first spent summers in a fieldstone boathouse built by Sam Nardone about 1914 in Musicolony (now Shelter Harbor). He later hired Harden Pratt to design and oversee the building of the main house which featured stone work on the inside as well as the exterior.

The granite for "Stonehenge," completed in 1925, was quarried right on the site with the exception of the two pillow stones supporting the fireplace arch, which were specially cut at the Smith Quarry. Pieces of stone are lying on the ground as the house is being constructed.

Bill Rhodes posing for picture on top of stones he has quarried on site. His rather formal attire of white shirt, tie, and vest is protected by a set of sturdy overalls.

Dr. Swanson (left) and William "Bill" Rhodes, the stone cutter and mason, with backyard quarry rig. Stone has been taken from the hole on the right.

STONE CHIPS

Narrangansett Weekly. January 10, 1890 ~ Some idea can be formed of the quarrying business, when it is known that one branch of it alone – that of paving stones—has shipped eighteen thousand tons to N.Y. during the past season, to say nothing of the large quantities sent elsewhere.

Narrangansett Weekly. October 20, 1892 ~ Stonington, CT (following a strike) The resumption of work at the Westerly Quarries has already affected business here, as two schooners were loaded with paving blocks for New York at one of our wharves during the past three days.

Narragansett Weekly. January 19, 1893 ~ The work of a paving cutter … is invariably done in the open air. It is not to the advantage of the cutter to work during severe weather, as he receives pay for the number of blocks cut, and his exposure to the cold and cutting winds might result in that dread disease, pneumonia. . . . The paving cutters [nearly one hundred] are usually young men, and unmarried, and they collect their tools and start for warmer climates in Georgia or other Southern States …. Others return to the old country, as Scotland is commonly called by them, live in leisure upon their wages earned in this country, and when the blue bird appeareth and tells them of the approach of spring they come to this country again.

Narragansett Weekly. June 13, 1872 ~ Immediately after the forced suspension of work on the Masonic Temple in New York, by the New York Stonecutters' Society, a squad of men were sent forward from Westerly, composed of three Italians who could not talk English and three apprentices who could. As one of them, while at work, was accosted by a swaggering stranger, who in a characteristic way asked the apprentice who he was working for, he replied, for "his family, himself, and J.G. Batterson," and that he had better be doing the same thing, instead of "loafing around, meddling with other people's business." The stranger proved to be the President of the New York Society.

The posts around Elm Street School (now St. Pius X School) were cut by hand circa 1865. The steps and buttresses of the east and west entrances of the school and the old Stonington Borough School are exactly the same.

CREATING A MONUMENT: AN OVERVIEW

At the height of the granite business, the emphasis had transitioned from the practical to the artistic. A great monument, however, was not the product solely of a talented sculptor and carver, but rather of a team of specialists who worked at various stages of the manufacturing process. Each specialist had his own set of tools and many faced particular hazards. Today some of the work which originally required brute strength and basic machines can be done more quickly and easily with the aid of power tools, but a team is still required.

Often a salesman or company agent helped a customer select a design from drawings done by a draftsman. Once the customer had placed the order, a record of the monument's progress was begun in the order book. Management then submitted the rough dimensions needed for the monument to the quarry foreman. The quarrymen then freed the stone, riggers lifted it, and lumpers moved it.

In the shed, stonecutters cut the stone to specified dimensions. Polishers used polishing mills to give a stone its desired appearance. Letter cutters once cut the inscription with chisels; today sandblasters, using stencils, create the design and lettering. Carvers might have added exquisite details and statue cutters carved figures from a designer's model.

Without a supporting team, the product could not have been made. Toolboys carried tools to the blacksmith who sharpened the tools the way the carvers wanted. Derrick operators and engineers moved the stone as needed. Carpenters boxed the finished product for shipment. Company farmers took care of the oxen. Teamsters drove the oxen in the early days and were replaced by railroad engineers, who drove the locomotives to the main railroad line, and who themselves were later replaced by truckers. Setters traveled to the site to erect the finished piece. The apprentices spent their time learning the trade.

Frequently, we attribute a glorious monument to the statue cutters for they had truly enviable skills, but it behooves us to remember that the finished product was the result of many men doing the very best job they could.

The plaster model of the Bowdoin College bear is in the background and the granite from which the bear will be cut is wrapped in heavy chain in the foreground with Edward W. Smith, part owner of the Smith Granite Company.

STONE CHIPS

On carving the Bowdoin Bear: "And then Comolli would carve it [using the plaster model] — from a big hunk of granite. He'd start, you know, and you'd say to yourself, 'Is he going to come out right?' By God, I'm telling you, unbelievable! Perfect! He had that arm. Every once in a while he'd put it up there to make sure the eyes were the same on that, make sure the nose or the mouth, or the chin, you know, he'd set that thing up and he could move it down where the bear's paw was."

Arthur Ferraro

opposite page: Smith Granite Company stone cutting shed in 1889. The picture was posed; the shed floors were usually covered with granite chips.

CREATING A MONUMENT
DESIGNING

When a potential buyer decided to purchase a monument, he often sought a salesman from a Westerly granite company which might have offices in New York, Philadelphia, Providence, Cleveland, and Boston as well as in Westerly.

Often the customer would have a design in mind, but salesmen were always prepared to offer ideas from their promotional material. Frequently, the salesman would have rather elaborate drawings done in chalk, pastels, or colored pencils by company draftsmen and designers. The salesman would then try to match the clients' wishes with their budgets, the requirements of the cemetery lots or public places, and the capabilities of the company. They agreed on a contract which contained both a preliminary design and the specifications for the final monument.

If the monument called for a statue, the sculptor would begin his work. First with sketches and then with clay, his design would take shape. He would sculpt a statue, often life-sized, in clay, perfecting the proportions and details. Then a mold was made and a plaster cast was poured. When the plaster was set, the mold was removed, leaving a plaster copy of the sculptor's design. Later, the statue cutter would use these casts with a pointing machine to create an exact copy in granite.

A draftsman would design the monument's other components, indicating the dimensions of the base(s), die, cap, and other "non-statue" features and lay out the lettering in life-size drawings for the inscription. Stonecutters and letter cutters would use these drawings to faithfully reproduce the design in granite.

The order books for the Smith Granite Company show detailed sketches of every component of the monument with each dimension carefully specified. The drawings are works of art in themselves and foreshadow the beauty of the finished product.

When courting a wealthy, potential client, the company would commission an artistic rendering as a powerful sales tool. This picture of the Sotter mausoleum was probably done by Alvin (?) Andrews who was a draftsman/artist for the Smith Granite Company from the 1920's to World War II.

STONE CHIPS

As a child: "One day . . . I got into the modeling shed . . . I opened the door and stepped in, you know. For some reason or another, I was all alone. And, by God, I was just inside the door and there was a guy with a goddamn gun with a spear on the end of it aimin' it right at me! You oughta seen me coming right out of the building! I never got in there again! Scared the gizzards right out of me! I was nothing but a kid, see?"

John Keena

John Coduri tells a similar story about being a young boy and scared by the plaster model of the statue of Columbus inside his family's shed.

Sculptors' studio at the Smith Granite Company which employed four sculptors: Edward Pausch, Stanley Edwards, Robert Barr, and J.G. Hamilton. By dating the works in the background, it is hypothesized that Edwards is standing and Barr is seated.

The sculptor Charles Pizzano putting final touches on the plaster model of the statue for the Columbus monument cut by Joseph Coduri Granite Company in 1949.

WE DEPRECATE DUPLICATION OF DESIGN. IT BELITTLES YOUR MEMORIAL AS WELL AS THE ONE FROM WHICH IT WAS COPIED, AND GIVES MONOTONY TO THE APPEARANCE OF OUR CEMETERIES. BY AVAILING YOURSELF OF THE SERVICES OF OUR SKILLED SPECIALISTS IN MONUMENT ARCHITECTURE, THE CHARM OF ORIGINAL AND CORRECT DESIGN IS ASSURED. WITH A KNOWLEDGE OF YOUR EXPRESSED PREFERENCE FOR A CERTAIN TYPE AND OF THE APPROPRIATION AT YOUR DISPOSAL, OUR DESIGNERS WILL VISIT YOUR CEMETERY LOT, NOTE ITS TOPOGRAPHY AND SURROUNDINGS, AND THEN PREPARE FOR YOUR CONSIDERATION DESIGNS WHICH EMBODY YOUR IDEAS AND ARE DISTINCTIVE AND ARCHITECTURALLY CORRECT. SUCH SERVICE IS ESSENTIAL IF GOOD WORK IS TO BE PRODUCED. WE DO NOT DICTATE, BUT ADVISE, AND YOU ARE NOT OBLIGATED IN ANY WAY BY CONSULTING US.

A page from a promotional booklet of the Smith Granite Company circa 1920. This page encourages the potential customer to select an original design.

This drawing by Lido R. Mochetti shows the dimensions of a proposed monument. Mochetti worked as a draftsman/designer for Presbrey-Leland, a national monument dealer, and then for Fraquelli & Brusa in the early 1940's before he was killed in WW II.

Drawing of a poppy, a design element, by Lido R. Mochetti

Plaster model of a design element for a monument cut at Bonner Monument Company

Alex Thompson (1880's – 90's) was a draftsman and designer who worked out of a New York City office and, coincidentally, married the boss's daughter, Sarah Smith, daughter of Orlando.

Calvin Thurber (1880's and 90's) worked independently and for various companies and often added the scenery behind the drawings done by draftsmen. He is the probable artist of a painting of the Gaspee which hung in the Smith Granite Company office and now hangs in the Carriage House of the Babcock-Smith House Museum.

Alex Austin (1920's – 30's) was an excellent draftsman who both designed and did working drawings.

William Bell (1930's – 50's) worked as designer/architectural engineer for the Joseph Coduri Granite Company.

Marcia Thompson (early 1960's to 1977) was a draftsman for Bonner Monument Company.

THE ORDER

A page from an order book of the Smith Granite Company reveals much about the production of the monument that Lizzie Borden ordered for her parents on July 2, 1894.

1. Top center: name of the customer

2. Upper left corner: the order number and the contract price

3. Upper right corner: sales agent

4. Beneath the red line: type of granite, order date, and cemetery

5. Left side of page: a sketch of the monument, indicating the number of separate stones required. The stones are numbered from the bottom up and the dimensions of each stone, the inscription, and the type of lettering are indicated.

6. To the right of the sketch, there are columns indicating the number of the stone, the date that the stonecutter finished, the name of the man who cut that stone, the cost of the stock and the cost of the labor. It is hard to believe that it cost only $13.23 for Tom Holliday to cut to dimension the cap at the top of the monument.

7. Beneath the list of numbered stones is a list of specialties required and the number of the stone on which the work was done, the date completed, the name of the specialist, and the cost of labor. As expected, the most expensive specialist was the carver L. Galli, who carved the #4 stone (the most elaborate stone next to the top) at a cost of $230.79.

The bottom of the page documents similar information about the four headstones. The shipping date, January 1895, is in the bottom center.

The finished monument stands in Oak Grove Cemetery, Fall River, MA, but the order books tell the complete story.

① E. L. and L. A. Borden.   ③ Vault ✓

② Order No. 195
2124

④ Statuary Granite   Ordered July 20/94 delivered and set up
Oak Grove Cemetery.

⑥
1	Nov 26	Cat Holliday	30 3	57 44
2	Oct 9	Jas Brown	30 21	73 88
3	Oct 1	Mike Burke	22 4	58 58
4	Oct 21	Jas Dower	12	13 17
5	" 10	Tom Holliday	29 9 16	13 23

⑤
A. J. BORDEN
R + P FRONT & REAR.

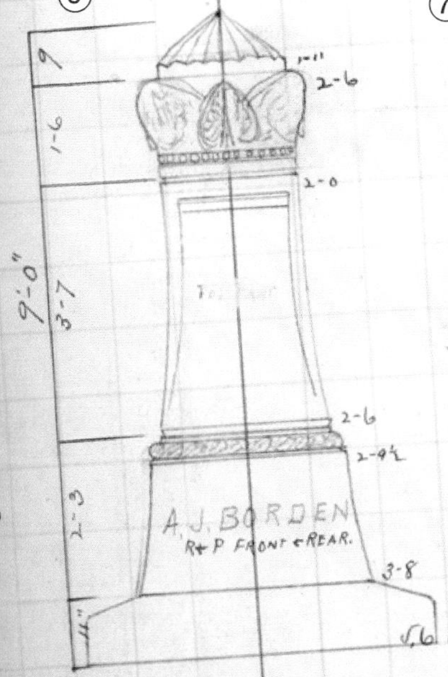

⑦
Polish 2 Nov	Geo Rae		46 7
Framer Dec	P Straddick		32 44
Carving " "	F Pollette		87 60
Panels 3 "	J D Straddick		38 75
& Ins " "	Joe Fraser		9 36
Carving 4 Jany	L Galli		230 79
Trim & Dec	Dan Kelliher		7 20

Die 2nd Trim June 4 James Blake   60 99
Panels Oct Ira Norman   39 35
& Ins " Joe Fraser   86 4

Geo d Brown   2 6   3 21

Lizzie Borden (circa 1889) Accused of killing her father and stepmother with a hatchet on August 4, 1892, Borden (1860-1927) became the subject of one of the most sensational trials in history. She was acquitted, but remains infamous in folklore.

LIZZIE BORDEN

In 1894, Lizzie Borden and her sister Emma ordered a monument for their parents. *The Fall River Herald* on January 12, 1895 reported their visit to the cemetery as the stone was being set.

"The stone was built by the Smith Granite Company and the company's workmen set it in place, under the supervision of Superintendent Morrill. Emma and Lizzie Borden, children of Andrew J. and Sarah A. Borden, visited the cemetery while the men were at work. A small knot of curious spectators was hanging about at that time. The sisters went to the cemetery in their carriage. They alighted to view the work, Lizzie glancing at the stone, and immediately re-entering the carriage. Emma viewed it critically, gave directions to the workman, and soon rejoined her sister in the carriage, leaving the cemetery at once."

The completed Borden monument and head stone.

STONE CHIPS

Stonington Mirror. May 8, 1879. WESTERLY WHISPERINGS... Perhaps to no other single industry is Westerly so much indebted for her prosperity as to the famous Rhode Island Granite Works. Started in a small way, they have steadily increased in strength and efficiency until now ranking among the finest of their class in the country. They are now running 325 men, and yet this great force is insufficient for the work under contract. Through the winter they have employed 275 men, and got off a vast amount of fine work ready for the spring shipments. For the attainment of such wonderful results over the crude and seemingly valueless rock mined out of mother earth, success is due to that master spirit, Batterson, a name that is familiar all over the civilized world in connection with fine granite and marble architecture, supplemented by the scientific corps of artistic managers in direct command. At present they have rising of a hundred monumental designs under contract to be delivered the coming fall, a portion of which are not commenced, and additional orders are accumulating daily. Below we append a brief description of a few of the more important designs. The Heath sarcophagus promises to be the most magnificent affair of the kind ever wrought at these works. The dimensions of base are 10 ft. 4 in. x 5 ft. 8 in. height of structure 11 ft. The design is Gothic, and every conception is of the most elaborate grandeur. The polish and finish will reflect the highest credit on this department of the cutter's art. Another somewhat similar but inferior structure is for the Perry family, both destined for western cemeteries. Dimensions of lower based, 10 ft. 9 in. x 7 ft. 2 in., and 1 ft. 7 in. thick, weighing 9 tons; height of structure 11 ft., to be crowned with an elegant group of statuary. The work includes carved and polished columns, capitals over die, and frieze with polished text. Total weight 30 tons; cost about $10,000. An elegant monument is under way for the late Mrs. Cross, daughter of Commodore Vanderbilt, to be erected in Woodlawn by her devoted husband, James M. Cross, Esq., of Westerly. It will tower 34 ft. high, weigh from 30 to 35 tons, and cost about $4,000. The design is Egyptian, and the drawings promise a very elaborate affair. The base is 7 ft. 5 ins. square; shaft 25 ft. high by 2 ft. 8 in. square. The Shipman monument for the West is of full Corinthian design, and lifts its crown 44 ft. above the ground. The base is 7 1/2 ft. square, on which rests a fluted column 15 1/2 ft. high by 2 ft. 7 in. square, surmounted by a really elegant and elaborately carved statue. This imposing structure will weigh some 40 tons, and will cost about $7,000. Another massive monument goes to Denver, Col., for the Cliff family. The lower base is 9 ft. square, 2 ft. high, and weighs 14 tons; die 4 1/2 ft. square, 10 ft. high and weighs 17 tons, for which a special locomotive car will be required to transport. Total height 33 ft. weight 50 to 60 tons, and costing from $8,000 to $12,000. The Dixon monument for a Western city, is 32 ft. high, weighs 30 tons, and is worth from $4,000 to $6,000. The base is 7 ft. square, shaft 6 ft. square tapering to 2 1/2 ft. at the top, and 21 ft. high. It is to be of blue granite, and in design is an Egyptian obelisk. The Rhode Island works are cutting two imposing soldiers' monuments, the largest for Wheeling W. Va., to have the enormous weight of 70 to 80 tons. It is of oblong architecture, and is 18 ft. in the pedestal, crowned by statue of Union soldier. Two other statues are to stand on either side near the base. The statues are artistically designed, and in every detail true to life in their military bearing. The die is 5 ft. square and weighs 10 tons. The cost of this graceful yet mammoth monument will be from $8,000 to $10,000, and will form a fitting tribute of the people of Wheeling to their dead soldiery. The people of Wolcottville, Conn., animated by like patriotic prompting, have contracted for a monument to commemorate the lives and virtues of their fallen Boys in Blue. The base is to be 8 ft. square, and total height of monument 18 ft. A life size statue of Union soldier crowns the whole. Cost $4,000 to $5,000. We could refer to other designs fully as grand, but this brief sketch must suffice for this occasion. The people should not fail to visit the works at this time and see for themselves these magnificent designs of artistic skill.

CREATING A MONUMENT
QUARRYING

The quarry foreman, having received the rough dimensions for each stone in the monument, then had the responsibility of finding the location in the quarry which had granite of the appropriate size and quality needed.

In the days of the first Orlando Smith, granite quarrying and cutting were rough and rugged tasks. All power originated in the muscles of man and beast; all tools were coarse and rudimentary. Drills, chisels, hammers, wedges, crowbars, picks and shovels were the tools of the trade. Iron chains were used for slings and hitches, and hemp ropes were used for hoisting. Oxen were yoked up for heavy pulling and hauling.

Granite is found in strata or layers which the quarrymen worked. In order to free a large piece of stone, a three-man team—one holding and turning a heavy drill while two others struck alternately with heavy hammers—drilled large holes that were later filled with blasting powder. To quarry smaller pieces, they split out the granite by drilling holes and driving wedges. Small holes were drilled about six inches apart along the line. A small wedge and two half-rounds were placed in each hole and the wedges driven until the stone was split. Large flat wedges were driven into the crack and into the bed underneath the stone until the stone was separated and raised enough to get a chain sling around it. The process was a great demonstration of the power of the wedge.

Steam boilers were operated on the surface and live wet steam was piped into the quarry hole to drive the pumps and drills. Later, air compressors were installed which provided the power to drive faster and bigger drills which freed more stone with less waste. One man with a pneumatic drill could drill more holes than ten men by hand.

The first derricks were shear poles—two big timbers mounted in granite socket holes, chained together at the top with guy wires on the front and rear sides. The upper hoisting blocks were hung just beneath the joined top with many parts of hemp rope run through both the top and the bottom block, which was lowered into the quarry. As a quarry hole got deeper, a wooden brow or skid-wall, was built vertically below the shear poles to protect the granite stones as they were dragged up against it. Once above the edge of the quarry hole, the rig swung away from the hole and lowered the stone onto either a wagon (small stones) or a "big wheels" rig (larger stones).

The shear pole derricks were gradually replaced by more sophisticated boom derricks which gave more flexibility in lifting the stone. The mast along with the boom could pivot using the bull wheel to reach a greater area. The end of the boom could be raised or lowered to accommodate the weight of the stone. It was a faster rig with greater capabilities.

Better and more complex hoisting engines were used first with steam power and much later with electric drives to make hoisting the granite more efficient.

STONE CHIPS

On removing large stones: "Oh, down at Sullivan's you ought to see the pieces of stone they used to get out of there. " . . . they wanted a hunk of stone . . . oh hell, as wide as this house, let's put it that way. They'd drill the holes here and line up the holes and they'd put powder in there with a cap; then they'd touch it off with a battery . . . and that powder would go "bump" and it wouldn't damage your granite if you knew what you were doing and it'd push that darn stone forward. Loosen it right off the bed and push it forward."

Patsy Capizzano

Deep layers allowed the quarrying of a large piece of granite in New England Granite Works hole.

Pump house in Smith Granite Company East quarry, circa 1921, adjacent to water collecting in the depths of the hole. In a hole lower than the water table, water had to be pumped out in order to work the quarry. After a heavy rainfall, pumps often had to be run through the night to insure quarry availability on the following morning.

Steam drill in Smith North quarry

STONE CHIPS

"We had pumps going 24 hours a day. My father's job [was to go] weekends, when no one was working, holidays. His job was to go and grease those machines. . . . They had several pumps you had to check on. If anything happened, you had to call up DeFanti, cause he was the machinist. He'd go there and find out what the problem was. Otherwise, when they went to work Monday morning, they couldn't go to the quarry. The quarry'd be full of water."

Arthur Ferraro

Shear poles and vertical, wooden skid-wall at the Smith Granite Company

Rick Jacobson, North quarry derrick engineer, operating the engines for the hoisting derrick, circa 1940

Boom derricks at Sullivan quarry

STONE CHIPS

Another method of getting stone out: A cable and derrick would be used. Railroad ties would protect the cable. Later on in the process, with the steel balls under it, "they would drill it to the size they want. Whatever they needed. You'd cut it. Just slice it off and they used to put jackhammers in the holes … because a lot of beds were awful thick up to Sullivan's. When we got through before four o'clock drilling the stones, we'd get water and fill the holes up with water. The next morning, this is in the winter now mind you, why that water would crack the stone open. So the men wouldn't have to pound their head off cracking that stone with a sledgehammer. That water used to freeze and open that stone right up."

Patsy Capizzano

QUARRYING THE HALL SHAFT

Once the order for the Hall obelisk was placed with the Smith Granite Company in 1895, the company purchased special equipment and developed operational procedures to meet the challenges of quarrying.

About fifty feet below the surface, a granite ledge large enough to quarry a piece 50' 7" long and 10' 4" high was found. The ledge was cleared of the over-burden (dirt and stone covering the chosen ledge) to make it accessible to quarrymen and their equipment. Because of the size of the stone required, blasting was eliminated as a method of quarrying, because it might result in cracks or breaks in the stone.

The following photographs from 1896 document this challenging process.

The Hall obelisk, made up of several bases, a die, and a large shaft, was simple in design, but bold because of its dramatic size. The completed monument, set in Woodlawn Cemetery in the Bronx, measured 57 feet high, the height of a five story building.

The freeing of the stone began as channels were drilled the entire length of the block to insure safe and accurate separation of the block from the ledge. These channels were cut by a large steam-drill (like the one pictured) and core-cutter (called a channel bar).

When all the channels were cut, and the block was freed from the quarry ledge, chains were wrapped around pins on the top of the stone and attached to blocks and tackles to turn the stone on its side. Piles of wooden logs were placed in front to make "pillows" for the block to land on so it would not be damaged.

After the block was turned on its side, a series of deep holes, which would assure a straight break from top to bottom, would be drilled the entire length of the block in order to split it in two lengthwise.

Once the granite block was split, one of the blocks was separated and shaped to within eighteen inches of the shaft's finished dimensions. By removing the excess granite, it became light enough (seventy-seven tons) to haul to the surface. The remaining block was cut into smaller pieces for the bases and die.

Extra large iron chains then were wound around the shaft with large pieces of wood between them and the stone shaft to prevent the chains from touching and possibly damaging the granite. It was dragged to the wooden skid-wall in preparation for lifting.

The top of the shaft was raised so it could be seen over the brow of the quarry. Hoisting continued until the shaft was at the very top of the shear.

The guys were tightened so the shear poles could not move. Then one set of guys became taut and other set fell slack as the shear poles leaned away from the edge of the quarry hole. Finally, the shaft was slowly and safely lowered to the ground.

STONE CHIPS

On life on the Chase Hill Farm: "I don't know how my father managed when we bought the farm . . . it was all brush land and swamp and he built it so that it was very well landscaped, but how he did that and work in the quarry too . . . and my sister used to go with Pa to plow the gardens, carry the lantern and lead the horse . . . and he would do that after he came home from work."

Thelma Hill Gardner

On work in the winter: "That's when my father did all the repairing, you know, a bunch of kids—their shoes need to be taken care of. You kept the shoes. You didn't go to a cobbler. And the harnesses and anything else needed to be repaired."

Hannah Hill Robinson

"I can see the quarry now. I can see the sloping granite down there and there used to be a place, one of the bluffs, they used to call 'Chain Rock.' And all the kids, boy, if they didn't jump off that, they were chicken. So I went up there and looked down off it one day. And I looked down. 'I'm chicken. I'm not going to jump off this bugger.' Some of the guys used to do one and half back gainers and everything. Crazy. Then there were women down there. The fellas used to swim in the nude. Women artists down there taking pictures, drawing pictures and drawing pictures of the boys swimmin' in the quarry."

Tony Morris

On the dangers of blasting: "It wasn't too long ago, maybe what 15 or 20 years ago, Sam Cherenzia, he used to make the holes in the stone and then use powder to blow it with a cap. Well, they blew it and the stone did come apart, but there was one hole that didn't blow, for what reason, we don't know. So he says something . . . I don't know if he started to drill it or started to dig it out. What it was I really don't know, but when he hit the point where the cap was, the thing come up and killed him right there."

More danger: "Then you get them poor guys with the sledgehammer and wedges and raise it up. [Then steel balls about four inches would be wedged in.] Well, when we got the ball under there, then we'd get five or six men . . . oh, we had a heck of a big crew. We'd get a place made in there and the whole bunch of us used to go "bump, bump" and hit it and you'd see the stone move. This particular day, oh, God, I felt sorry for that man, Bill Collins his name was. As we were doing that, the stone went ahead and he fell in between the stone and geez . . . oh, he didn't get killed, but brother, I felt he was a dead man. You see the spring of the bar threw him right in."

Patsy Capizzano

CREATING A MONUMENT
PRODUCING THE MONUMENT

Once the stone had been hoisted to the surface, it was moved by **teamsters** to the sheds for cutting. In the early days, an ox cart with high wheels, as much as twelve feet in diameter, transported it. Later a steam locomotives or trucks were used.

Cosmo Ruga's tool box. The contents of a stonecutter's tool box, located next to his banker, told a great deal about him. A large variety of tools reflected a greater proficiency.

A small high-wheel ox cart was used to move unfinished granite to the sheds. The driver backed the cart so that the wheels straddled the stone. Chains that had been laid under the stone were then connected to the cart. Using the large lever on the top of the cart, the chain was wound up until the granite was no longer resting on the ground. The oxen would then haul the cart, with the granite suspended beneath it, to the appropriate location.

Once the granite reached the sheds, a different crew of men took over. Each stone might be worked on by several different men .

A **lumper**, a man with the skills to move the heavy block of granite without causing damage, would set the stone on the banker, the stone cutter's work station.

The **stonecutter's** job was to cut the stone ultimately to the design dimensions. He used strong and heavy tools for the initial rough cutting, and finer, lighter and sharper tools for carving and lettering. His tools included his

Robert Greene, stonecutter at Bonner Monument Company, circa 1990

hand hammer, hand set, point, big chisel, small chisel, calipers, a bevel, a peen hammer and several bush hammers.

Using a system with winding blocks, a straight edge, and geometry, the stonecutter determined the planes needed. Slowly and carefully, using a pitching tool and finishing with a chisel, he cut away stone

to make sure that he had parallel edges and even corners. To check to see if the surface was exactly the same height, he put chalk on his wooden straight edge and rubbed it over the surface. The high spots would be marked with the chalk and the low spots would remain clean. Using a bush hammer on the high spots, he repeated this process until the whole bed was covered with chalk. Then he knew the entire surface was in a single plane.

A stone was set up on a wooden horse called a banker. On top of the stone are the winding blocks and straight edges which the stonecutter used to determine the plane of the surface of the stone.

Later, power tools would make the stonecutter's life easier. Pneumatic hammers were first used by the statue cutters, carvers and letter cutters and then by all cutters. Instead of stone being quarried to rough dimensions according to its final use, great chunks of stone could be removed and put into a

Stonecutters in the shed of the Joseph Coduri Granite Company circa 1930
back row, 5th from left, Charles Harman

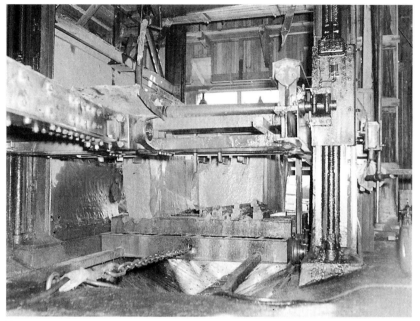

The "gang saw" drove up to eight parallel blades back and forth over the large block of granite. The blades were fed with water and steel shot until a vertical cut was actually worn down through the stone. The blades, preset to the required dimensions, would reduce the block to slabs 8, 10, or 12 inches thick.

"gang saw," which sawed it into multiple pieces. There was much less waste and a sawed face had nearly a finished surface. Later, the "carbo" and diamond circular saws were used on a high speed wheel which was guided back and forth across a stone, usually after at least one face was finished, going deeper each time. A wire saw in which a small twisted wire rope was guided across a granite block at sixty miles per hour was used for thicker stones.

Richard Comolli circa 1970 cutting raised letters with a pneumatic chisel

When the stonecutter finished his work, the lumper moved the stone to the **letter cutter's** banker. He had a full-sized drawing on tracing paper of the letters to be cut. The **draftsman** had carefully spaced the letters depending on the font and the arrangement of the letters. The letter cutter marked the center line of the stone on the letter pad and then made a thin watery coat of plaster of Paris to adhere the tracing paper to the letter pad. Using a sharp chisel, he marked the location of critical points of each letter. Cutting away all the background (in the case of raised letters), he would complete the lettering using small drills and sharp chisels. Later, small air hammers would be used to drive the cutting tools.

Today **sandblasting** is used for both lettering and some carving. Fast and inexpensive, it can produce deep and very legible letters and designs. Sandblasted carving is basically limited to low relief ornamentation. A special rubber sheet is cemented to the face of the stone, the layout of the work is transferred to the sheet, and a stencil cut out with a knife. Then the stone is placed in a booth and a blast of "sand" is blown from a nozzle by compressed air and directed into the stencil area. The sand bounces off the soft rubber surfaces, but cuts away the exposed granite surfaces. When the proper depth has been reached, the stencil is removed and all cement traces are cleaned off.

Harold Buzzi cutting a sandblast stencil in 2010

For monuments with a statue or lavish carvings, the **statue cutter** or **carver** took over after the stonecutter had removed much of the excess granite. The statue cutter or carver worked from a model, usually full-sized, which the company's **sculptors** had prepared. For the statue cutter, the model, placed horizontally, face up, was positioned next to the stone. The statue cutter studied the stone to determine how it would cut, assessing it for weaknesses which he would not want to have in a delicate area of the statue. He then marked the stone with reference points to locate the various features of the statue and roughed out the dimensions. Using a pointing machine (a framework of metal arms which could be fitted around the model to measure the relationship between given points on its surface), he transferred these measurements to the roughed-out section of stone to help him determine the correct proportions for various parts of the statue. He would repeat this process over and over for many points around the statue, turning it as required. Once he had a sufficient number of points to determine the shape of the head, face, arms, and other parts, he would use his artistic eye to cut the fine details. The stone would be turned and the process repeated for as many as sixteen to twenty times. This entire process was done with the figure lying down. Each time the statue cutter would get closer to the finished statue.

In the Smith Granite Company statue cutting shed, Charles Lena, center front, is using the pointing machine to compare the dimensions on a nearly finished statue to the plaster model lying adjacent to it.

At the next banker, Edward Fuller evaluates the rough stone to determine how best to carve the statue from the unfinished block. The model he is working from is just to the front of the rough stone.

Additional bankers are in the rear of the photograph. On the walls and shelves are plaster models used in the past and available for the future.

TOOLS
Tools to Shape the Stone

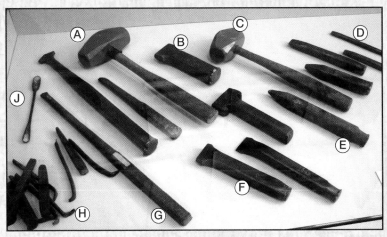

A. The 2 1/2 pound hammer was used with drills and pitching tools.

B. The pitching tool was used to take off big chips of granite from the sides.

C. The 1 pound hammer was used with points and chisels.

D. Chisels with a straight cutting edge were used to finish edges; small, fine chisels with a curved cutting edge were used for carving, statue cutting and letter cutting.

E. The point, a roughing tool, was used to approximate a surface.

F. The chipping iron was used with a straight edge to determine the finished edge.

G. Drills were used in the quarry to make holes in the stone.

H. Wedge and feathers were used in the quarry to split stone.

J. A scoop was used to remove stone dust from drill holes.

Tools to Finish the Surface

A peen hammer, a hammer with one cutting edge, was used to begin the job of finishing the surface. The entire edge hit flat against the surface in various directions to achieve a uniform surface.

A four-cut bush hammer with four edges per inch was used next. It, too, was used with its cutting edges flat against the surface and would create a somewhat smoother surface. Finer and finer bush hammers (with more and more cuts per inch) were used until the desired finish was achieved.

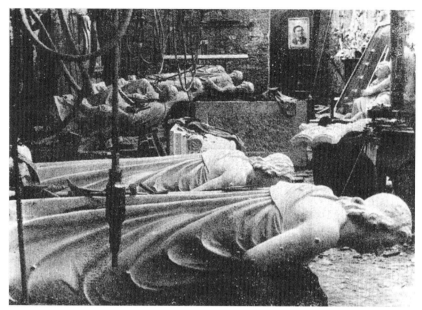

In the statue cutting shed, statues are lying adjacent to the models. A pneumatic tool hangs in the foreground.

Alex Shanks, turner, using a lathe to cut a small column at the Smith Granite Company. Note the cutting disk and air collection system. 1940's

When the statue was complete, it was put into an upright position and studied from all angles in the north light to see if there were any imperfections to be removed or areas that needed to be touched up. Of the hundreds of stone cutters employed by the Westerly granite industry, only a few were gifted enough to work as statue cutters.

Other specialists were required to produce monuments with special shapes or surfaces.

If there were columns or curved pieces to be cut, **turners** used a steel lathe. The cutting tool was a beveled steel disk mounted at an angle to the work. Because this machine produced an inordinate amount of dust, it was one of the first fitted with a dust removal system.

Polishers used an iron scroll wheel with an abrasive pad. The wheel was turned by power and moved over the granite surface by hand. In the early days, sand was used as the abrasive; later, steel shot and carborundum were used. The grinding process was wet, so that water, mud and abrasive material flew around in all directions. The final gloss, for a highly-polished surface, was brought up by using "putty powder," mostly tin oxide, under a felt wheel and run nearly dry. Small areas in tight corners were laboriously polished by hand. Round work such as columns or urns were polished on a special lathe where the work turned and the abrasive blocks were fixed.

Thomas Lynch, polisher, using the polishing mill to bring the finish to a high gloss at the Smith Granite Company circa 1940's

STONE CHIPS

"The task of stonecutter was oversimplified by an idle onlooker who stated that all that a stonecutter had to do was to knock away what was not wanted. Any cutter knew how to take care of such an idler. He aimed a few chips in the direction of such a smarty and mighty soon the onlooker departed."

Isaac G. Smith, Sr.

"The cutter also had to retain what was wanted, including all surfaces, edges and corners. A starting apprentice was carefully instructed to save the corners. The struggling beginner knocked off plenty of them but he saved them all—in a tin can he brought in to hold them."

Isaac G. Smith, Sr.

On his apprentice days: "We started cutting these rock face markers. They were 2 foot, by a foot, by 8 inches high. Of course, we'd go down and we'd knock a corner off. So the foreman would come over and he would put new lines on and instead of being 2 foot long, it was 20 inches long. Sometimes we ended up with one … only 8 inches long by 6 inches wide. [The foreman said] 'Okay, you put that right down by your tool box and every time you think you're getting pretty good, you look at that marker and remember how many [corners] you knocked off before you got there.'

One of the stories goes that an apprentice was told to 'save the corners.' So every corner he took off he threw in his tool box. He couldn't get any tools in, he got in so many corners."

Isaac G. Smith, Jr.

STONE CHIPS

Regarding the skill progression in sharpening tools: "In sharpening you graduated to the carver's tools because they were the fussiest ones. Everything had to be just so …. Sometimes it was to their advantage that they complained because it gave them a chance to get away from the stone and all that stone dust. They would go and grind, sharpen, their own tools. By finding fault with it, it would give them a chance to get away from it."

Arthur Ferraro, who had been a tool boy and later sharpened tools for Dick Comolli's father, Ferruccio

On what happens if a stonecutter made a mistake: "Well, they would start all over again. Sometimes you would spoil that stone and, of course, if you spoil it, it runs into money. The company pays for that. Of course the company buys that stone … and sometimes it happens and the company takes a licking and sometimes … there is a trick to it. They would patch it up, but you wouldn't know it for a while, but after awhile you can see there is a patch there. Probably drops out, but after years, you know. … The foreman would come to the blacksmith to put [the stone] over the fire . . . the same color … and of course they would put it in and you would know that stone was patched."

Frank Turco

The Narragansett Weekly. May 9, 1872 ~ The apprentices at the R.I. Granite Works are to have new uniforms. Samples were submitted for consideration from which was selected one furnished by I.B. Crandall & Co. The selection made does credit to the taste of Mr. Palmer, who also manifested his generosity by presenting it to an apprentice. It was very greatly accepted.

On tempering tools: "They [the blacksmiths] used to finish sharpening the chisel and they'd lay it down for a few minutes, then they'd pick it up. Your temper on your chisels runs as it cools off; it runs and then ….they would just look at it because they could see it running. When it became a straw color, a certain amount of the chisel "boom," they'd dip it into salt water that held the temper right there on that chisel … points rather. [They added salt to the water.] They probably could go down to the beach and use that salt water and it would be the same thing, but they never did. They had a fifty gallon drum cut in half … that's where they used to dip them in."

Patsy Capizzano

"I was a young kid; . . . I used to eat like a horse. And I used to sneak, 'cause if you got caught eating a sandwich, they'd give you holy hell because you're wasting time. So I remember when I first went to work, I'd grind with one hand and eat with the other one! And I was situated so that I could see the boss. I put up a mirror and, if he were coming, I hid the sandwich. … You wouldn't dare get caught eating a sandwich. There was only one time you ate and that was when the whistle blew."

Arthur Ferraro

On the stress of carving: "There was a story of man who was finishing up a statue and was practically done and an accident happened. A finger broke off or hand broke off and these people would be very upset. This particular man, he just wanted to be alone and went into the woods. They would find him and take a blanket out and cover him up at night and bring him a glass of wine or a cup of coffee and sit with him for whatever time it took. I think in this particular case it took 2 or 3 days. Then he would come home and get straightened out. He had to get this worked out to be of any value later on and to come back and do the great things he was capable of doing."

Isaac G. Smith, Jr.

Nineteen quarrymen at the Sullivan Quarry in Bradford stand atop one of the huge stones for the Andrus mausoleum in Valhalla, NY. The railcar went on to the cutting shed of the Joseph Coduri Granite Company in Westerly where the stone was cut and finished.

CREATING A MONUMENT

OCCUPATIONS IN THE GRANITE INDUSTRY

Agent: a company salesman who secured orders for monuments. Salesmen for Westerly companies were located in major cities across the eastern United States.

Apprentice: a young stone worker in training. A young boy began his training by getting tools and materials needed by the master craftsmen. As he handed over the tools, he watched the experienced men use the tools. He imitated the way the tools should be held and used. The more he imitated the master craftsmen, the more proficient he became in using the tools. Eventually the apprentice acquired tools of his own and worked independently.

Architectural Engineer: a highly-trained specialist who took into consideration the load-bearing members in the structure of the monument and made certain that the monument was structurally sound. He also designed the hoisting mechanisms for lifting and transporting very large pieces of stone.

Artist: a creative worker who used colored pencils, pastels and watercolors to create two dimensional pictures of monuments—most often for sales presentations.

Blacksmith: a worker who shoed oxen and horses, mended chains, shaped iron tires for wooden wheels and struck them on. There was one blacksmith for every twelve granite cutters. He sharpened tools by forging, hardening and tempering the edge and he also made new tools. The Smith Granite Company blacksmith's shop, with a higher center section, had a lifting device to hoist oxen in order to shoe them because oxen, unlike horses, are not able to stand on three legs.

Blaster: a quarryman specially trained in blasting techniques. The amount of black powder used was critical. Not using enough would not free the granite block; using too much powder would result in waste due to broken and cracked stone.

Carpenter: a tradesman who boxed finished work to protect it for shipment. He also built and repaired buildings and other wooden objects.

Carver: a highly skilled stonecutter who specialized in cutting the floral, geometric, and classical designs and moldings on monuments.

Designer/draftsman: an artist who created the conceptual design for the monument and presented it to the customer for approval. He then made detailed drawings which were used by the stonecutters in producing the work.

Driller: a quarryman who specialized in making drill holes. In the early days drilling was done by hand; later drilling was done with a steam drill.

Engineer: a man who operated the engines for the hoisting derricks and cranes and the railroad locomotives.

Farmer: a worker who cared for the horses and oxen and was responsible for the barns.

Fireman: a worker who ran the boilers to produce steam to run the power equipment.

Letter cutter: a skilled stonecutter specializing in cutting the letters on a monument.

Lumper: a quarryman who moved or turned partially finished or completed work.

Mechanic: a specialist who kept the engines and machinery in working order and operated air compressors.

Paving Cutter: a stonecutter who cut paving stones to dimension.

Photographer: a worker who documented on film the work of the granite industry.

Polisher: a craftsman who used increasingly fine grit to bring the finish of a monument to a high gloss. Large areas were polished by machine. Small areas and areas around intricate details were polished by hand.

Quarryman: a worker who drilled, blasted, and hoisted granite from the quarries and moved it to the nearby sheds

Railroad man: a worker who ran and maintained the railroad tracks and equipment

Rigger: a quarry worker who erected derricks, and designed pulleys and chain mechanisms to lift and move the heavy slabs of granite.

Sand blaster: a stone cutter skilled in using the sandblast machine to carve letters and designs.

Sawyer: a man who operated the saws to cut large blocks of granite to the approximate size required for the monument. Before the use of saws, granite was cut to rough dimensions in the quarry.

Sculptor: an artist who designed and created the clay representation of the statue or design. After the clay work was completed, a plaster version was made to serve as a model for the statue cutter or carver.

Setter: a member of a team which was responsible for erecting the finished product on its permanent site.

Statue cutter: a highly skilled stonecutter who used the plaster model as a guide in cutting the statue in granite.

Stonecutter: a journeyman craftsman who cut the stone to the final size and shape, and finished the hammered surface as required.

Teamster: a man who drove oxen, horses, and eventually trucks to move materials.

Tool boy: a boy who carried dull tools to the blacksmith and later returned them sharpened. He kept track of which tools belonged to which craftsman.

Turner: a stonecutter who used a lathe to cut round components of the monument.

Wheelwright: a worker who built and repaired wooden wheels. (The high wheels on the ox carts were about 12 feet in diameter.)

STONE CHIPS

Narragansett Weekly. 1886 ~ William Oppy was granted a patent for a bush hammer for use in the granite industry.

Narragansett Weekly. n.d. ~ Joseph C. Burdick retired as "Boss" Blacksmith after 52 years with Smith Granite Company. He was given a gold-headed cane in recognition of his service.

Narragansett Weekly. 1887 ~ Jerry Dodge, an oxen driver for Rhode Island Granite Works, has a team which weighs in at 3,770 pounds.

Narragansett Weekly. 1877 ~ Albert Peach, an oxen driver for Rhode Island Granite Works, has a team which weighs in at 4,160 pounds.

CREATING A MONUMENT
WORKING WITH HAZARDS

Both granite workers and companies were concerned with safety. Although granite workers did their best to protect themselves, injury or death could easily be the result of accidents or environmental conditions. Companies were equally safety conscious, not only for the welfare of their workers, but also for the protection of their investment in equipment and materials.

The quarry holes presented a myriad of dangers. Uneven ground and loose stone made footing difficult. Wooden ladders which provided access to the quarry holes as deep as 160 feet were primitive and built on site. Blasting meant dangerous flying debris. Moving the stone and lifting it out of the hole put strains on derricks, chains, and cables which could break.

A free-moving piece of granite was very dangerous and nearly always resulted in loss of equipment and often in injury or death.

Although granite workers wore sturdy clothing and heavy duty shoes for protection, in the sheds they added denim aprons to try to protect their clothes. Gauntlets or gloves protected sleeves and arms from flying stone chips. Stonecutters wore goggles with slits to minimize the possibility of getting stone chips in the eye. If a workman did get a tiny chip in his eye, another workman might hold his head up against a pole to keep his head still while a third workman used a straw from the broom to get the chip out.

Stonecutters often put lamb's wool in their nostrils to filter out the fine dust. As the industry became more mechanized, finishing machines created larger concentrations of dust, making the men very susceptible to silicosis (white lung disease). The lathes and the surfacing machines were the first machines to be fitted with a dust-collecting system and eventually each stonecutter's bay had a dust collector.

During the winter the only fire in the unheated shed was not for the comfort of the men, but rather for warming the tools. Working with cold tools could actually lead to frostbite.

Blasting of the surface stone at Smith's East quarry

Inexperience contributed to accidents. For example, new apprentices were easily identified by their bruised and bloodied knuckles, resulting from the hammer's missing the chisel.

Hoisting a granite block

"I THOUGHT IT WAS HIS GHOST."

This story was told to Mary Bray's great nephew, Lonnie Foberg, when he was visiting her in the 1940's.

Great uncle Joseph Bray worked for the Smith Granite Company as a crane operator. One day while he was operating the crane, his supervisor asked him to pick up a slab of granite that was too heavy for the crane. The boss insisted that he proceed, which Joe did with almost tragic consequences. Joe was lucky to escape out of the crane before it crushed him.

Upon escaping from the fallen crane, he went behind a nearby shed and sat down on a bench to gather his thoughts. He said, "I was shaking like a leaf." In the meantime the other workers and the boss thought he was trapped and crushed to death under the crane! The supervisor went over to his house, just across the way at 131 Granite Street, to inform his wife what had happened.
Later that day, a little after dark, Joe decided to head home. When Joe entered the house, he scared his wife half to death. She said, "I thought it was his ghost."

Difficult footing in the quarry

Access to the quarries was via primitive ladders.

Stonecutter Carl Carlson wearing his stonecutter's apron

STONE CHIPS

Referring to the lack of safety glasses: "They all had steel in their eye. Little pieces that flake off. I've seen my father take a piece of steel out of the old man —- an old blacksmith up at Sullivan quarry. His eye was just like a red golf ball. They both take a shot of whiskey, my father takes his knife out of his pocket ..[sounds of the knife removing the steel]. . . and they take another shot of whiskey … both of them."

Carl Myllymaki

On accidents in the quarry: "Good Lord, I can remember at least a half dozen accidents right up here at the quarries, local people that were killed. Lot of them were killed up there. It was dangerous lifting those stones up. Chain would pull out and slip off and come down. Oh, man, it was bad. Well, it wasn't an everyday occurrence and they had a foreman there that was supposed to check on it. Of course, they did the best, but all I can say is it was dangerous, dangerous work. Occupational hazard."

Thomas Barber

The Narragansett Weekly. March 9, 1871 ~ MR. EUGENE DRISCOLL, employed at Smith's Quarry, met with a painful accident, on Friday afternoon. While standing in the engine house, in company with several of the workmen, he slipped and caught his left foot under the piston rod of the engine, smashing two of his toes so badly that the whole of one, and a portion of the other, had to be amputated. He was immediately conveyed to his residence at White Rock, where the requisite surgical aid was promptly rendered by Dr. Wilbur.

On the dust: "All the dust they made they either breathed it in or it was in the air. When the sun shines, you could cut it with a knife—that's how thick it used to be."

Arthur Ferraro

"Most of them used to have little sponges. They'd wet the sponge and stick it in their nose. Every once in a while they'd take the sponges and wash them out and stick them back again."

Arthur Ferraro

On the dangers of free-moving stone: "One day, a stone on the boring mill broke loose and moved toward me. I scrambled up the nearby staging. My clothes were torn and I was shaken up, but was very lucky not to have been hurt more seriously."

Isaac G. Smith, Jr.

On becoming a stone cutter: "I wasn't crazy to learn about it but I'm glad that I did because I liked it. [I thought] well, okay, I'll try anything. I can quit. What a hell of a time I had, trying to get going. My hands where I used to miss with the hammer [were] cut, black and blue, and bleeding all day. They would heal over at nighttime a little, stop and clot you know . . . next morning go "bump" hit and oh, Jesus. Then, after a while, you got used to it. You never missed no more. You can close your eyes and go automatically."

Patsy Capizzano

On working conditions and pay: "[Forty or fifty years ago] the granite cutter was getting the top wage of any trade including machinists at Cottrells. A good steady working stonecutter worked 10 months of the year. It was only the carver or the statue cutter that worked 12 months a year because they had facilities to work in cold weather. The others worked until they couldn't hold the steel or it froze. I worked one winter and I froze my fingers. I can't go swimming today that they don't turn white now."

Isaac G. Smith, Jr.

STONE CHIPS

On his father's death in a quarry: "He was down there one day, poor fella. I don't know how it ever happened, anyway, but there was a few new men down the hole. Nobody ever knew who hooked up that big rock they were taking out of the hole, the great big one. . . . And they put a chain on it to hoist it out of the hole where there was a flaw in the chain, or it wasn't balanced right. It go out of the sling, anyway, where it was hooked up. And it came right down and dad and the rest of the men . . . of course they all was vacated; they never stayed underneath the stone when they were hoisting them out. They're all scattered all over the place. Well, dad didn't get far enough away, see? And a big chip came along after it struck the bottom, broke it up in a hundred different pieces and, God, he was hit. He was all cut up.

[at the funeral parlor] I can remember him there, his face all plastered up with this plastic stuff, coverin' up the cuts and bruises. You couldn't recognize him. He never knew what hit him. Killed him immediately. Nobody, you know, nobody knew who hooked up that stone. And nobody was supposed to. That was the orders by, you know, the big boss, Orlando Smith. He wouldn't let anybody say a word. Now who killed Andrew Keena? Everybody was mum. Nobody knows today who done it."

John Keena

Open pit quarries could not be worked safely in the winter. Ice on ladders made access to the quarries unfeasible and ice underfoot made working dangerous. Cold weather made granite so brittle that splitting the granite in a controlled fashion was impossible. To prevent the large pneumatic valves from freezing and subsequently breaking, boxes packed with cow manure were placed around them.

DELIVERING THE MONUMENT

Once the monument had been completed, the pieces were numbered to aid in the setting. Then the carpenter boxed the stones for protection on the journey to the permanent location. In the case of a vault, the first shipment contained the stones in the bottom course and the final shipment contained the roof stones.

To move a finished monument, a low bed wagon was used, drawn either by horses if the piece was relatively light or by oxen if the piece was heavier. In the early years, finished work had to be hauled down Granite Street hill, through Dixon Square, up High Street to the Westerly railroad station. Going downhill, two oxen were in front of the cart to provide steering, but as many as ten pair were behind the cart to hold the load and prevent it from going downhill too fast. Large blocks of granite were dragged behind the cart to further slow it. Once loaded on the train, the piece could go anywhere the railroad went.

The monument on the right is boxed for delivery. The wheels on the large high-wheel cart on the extreme right were twelve feet in diameter. These oxen are at New England Granite Works, looking north. Houses in the background are on Ledward Avenue.

A spur from the main railroad line was first brought into the New England Granite Works around 1870 and extended in 1892 into the Smith Granite Company, making it no longer necessary to haul granite down the hill to the station. A company-owned locomotives loaded boxed work onto a railroad car and brought it to the main railroad line. It was a great advantage for Joseph Newall & Co. (and later the Joseph Coduri Granite Company) to be located on Oak Street right next to the railroad tracks where a special spur line ran right into the cutting shed.

When trucks became readily available, moving granite around the plant and shipping it became much easier. The finished work could go directly to the site without transfers, saving time and reducing the chance of damage during shipment.

The Hall shaft, boxed and on a railroad car, ready for the railroad trip to New York City. This monument was so long, nearly 50 feet, that the end of the monument overhung the railroad car; an empty car had to be coupled to this one to accommodate the swing.

Smith Granite Company locomotive circa 1932 moved the railcars with finished monuments via the spur to the main railroad line. Grafton Palmer, engineer

This fourteen-horse team, loaded with a 25-ton monument on a low-bed wagon, hauled it from the Boston
freight yard to Forest Hill Cemetery in Jamaica Plain, MA on June 2, 1896.

CREATING A MONUMENT
SETTING THE MONUMENT

In preparation for the arrival of any multi-pieced monument, the cemetery superintendent would have hired a local contractor to build a foundation. In preparation for a vault, the most complicated to set, the foundation would have sat for about six months in order to cure. A team of setters, with a railcar packed with 10 tons of tools including the derrick and rigging, arrived from Westerly. The setter boss would have developed a detailed plan for setting, taking into account many contingencies. No stone was moved, no equipment used, no task undertaken without the express orders of the setter boss who had complete responsibility.

Local teamsters moved the stones from the freight yard to the cemetery. Derricks placed the pieces needed first closest to the site and those needed last farthest away.

Next, the foundation was checked to make sure it was perfectly level and square. Beginning with the first course, the stone was lifted and then gently lowered into place on a bed of mortar. A day's work might consist of setting the stones on one side of the vault. The entire course on all four sides was set and allowed to cure for a couple of days before the next course was begun. At the end of each day, the joints were "struck"; that is, mortar was added to the joints to ensure that the vault was weather-tight. The floor (often marble) was set before the walls were built and then boxed again so that it was protected from damage during the remaining construction. The walls had to be square and plumb since small mistakes at the bottom would be magnified in the upper levels. Staging was built around the vault as the work progressed so that the workers could guide the stones into place. Columns had to be set plumb and level so that the next course would rest evenly on all the columns.

Setting the large heavy roof stones presented the final challenge. A crane lifted the roof stones into place and they were set with mortise and tenon to prevent slippage. Setting the center roof stone was the final test of the setting job. The derrick lifted the stone and

lowered it to just above its final position; then it was lowered into its final position with jacks. If all had been done correctly, the final stone slipped into place and the vault would be straight and true forever.

Donald Bonner, Tony Broccolo and Richard Comolli (l to r) setting the Westerly-Pawcatuck War Memorial in 1978

Presbrey-Leland setting crew pictured in a promotional brochure

The Gould mausoleum contained 450 granite pieces, some as long as 33 feet, which had to be individually numbered, boxed, shipped, and assembled in Woodlawn Cemetery in the Bronx. Produced by the Smith Granite Company from Westerly blue granite in 1893, it features 30 Ionic columns, each 18 inches at the base and 18 1/2 feet tall, on all four sides, 32 crypts, and two levels inside.

Setting the center roof stone on the Whitmore mausoleum, Norwich, NY (1903)

STONE CHIPS

On temporary railcar lines in Bradford: "I can remember vividly if Sullivan hit a big job, you know a huge piece of granite, they'd have to take and I don't know how the hell they got the flatcar up there, to tell you the truth. They'd put it on a flatcar and build a temporary rail line from the stone . . . they'd bring it right on the street here. They'd put on two or three sections, rail at a time, and they built a moveable railroad. It had to be fastened down 'cause it had this tremendously big stone on it. That happened quite frequently here. They'd lay the rail along the street here, and, of course, they had it all blocked up and then they'd take and move it ahead and then take the rail up and move it ahead, kept moving it that way. Take off and piece on. Take off and piece on. Right down here to the railroad."

Thomas Barber

On oxen and their drivers: "The oxen would bring the rough stone into the stonecutter's shed where they had to cut it. They'd be an old Irishman or an old Yankee or an old Finlander or whatever he was. All nationalities drivin' those oxen. And every man knew his own oxen, see? If he got somebody else's pair of cattle, you know, he might just as well be tryin' to make that chair do something for him. The oxen wouldn't do nothing for him. He had to have his own driver. . . . If he was off on a drunk for a couple of weeks, the oxen stayed right in their barn. They never went out. Nobody could drive 'em."

John Keena

Narragansett Weekly. November 17, 1892 ~ The first consignment of paving blocks that has been shipped by water since the settlement of the recent granite difficulty, was on one day last week, when the schooner Emma Paul sailed with a cargo. The Smith Granite Co. ship all their blocks in this manner, while the other manufacturers, especially those who operate quarries near the railroad, ship their blocks by rail to Stonington, where they are transferred to sailing vessels.

Once when there was no carpenter available to box a stone, Isaac Smith, Sr. had to box a 12-foot octagonal base weighing over 10 tons. He had help, but no plan. They protected all the sides and the finished parts on the top. Then, it being too wide to ship flat on a railcar, they built some brackets of 8 by 8 foot timbers, which held the boxed stone in a sideboard car at an angle which would keep it within the allowable width. More timbers were spiked in the car to keep it from sliding or rolling off the brackets if the car were ever bumped in switching.

Isaac G. Smith, Jr.

It was quite a trick for a blacksmith to fashion an iron tire to a true circle for a twelve foot wheel, heat it all at once, have it carried to the wheel and fitted in place with a full circle of men with tongs, have it cool to shrink so that it would not come off the wheel, and put out the fire before the wheel burned up.

Adapted from a 1972 paper by Isaac G. Smith, Sr.

Narragansett Weekly. April 19, 1888 ~ THREE STONE CUTTERS in the employ of the Smith Granite Company left Westerly Sunday night, on the mail train, for Gettysburg, Pa., where they are to set up a number of monuments as mementos of regiments which took part in the battle once fought there. They were John Brines, Joseph Thompson, and Edward Kelleher. It is probable that they will be gone two months or more.

Narragansett Weekly. 1896 ~ Ed. N. Burdick returns from Woodlawn Cemetery in New York City where he has been photographing for Rhode Island Granite Works.

STONE CHIPS

On oxen moving monuments: "There were forty pair of them . . . You could see them going down over Quarry Hill with one of them danged big monuments, half the size of this house here, all cased up. A pair of bulls on the tongue of the wagon. Wheels, you know, higher than this ceiling! Great big wheels with tires on them that wide! Pair of oxen, guiding it, steering it. He'd be on the wheel, see, to guide it going down over the hill and then, many behind it, holding it. By God, a string of oxen behind, almost pulling the horns right off of them. The yokes would be right up against their horns, see? And the bull drivers wheeling the devil out of them, making them pull back . . . If them fellas didn't hold back, that danged big monument'd push 'em all right down into the river, I imagine."

John Keena

"We always talk about the man who was a teamster; he drove his oxen. There was a great vertical drop into the quarry and he backed the oxen up underneath the shear poles and they kept going and they went right over the shear down into the quarry. The oxen were killed. So they got the butchers in town [who] went right down and butchered the meat right in the quarry hole and brought the meat up and did whatever they do to preserve it. From that day on that man was always known as Butcher Shea and he was a teamster at the Smith Granite Company for many, many years."

Isaac G. Smith, Jr.

The Priore family monument, cut and carved by the Joseph Coduri Granite Company, was set in St. Sebastian Cemetery in Westerly, RI.

CREATING A MONUMENT
MAINTAINING THE MONUMENT

Granite monuments, whether close to or far away from the water, in the shade or sun, big or small, are not immune to staining and unsightly organic growth.

When one buys a cemetery plot, approximately 40% of the cost goes to perpetual care which includes mowing, tree and grounds maintenance, and the repair, straightening and maintenance of stones by the cemetery staff as time permits. Their goal is to maintain a pleasing natural landscape.

Maintaining and cleaning individual stones is primarily the responsibility of the family. There are several choices when it comes to cleaning granite monuments which are not stained or damaged, but have just dust, grime, and organic material on them. A family can come equipped with bleach, a brush with hard bristles, and elbow grease and start scrubbing from the bottom up to avoid streak staining. Several reputable internet sites recommend a soft-bristled brush with nylon or natural bristles, a toothbrush, lots of water, and a non-ionic detergent such as Photo-Flo, a Kodak product. One should not use regular household cleaners and nothing should be done which cannot be undone. Stained or marble monuments require a different approach.

For larger or more complicated granite monuments, professionals recommended by the cemetery staff can be hired to use a power washer and a product which eats the organic material. A cloudy day between April and November is the optimum time since the material a professional uses has to stay moist for 15 to 20 minutes. In 2011, cleaning a small marker cost about $30.00. An average headstone was about $150, and a complicated monument such as an angel was between $600 and $700. A professional cleaning should last about ten years.

This monument is so covered by organic growth that the names are no longer visible. Cleaning the monument would restore it to near-new condition.

Sarah A. Madison cleaning her parents' monument in the River Bend Cemetery. She used only water, a scrub brush and "elbow grease."

One of the two lions guarding the 70-year-old Coduri mausoleum in River Bend Cemetery. The mausoleum was professionally cleaned three years ago and looks brand new.

STONE CHIPS

"Friday night he'd [Myllymaki's father working in New London] take his toolbox home. A taxicab driver stopped to give him a ride. [His tool chest was on the sidewalk.] Taxicab driver says, 'Well, I'm a younger fellow, I'll put them in the car.' My father said it didn't even move off the sidewalk. Couldn't even lift it up. You realize that's all solid iron!"

Carl Myllymaki

On changing jobs: "I was a young man . . . eighteen or nineteen . . . and I had a sore back and I figured it was from lifting . . . them big chains. I says, 'Let me get out of here; let me go up and see Smith.' Ed [Smith] says, 'Where'd you work?' I says, 'Sullivan's Granite.' 'Well,' he says, 'let's see now, what kind of a job can I give you?' Just like that. He was a nice guy; he was very good to me. He says, 'How about being a truck driver for a while until I decide what to give you?' Just like that. He gave me a big bulldog Mack. Then came winter. Cold weather, snow, rain. You couldn't get in them holes. You know, wet ice, no ladders to go down. So they closed down. They laid off everybody just like that, but he didn't say anything to me. [Others asked him if he had been laid off, but he didn't know, so he went to ask Ed.] 'Am I laid off?' 'Did anybody tell you you was laid off?' I told him no. 'Well,'

he says, 'Monday morning you come in here.' I says, 'What do you want me to do here on Monday morning?' He says, 'You go in that shed and work with the stonecutters.' Just like that." [And so he learned how to operate the overhead crane. and later became a stone cutter.]

Patsy Capizzano

"We had those big saws, I guess, you maybe heard them? We used to hear them when I first moved up here on Bellevue Avenue. You could hear them going all night. They had a saw cuttin' through that stone, you know, cuttin' and cuttin' and cuttin' right through it."

Peter DePerry

Every quarry and every stone shed had its own whistle and you could tell who was going to work at what time by the time the whistles blew and who was late and who was early. Smith Granite Company had two whistles, one on the stone shed . . . and the other . . . in the quarry so that the quarrymen could hear that whistle. There were danger signals when there was a problem in the quarry that they needed help. They would blow the whistle, short jabs on the whistle.

Isaac G. Smith, Jr.

Monuments

To appreciate the finished monument, we must examine the individual components and understand the different kinds of monuments.

Although we tend to think first of the beautiful monuments in our local cemeteries, the period following the Civil War gave rise to a great demand all over the country for both war and civic memorials as well as monuments for the rich and famous.

In Westerly, major downtown buildings and private homes serve a very practical purpose while also filling an aesthetic need. Ubiquitous structural elements, such as bridge supports and jetties, often go unnoticed, while the memorials, urns, fountains and monuments scattered throughout town provide beauty. By learning about our granite heritage, understanding what it took to produce these finished products, and opening our eyes to the granite world around us, we are better people.

APPRECIATION OF DETAILS

ANATOMY OF A MONUMENT

While each monument has a unified design that reflects its purpose, the details make its message unique and reflect more closely the values and tastes of the customer. Following is a sampling of the vocabulary involved in describing a monument. All examples in this section are in River Bend Cemetery, Westerly, RI.

Structural Parts

A: **Statue**: Carved three-dimensional figure.

B: **Cap**: Top-most piece of the monument. May contain more carving and molding. It may be peaked, rounded or irregular.

C: **Plinth**: Decorative member of the monument. It is usually located above the die and below the cap. It may contain elaborate moldings and carving.

D: **Die**: Major component of the monument. It often contains decorative carving and inscriptions.

E, F: **Base**: Bottom-most piece of stone in a monument. It is set on the foundation and provides a visual foundation for the rest of the work. Some monuments contain a second base to provide a more elaborate setting for the work.

Pollette monument

Morgan monument

A: Base: A one-piece base supports the monument and gives it stability

B: Die: Central stone in the monument, lettered with the name

C: Wings (2): The components which flare out from the die

D: Urns (2): Vase-like stones atop each post

E: Posts (2): Vertical components at the outside edge of each wing

SURFACES

A finished surface can vary from very rough to smooth to glossy.

Rock-face is the coarsest surface; the monument has been cut rough using a pitching tool to break the granite off in chunks.

Rock-face with margin lines is the next step toward a more highly finished surface. The margin, cut with a peen hammer, gives the monument more clearly defined edges. The rock face surrounds a central panel with the inscription.

A **stippled** surface is still rough but it has been tooled using a dauber to give a pocked texture.

A **bush-hammered finish** is made by pounding the surface with a bush hammer. The smoothness of the surface is determined by how fine a bush hammer is used in the final surfacing. A 6-cut hammer leaves a rough surface, usually used where the surfaces of two stones abut. A 10-cut leaves a smooth surface which gives a very attractive matte finish.

The most highly finished surface is **polished**. The sawn or hammered surface is rubbed with increasingly fine grit. The final rubbing is done with tin oxide using a nearly dry felt wheel which buffs the surface to a permanent high gloss.

For a **skin-work** finish, the entire surface is polished and then parts of the polished area are cut away to leave an intricate, polished design.

LETTERING

The lettering needs to be in harmony with the overall design of the monument. In the days before computers, talented draftsmen manually laid out the inscription for the letter cutter, taking into account the different spacing needed for various letters or fonts.

Examples of types of fonts:

Serif

Sans serif

Stylized

The designer of the monument also specifies the method of cutting the letters. When raised letters are cut, the stonecutter leaves a rectangular pad where the lettering is to be located. For polished letters, the pad is polished before the letter cutter begins his work. He then cuts away excess material and leaves the shape of the letters. Then he finishes the space between letters to match the finish of the monument. For sunken letters, the entire area is finished before the letter cutter begins cutting the letters into the surface.

In **raised polished letters** the letter cutter never touches the polished surface, but he must be careful to make the sides of the letter perpendicular to the surface of the monument.

Raised round letters require that the entire rounded surface of the raised letter be cut.

Square sunk letters are the most difficult to cut. The edges must be perpendicular to the surface. Great care must be taken not to break away the corners of the letters.

For **sandblasted letters**, a rubber stencil of the inscription is attached to the finished surface and sand is shot at high speed at the stone to cut the letters.

Letters following the curve of the molding

Letters beneath or interwoven with elaborate carving

MOLDINGS

Architectural moldings give a dignity and formality to a monument.

Bead

Greek key

Dentil

Egg and dart

STONE CHIPS

When the first sandblast machine came to town, nobody could or would run it and it stood idle for several years. Eventually Isaac Smith, Sr. tried it, worked out some of its problems, and cut some Greek frets and lines and letters at considerable savings. He then taught a few granite cutters who became experts like Patsy Capizzano. Ferrucio Comolli was the first carver who would use sandblasting as a preliminary for carving by chisel and his son Richard continues this process today.

Adapted from 1972 paper by Isaac G. Smith, Sr.

A GARDEN IN STONE

Often families chose flowers that had a special personal significance. These choices, combined with the skill of the master carvers, created a garden of stone in River Bend Cemetery.

The lily of the valley symbolizes innocence and humility. Fyffe cross

The poppy symbolizes consolation and eternal life. Newall monument

The passion flower symbolizes the last days of Jesus and especially his crucifixion. Stewart cross

Dogwood symbolizes the crucifixion. Isaac Smith, Sr. monument

The daffodil symbolizes rebirth. Gehmlich monument

The lily symbolizes chastity, faith, and purity. Bicknell monument

The iris symbolizes faith and hope. Franklin Smith monument

The rose symbolizes love and remembrance. Chapman monument

The thistle, the national symbol of Scotland, represents the suffering of Christ. Darrach monument

Bouquet on the Groppelli monument

TYPES OF MONUMENTS

For every customer there was a monument. The trained memorial craftsman required a broad knowledge of the many factors to be considered in helping a customer select the best type of memorial. Certain factors automatically limited the range of choice and simplified the problem—whether the memorial would be for an individual or for a family, whether the body would be above or below the ground, the size and location of the lot, the character of the monuments in the vicinity, the amount of money to be spent, and the personal taste and religious affiliation of the customer. Once these factors had been considered, memorial craftsman still had a broad choice of memorials to offer the customer, individualizing the final choice with personally selected design elements. Westerly craftsmen cut a wide variety of memorial types, many of which are illustrated here. All examples are from River Bend Cemetery in Westerly, RI unless otherwise noted.

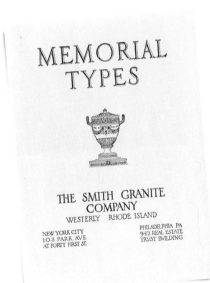

Booklets, pictures, and sales brochures such as the one pictured here (circa 1920) helped the memorial craftsman (salesman) advise his client in the choice of a monument.

The Relief

The relief monument, in which the figure projects from the background, is among the most dramatic and also among the most difficult to cut. It is meant to be viewed primarily from one direction as opposed to a statue which can be viewed from every direction.

Relief presented the greatest challenge to the talented statue cutters because of the restrictions placed on them. The statue cutter can work on a statue from any angle. Because of the presence of the background material, however, he must always cut the relief sculpture from the front of the monument, often forcing him into awkward and difficult positions.

The sculptor's position was restricted to the front of the stone in carving the **bas reliefs** on the Coduri mausoleum.

The two reliefs (one pictured) on the mausoleum, produced by the Joseph Coduri Granite Company in 1938 with stock from the Sullivan Granite Company, were carved from plaster models created by John Horrigan from Quincy, MA. It took Joseph Gervasini, carver, 188 1/2 hours for one ($235.32 or $1.25/hour) and 206 1/2 hours for the second ($257.50 or $1.25/hour).

In **bas relief** (pronounced bah relief) the figure extends less than halfway out of the background. In **haut relief** (pronounced oh relief) the figure extends more than halfway out of the background.

This excellent example of haut relief, in which the soldier emerges more fully from the stone, was cut by Columbus Zerbarini. The 16th US Infantry Monument at Chickamauga National Military Park, Fort Oglethorpe, GA was produced by Smith Granite Company from blue Westerly granite in 1893 for $1500.

The heroic-size (one and a half times life size), haut relief on the Stonewall Jackson monument in Charlottesville, VA was cut in 1919 by the New England Granite Works from red Westerly granite. It is unusual to see statues or haut relief cut from red granite; blue is the more common choice because of its fine grain.

The Cross

Latin and Celtic crosses have been familiar symbols of the Christian faith for centuries. Most Latin crosses have simple proportions and frequently have a "hammered" or smooth finish.

The Celtic cross includes a ring that travels completely around the cross intersection. The beauty of a Celtic cross frequently lies in the intricate carvings which may nearly cover the cross. These carvings, on one or more faces of the cross, might show important Biblical scenes or highlight elements of Celtic design and art.

above: The Orville Barber rock-faced Latin cross

right: The Stewart Latin cross with its hammered surface is simple in design and adorned with a passion flower

STEWART

The Neidel cross (1939), known as the Apostles cross with the figures of the twelve apostles on the lower part, demonstrates exceptional carving craftsmanship and detail.

A nearly-identical Celtic cross was done for Mrs. Dennis O'Brien, a resident of Watch Hill and New York City, and is located in Mt. Pleasant, NY. The stone for that cross was quarried at Sullivan Granite Company and was taken in a four-ton block from a vein of blue-white granite. George Stenhouse, of Fraquelli & Brusa, did the preliminary cutting of the cross and Nicholas Verzillo did the scrolled trimmings. Angelo Buzzi spent over two months carving the figures and other fine details and considered it one of his best works.

The central section of the Neidel cross is rich in symbolism. The holy mother and child with accompanying angels are featured in the very center. Surrounding them are symbols for the four evangelists. Matthew (top) is represented by the eagle; Mark (left) by the winged lion; Luke (right) by the winged bull; and John (bottom) by the angel.

above: Detail of the Ward cross: The Ward cross panels have a combination of design elements, some intertwined with snake-like figures. Each rosette is different and the scale pattern on each snake is unique.

The Ward cross is a two-sided Celtic cross carved at the Joseph Coduri Granite Company. Unlike most of the local crosses with carving on the front only, the nearly ten-foot tall cross has the family name and engraved panels on both faces of the monument. The faces are different and equally adorned so that either could be considered the monument's "front."

Some granite companies such as Coduri & Marzoli specialized in the carving of crosses. During the three year period from 1908-1910 they carved five Celtic crosses as subcontractors of the Smith Granite Company.

The Mausoleum

The mausoleum, the most complex and most expensive type of monument produced in the granite sheds, is a free-standing building meant to hold one or more bodies. Two common designs for mausolea are classical and Gothic and either may be embellished with statues, crosses or other designs. Sometimes a mausoleum contains burial vaults below ground.

Fourteen Ionic columns surround the Turner-Hooker mausoleum in Hartford, CT; note the position of the capital scroll of the corner Ionic column. This mausoleum was produced by the Smith Granite Company from blue Westerly granite in 1899 for $13,000.

Classical: The Hoxie-Middleton mausoleum is a classical mausoleum with its fluted Ionic columns on either side of the bronze door. The fine grain and uniform color of the granite gives a dignity to the columns and architectural details reminiscent of ancient Greece. To enhance the appearance of height, the columns are tapered with a smaller diameter at the top than at the bottom. Consequently, the flutes are not parallel but rather closer together at the top. Some mausolea had only two columns flanking the door; others had columns on all sides of the building. This mausoleum features both rock-faced and hammered surfaces. Designed by Orlando R. Smith, Jr., it was built by the Smith Granite Company in 1926 from blue Westerly granite for $26,500.

Gothic: The Richards mausoleum is a fine example of a Gothic design complete with steep roof, adornments and buttresses, which for this work are more design elements than structural supports. Located in Oakland Cemetery in Atlanta, GA, it was designed by H.Q. French of New York City for Robert H. Richards. The tower of the mausoleum rises nearly 33 feet, about the height of a three-story building. This front-view picture shows the arched doorway and window, the tower, and the granite wall surrounding the cemetery lot.

In a recent restoration, the cemetery staff used old photographs in the Babcock-Smith House Museum collection to recreate the original planting design. The stone no longer has the characteristic blue-gray color of the blue granite because it is soiled by dust from the red Georgia dirt. The mausoleum was cut by the Smith Granite Company from Westerly blue granite in 1899 for $13,500.

Intended to frighten away evil spirits, the gargoyle features a lion head, bat wings and talons.

Inside, the focal point is a semi-circular bay with five stained glass windows. On the windows is written: "I am the Resurrection and the Life: he that believeth in me, though he were dead, yet shall he live." John 11:25. Wrought iron urn is in the foreground.

The Obelisk

The obelisk is impressive in its stark simplicity and height. Most effective when the height exceeds twenty-five feet, it is a tall, narrow, four-sided, tapering monument with a pyramidal top. Many obelisks have a concave pedestal supported by one or more bases. Although many obelisks, like the Washington Monument, are made of many stones and can have interior spaces, obelisks made by the Westerly granite industry were most often monolithic, meaning that the shaft is constructed from a single stone. The obelisk provided challenges in quarrying.

Dominating the small cemetery in Curwensville, PA are two obelisks: the Patten (22' 6") and the taller Swoope (25'7"). In 1904 and again in 1918 it was a challenging task for the Smith Granite Company to transport the long granite shafts from Westerly to Curwensville—a distance of over 350 miles. The final leg of the journey was perhaps the most challenging because the cemetery is atop a steep hill accessible by a narrow road with hairpin turns—not at all conducive to transporting a long granite shaft.

One wonders if the taller Swoope obelisk, built 14 years after the Patten, carries on a tradition of one-upmanship between the two families.

The Sarcophagus

Not the most expensive or the most dramatic of monuments, the sarcophagus was very popular in the Westerly granite industry; the order books of the Smith Granite Company alone document nearly 900 sarchophagi. They can range in size from medium to tremendous, in a finish from rock-faced to polished, and in design from simple to elaborate.

The word "sarcophagus" comes from a Greek word meaning "flesh eater." The ancient Greeks called the outer coffin a sarcophagus because it was often made of limestone, which, they thought, helped dead bodies to decompose. On the other hand, in ancient Egypt, a sarcophagus was a stone coffin into which the mummy was placed for preservation.

In modern times a sarcophagus is a monument that looks as though it would actually contain a body, but, most of the time, the body is actually buried below it.

Massive, ornately carved sarcophagus in Forest Hills Cemetery, Boston, MA

ADVENTURES AT THE VATICAN

John B. Sullivan's story of getting the measurements of the Scipio Sarcophagus

John B. Sullivan (1845-1911) founder and first president of Sullivan Granite Company

"As I was looking at this Sarcophagus the thought struck me, now is my chance to make some measurements. I had not more than touched it with my rule when the guard stepped up and talked very volubly in Italian. I could not understand a word—whereupon he rushed into another room and soon appeared with another man with considerable gold braid on his coat and cap. The gentleman with the gold lace said something in French— I said 'no French, I am an American.' Then he spoke English and said 'the Vatican Board of Directors positively forbade any one to copy, measure or take photos of any monument, picture or work of art within the confines of the Vatican.' Then he referred me to the proper authorities to get a permit.

I told him I made monuments in my own country, and I could make a sketch for the monument and take measurements in half an hour. I slipped a fee into his hand, and he smiled, made a bow, and said 'go ahead, it is all right.' I thanked him for the privilege and went to work. The guard that had first spoken now came to my assistance with a long stick, something like a yard stick but not spaced off. I thanked him, gave him a small fee and said that I could get along with my two foot rule. He stayed until the measurements were taken and was as fine and obliging as could be, and we parted on the friendliest terms."

The original sarcophagus at the Vatican of L.Cornelius Scipio Barbatus who died in 980 B.C.

The Sullivan sarcophagus in Mt. Pleasant Cemetery in Taunton, MA is a copy of the Scipio sarcophagus.

The Statue

Statues are the most evocative of all monuments and the ultimate showpieces of a skilled statue cutter. Whether designed to be realistic or allegorical, statues often communicate hope, trepidation, solace, or the complex relationships between two individuals. They frequently take the form of idealized women dressed in flowing classical garb, angels with outspread feathered wings, mothers with an adoring child, battlefield heroes in heroic poses, or great political leaders. Often focal points in town squares or in the cemetery, statues viewed from a distance instantly communicate a unified impression. Viewed closely, however, the fine details of faces, fingers, and feathers may send a more personalized message and also speak of the statue cutter's skill.

The rock-face cross emphasizes the highly finished statue of a woman with flowing robes and lilies. Graf monument, River Bend Cemetery, cut by Columbus Zerbarini

Faith and Hope, standard models at the Smith Granite Company, were used to help the bereaved declare their faith in eternal life. Both models featured graceful hands and artfully draped garments. Hope held an anchor and Faith held a cross either of which could be plain or decorated. The degree of decoration would affect the price of the monument. Hope (left): Austin monument in Syracuse, NY carved by Charles A. Pinardi. Faith (right): Sanders monument in Evanston, IL carved by James Pollette.

This group statue sentimentally portrays the love between mother and child. The Milner monument, cut by New England Granite Works, is in River Bend Cemetery.

The four statues on the Ohio monument, Missionary Ridge, Chattanooga, TN showcase the talent of the sculptor and statue cutter to individualize each soldier from the young drummer boy to the seasoned veteran. The statues surround an obelisk and were cut from blue Westerly granite by the Smith Granite Company in 1902. At least one of the statues was cut by James Richards; the other statue cutters are unknown.

The sculptor and statue cutter were attentive to the smallest details. The hem of the dress, the toenails, and the individual flowers on the lily of the valley can all be admired as individual parts of the whole statue. The Loveland-Langworthy angel in River Bend Cemetery was cut by Angelo Zerbarini at Joseph Newall & Co.

Other Types

Although a mausoleum reflects affluence, a huge obelisk is impressive, a statue can evoke emotions, and a cross is a statement of faith, some customers wanted something different. Here is a gallery of some of the options that were available from the Westerly granite companies.

Colonnade: a series of columns supporting an entablature which is the upper section of a classical monument. Atwood colonnade, Evergreen Cemetery, Stonington, CT

Balustrade: a railing with supporting balusters which are short vase-shaped columns. Castritius balustrade

Bench: a long seat with no back. Atherton bench

Column, broken or fallen: a symbol of a broken life. Collins column, Maysville Mason County Cemetery, Maysville, KY

Boulder: a rough-hewn monument. Shotwell boulder

Cradle: reminiscent of a bed, a symbol of a final resting place. Smith Chapman cradle in the Smith plot

Ledger: a stone slab that completely covers the gravesite. Elm Grove Cemetery, Mystic, CT

Table Tomb: a raised ledger supported at each corner by small columns standing on a landing stone. Mallory table tomb, Elmgove Cemetery, Mystic, CT

Marker: a small stone indicating an individual grave often located near a family monument. Markers may have varied styles: ornate, simple, round top, slant, flush, etc. Brown monument and markers, Elm Grove Cemetery, Mystic, CT

Tablet: the most common type of monument. Slab-like in form, with or without a base, it ranges in design from simple and inexpensive to imposing and ornate. Smith tablet

Stele: an upright stone or slab with an inscribed or sculptured surface. Boardman stele

Urn: a vase of varying size and shape, usually having a footed base or pedestal; it may be on top of the cap of the monument or freestanding. Pierce urn

NOTABLE MONUMENTS BEYOND WESTERLY

From coast to coast, the fine craftsmanship of Westerly's granite workers honors a wide range of people from politicians to businessmen, from creative artists to military heroes. Impossible to list the thousands of monuments that were produced in Westerly, the following gallery augments those already cited.

Theodore Roosevelt (1858-1919), 26th President of the United States. Best known for being a Colonel of the Rough Riders in the Spanish-American War before becoming President, he assumed office following the assassination of McKinley and was subsequently elected in 1904. He became known for "a square deal" for the average citizen and the policy of "Speak softly and carry a big stick." His love of the outdoors, hunting, and of travel resulted in a program to protect America's natural resources which became our national park system.

This tablet was cut from Sullivan blue-white granite by the New England Granite Works around 1920. Oyster Bay, Long Island, NY

Franklin D. Roosevelt (1882-1945), 32nd President of the United States. Elected to office in 1932, he was subsequently elected three times. Best known for the New Deal, his innovative programs to get the country out of the Depression, and for his involvement in World War II, he was beloved for his Fireside Chats which calmed a troubled nation.

The bust was designed by Gleb W. Derujinsky, carved from white Westerly granite, and was commissioned by the International Ladies' Garment Workers Union in 1947. Today the 27 1/2" tall bust, mounted on a black Swedish granite base, stands at Roosevelt's home in Hyde Park, NY.

The bronze statue of Standing Lincoln, designed by and completed by Augustus Saint-Gaudens in 1887, has been described as the most important sculpture from the nineteenth century of **Abraham Lincoln (1809-1865)**, 16th President of the United States. The steps, pedestal, and exedra, designed by Stanford White and located in Chicago, IL, are Westerly granite probably done by New England Granite Works.

Lincoln Address Monument, Gettysburg, PA marks the site of Lincoln's famous Gettysburg address.

This impressive monument was cut by the Smith Granite Company from red Westerly granite in 1912.

Prospect Terrace in Providence is more than just another tribute to Rhode Island founder, **Roger Williams (~1603-1683)**; it is his final resting place. His gravesite was moved multiple times before his remains were finally interred at the base of this monument in 1939. The sculpture shows Williams blessing the city from the bow of a canoe.

Harold Buzzi shared a story about the involvement of his father Angelo with the fourteen-foot statue of Roger Williams cut from Westerly granite. Evidently the statue was being carved in the Joseph Coduri Granite sheds when some sort of impasse occurred and Angelo Buzzi was called in to see whether he could finish carving the statue. Finding the statue lying on the ground with the front completed, Buzzi said, "Please stand it up."

The crane operator said that he could not because there would not be clearance for the overhead crane. "Then dig a hole." And a hole was dug. It was when the statue was raised that Buzzi discovered a problem. The hunk of stone was lacking 7 or 8 inches from what was needed to complete the back of the statue. The designer, when called in, said "Just do the best you can." And Buzzi did. His son said, "If you look at him (Williams) sideways, he looks as if he went to Weight Watchers."

Part of the Freedom Trail, the **Declaration of Independence Plaque** was erected on Boston Commons in 1925. The bas relief by John F. Paramino was based on a mural by John Trumbull in the Rotunda of the Capitol building in Washington, DC. Cut by the Smith Granite Company from Westerly dark pink granite for a cost of $3725, it features a bronze plaque on its face.

Minute Man, also known as Revolutionary War Soldier, was designed by Carl H. Conrads of the New England Granite Works. Cut from white Westerly granite, the statue was based on a model Conrads had previously made for a marble statue in Washington, DC.

The five foot figure is standing on a 6-foot tall white Barre granite base and was dedicated on April 21, 1905 in Union Square in Elizabeth, NJ.

This larger-than-life-size statue depicts the eminent statesman, **Alexander Hamilton (1757–1804)**, a strong supporter of a powerful federal government. He was a representative to the Continental Congress, co-authored many of the Federalist papers, became the first Secretary of the Treasury, set fiscal policies which still stand today, and, most famously, was fatally wounded in a duel with Aaron Burr.

Donated by Hamilton's grandson, John C. Hamilton, to New York City in 1880, the monument is carved from blue Westerly granite. Sculpted by Carl H. Conrads of the New England Granite Works, the 15'5" sculpture stands along Central Park's East Drive at 83rd Street near the Metropolitan Museum of Art in New York City.

The first monument to be placed at Gettysburg was the **Soldiers National Monument** which was placed at the center of the cemetery, promoting the Union victory and the valor of the fallen soldiers. The graves were arranged in a series of semicircles around the monument.

The monument was designed by the Batterson-Canfield Company, later New England Granite Works, and the statues were sculpted by Randolph Rogers. The cornerstone was laid on July 4, 1865 and the full monument dedicated on July 1, 1869. The white Westerly granite monument provides the setting for the five allegorical marble statues.

This Union infantryman is depicted defending a log and stone breastwork, similar to that which existed on parts of Culp's Hill during the Battle of Gettysburg.

It is unusual for a monument to honor two units. Both the **78th and 102nd New York Infantries** had suffered heavy casualties prior to the battle and were considerably under strength on July 2 and 3. The following summer the two units were formally consolidated and for the remainder of the war fought together as one.

One additional feature, often overlooked, is the illusion of a lion, symbolizing the courage and bravery of the men defending the breastworks that day. Just below the soldier's left hand are the lightly carved features of the lion with the lower log resembling its paw.

Carved at the Smith Granite Company in 1888 from blue Westerly granite by statue cutter Joseph Bedford from a model by sculptor Robert Barr at a cost of $3000

Sergeant Ben Crippen's job as flag bearer of the **143rd Pennsylvania Infantry** was to keep the vital symbol of the unit visible where all could rally around it. Among the last of the unit to fall back, he made a point of turning around periodically to shake his fist defiantly at the advancing Confederates. His body is probably among the unknown in the Gettysburg National Cemetery. The survivors of the 143rd felt that he should be singled out for recognition on the monument that honored them all. Nearly two-thirds of the $1500 total cost of the monument was devoted to sculpting the bas relief likeness of Crippen standing forever in the pose that inspired and encouraged them. This is the only monument on the battlefield depicting a Non-Commisioned Officer.

Carved from blue Westerly granite in 1888-89 by Fortunato Zangrandi at the Smith Granite Company

The **Lee-Jackson Monument** is located in Baltimore, MD. Each year there is a ceremony to honor General Robert Edward Lee and General Thomas Jonathan "Stonewall" Jackson on the anniversary of their births. The ceremony also remembers and honors the thousands of soldiers who served the Confederacy during the War Between the States.

The bronze statues are mounted on a granite base and die, cut at the Joseph Coduri Granite Company. The original contract was awarded in 1936 but was delayed by the Second World War. The monument was officially dedicated on May 1, 1948.

The **Second Division Memorial** in Washington, DC honors the 17,660 men and women of the Second Division of the United States Army who lost their lives during World War I from 1917-1919. A wing on each side was added to honor those lost in World War II and the Korean Conflict.

The large open doorway symbolizes the entrance to Paris, and the fiery 18-foot golden sword symbolically blocks the Germans from occupying the city. The doorway is flanked by granite shafts with a wreath on each one carved in relief. The names of the battles in which the Division participated are inscribed on each side.

Located on the Ellipse south of the White House at 17th Street & Constitution Avenue, NW. Produced by the Joseph Coduri Granite Company in 1936

The Atwood Machine Co. was a Stonington, CT firm which, between 1876 and the late 1930's, manufactured the bulk of the world's silk-throwing machinery. By 1865, **Eugene Atwood (1846-1926)** had perfected and later patented a spindle, or sleeve whorl, a breakthrough in the development of thread-making.

The Atwood colonnade in Evergreen Cemetery, Stonington, CT was cut by the Smith Granite Company in the late 1930's.

Mathew J. Whittall (1843-1922) purchased several businesses and reorganized them as the Worcester Carpet Company between 1901 and 1906. By World War I, the Whittall mills in Worcester, MA had 350 looms in operation and employed nearly 1500 skilled laborers. The largest employer in South Worcester, the Whittall Carpet Company remained in business until 1950. After the death of Whitall's first wife, the family monument was produced at a cost of $6000 by the Smith Granite Company in 1898. Frank Gomena carved the statue from blue Westerly granite. Hope Cemetery, Worcester, MA

Colonel Edwin Drake (1819-1880), the discoverer of oil in Pennsylvania and the founder of the modern petroleum industry, was buried in Bethlehem, PA in a pauper's grave. In 1902 his remains were re-interred in Titusville, PA.

The imposing granite memorial cut by the New England Granite Works from Niantic (Bradford) blue granite marks the new burial spot. The monument features a variety of design elements including cut work, bas relief, Ionic columns, an exedra, and steps.

Jay Gould (1836-1892) was a financier and railroad magnate. His early career in land surveying and commodity speculation got him interested in railroad stocks, which were the high-growth glamour issues of the day. When he died, his fortune was estimated at $72 million, all of which he left to his own family.

The Gould mausoleum in Woodlawn Cemetery in the Bronx, NY was cut by the Smith Granite Company from blue Westerly granite for about $50,000 in 1883.

Richard Morris Hunt (1827-1875), an architect of great prominence, worked for the very wealthy during America's Gilded Age. Although he did much work in New York City, including the base of the Statue of Liberty and the facade of the Metropolitan Museum of Art, Hunt also had Rhode Island connections. Among the many Newport mansions which he designed are the Marble House and the Vanderbilt Mansion. Legend has it that, while on a final walk-through of one of his Vanderbilt mansions, Hunt discovered a mysterious tent-like object in one of the ballrooms. Investigating, he found it was canvas covering a life-sized statue of himself, dressed in stonecutters' clothes, all carved in secret as a tribute by the gang of stonecutters working on the house. Vanderbilt permitted the statue to be placed on the roof of the mansion.

Dedicated in 1898, the Hunt monument, cut by New England Granite Works from Westerly granite, looks west from Fifth Avenue into Central Park. The bronze bust was done by sculptor Daniel Chester French. The setting for the sculptures is an exedra with a statue at each end of the semicircular colonnade.

Joseph Schlitz (1831-1875) worked as a bookkeeper in a tavern brewery owned by August Krug. Following Krug's death in 1856, he took over management of the brewery and later married Krug's widow, changing the name of the brewery to the Jos. Schlitz Brewing Co. The company began to succeed after the Great Chicago Fire of 1871, when Schlitz donated thousands of barrels of beer to that city which had lost most of its breweries. He quickly opened a distribution point there, beginning a national expansion. He became one of the largest producers of beer in the world and his company became famous for their slogans "The beer that made Milwaukee famous" and "When you're out of Schlitz, you're out of beer."

This statue on the Gothic monument made from blue Westerly granite in 1887 was cut by statue cutter Joseph Bedford of the Smith Granite Company. Columbus Zerbarini, Frank Pasetti and John Scharphler carved the details on the rest of the monument, located in Forest Home Cemetery, Milwaukee, WI.

Entrepreneur **Benjamin Altman (1840-1913)** founded B. Altman and Company, a famous New York-based department store.

Altman's monument, located in Salem Field Cemetery, Brooklyn, NY, is an actual sarcophagus, unusual in that it actually contains his body. It is a replica of a sarcophagus in the tomb of Alexander the Great. Cut by the Smith Granite Company from blue Westerly granite in 1914

Samuel Langhorne Clemens (Mark Twain) (1835 – 1910) is perhaps the greatest humorist of the nineteenth century and one of America's greatest authors. Hemingway said that "all modern American literature comes from one book by Mark Twain called *Huckleberry Finn*."

This monument in Woodlawn Cemetery, Elmira, NY was cut from Westerly granite by an out-of-town granite company.

The polar bear became the mascot of Bowdoin College in Brunswick, ME, inspired in part by a 1917 gift of a full-grown stuffed bear from Arctic explorer Donald Baxter MacMillan, Class of 1898. This statue, known as **The Bowdoin Bear**, was designed by F.G.R Roth, and given by the Class of 1912 on their 25th reunion. Carved by Ferruccio "Frank" Comolli from white Westerly granite in 1937 at the Smith Granite Company

Father Duffy (1871 – 1932), a chaplain and the most highly decorated cleric in the history of US Army, served in both the Spanish-American War and World War I. He later was pastor of Holy Cross Church in Hell's Kitchen, a block from Times Square. Father Duffy was the ghost writer for Al Smith's famous statement of American Catholic patriotism arguing for the feasibility of a Roman Catholic's serving as President. In 1940, veteran character actor Pat O'Brien portrayed Duffy in the Hollywood film, *The Fighting 69th*; the film also starred James Cagney.

The simplicity of the statue of Father Duffy, dedicated on May 2, 1937, contrasts with the hubbub of Times Square. The pedestal and 17-foot Celtic cross were produced by the Joseph Coduri Granite Company.

Sayles Hall on the Brown University campus was given in memory of William Clark Sayles who entered Brown University in 1874 but died in 1876. His father, William F. Sayles, donated $50,000 to "build a hall which shall be exclusively and forever devoted to lectures and recitations, and to meetings on academic occasions." Interestingly, for a while, the baseball team practiced there.

Dedicated on June 4, 1881. Exterior is of rock-faced red Westerly granite cut by the Smith Granite Company; the trim is reddish-brown Longmeadow stone.

The **Henry B. Joy Memorial** stood on the Continental Divide in Wyoming until being moved in 2001. Henry Bourne Joy (1864 –1936) was president of the Packard Motor Car Company and a major developer of automotive activities such as the Indianapolis Speedway. He and his family summered at Watch Hill and his daughter Helen Joy Lee was a generous benefactor to local organizations.

Designed by Isaac G. Smith, Sr. and produced by the Smith Granite Company from red Westerly granite in 1939 for a cost of $750

The **Bethesda Fountain** in New York's Central Park was designed by Emma Stebbins and features an eight-foot bronze angel and four four-foot cherubs. Water from the fountain cascades into the upper basin and then into the surrounding pool.

New York Evening Post. October 10, 1872 ~ The Great Fountain in Central Park: the basin was contracted for by Mr. J. G. Batterson, of Hartford, Conn. The single solid stone from his quarry in Westerly, R.I. weighed in the rough sixty tons, and in the basin, as now set, weighs twenty-eight tons. In the past eight years Mr. Batterson has made three attempts to get out this stone—the first two proving scant in dimensions and otherwise defective; and in hauling the third out of the quarry, chains with wrought links of two-inch iron snapped like twine. These were some of the risks in getting this basin to Central Park, where, within a few days, it has been safely placed in position.

The Narragansett Weekly. March 30, 1871 ~. THAT BIG BLOCK OF GRANITE lately quarried in Westerly provokes the following sympathetic notice in the *Louisville Courier Journal*: "A block of granite weighing ninety tons has been quarried in Rhode Island for the basin of a public fountain in New York. Another block or so of the same size, and there won't be much of the State left."

WITHIN WESTERLY

Buildings

One of the oldest buildings in town, the **Hopkinton Bank**, constructed before 1850, is on Main Street in Bradford. Most likely, the fine blue granite came from a local quarry operated by Solomon P. Wells. The bank contained a "burglar-proof safe" weighing 3500 pounds and later served as a church, a quarry workers' meeting house, Universal food store, a saloon, and an art store. In this vintage picture the side windows have been mostly filled in with cement blocks, but the building retains its pleasing proportions.

The present **Watch Hill Lighthouse** is actually the second one on that site. Built in 1856 to replace a wooden one built in 1808, it is a ten-foot-square granite tower 45 feet tall. The granite for the tower was transported down the Pawcatuck River on the scow *Jason*. In 1858, the federal government allocated $40,000 to build a granite wall to protect the "Point." That granite, from a quarry owned by Orlando Smith, was brought down the Pawcatuck River and landed at a special wharf erected for just that purpose.

The first course (below the sill of the first floor windows) and the entryway of the **Washington Trust** building were made from red granite from the Chapman Quarry and was set by the Columbia Granite Company (Monti). The building was completed and dedicated in 1925.

Saint Pius X Church at 45 Elm Street was built in 1956 from several varieties of granite donated to the church by Angelo Gencarelli. The window trim is limestone.

When the church was built on this site, new gates were cut to complement the existing wall which was made of red granite from the Murray quarry in Pawcatuck, CT.

Christ Episcopal Church, built in 1891, achieves much of its beauty from the contrasting use of two types of granite with the same rock-face finish. The field, or main part, is constructed from blue granite while the trim work is made from red. This architectural treatment was a trademark of the Smith Granite Company and particularly of Orlando Raymond Smith. The reverse treatment was used in the receiving vault at River Bend Cemetery.

The use of buttresses, pointed arch windows, roofs with steep pitches is typical of Gothic design.

The cornerstone of the church is set off by its polished finish.

Built in 1894 as a gift from Stephen Wilcox and local citizens to honor Civil War soldiers and sailors, the **Westerly Public Library** features a majestic red granite entrance produced by the New England Granite Works.

The five engaged columns (#1) on either side of the door are cut from a single piece of stone. Likewise, the five stylized Corinthian capitals (#2) on each side of the door are cut from one stone. The arch is composed of fifteen pieces of granite. Each of these pieces (#3) includes part of every tier of the archway—each with detailed carved moldings. The challenge was to cut the stone to fit precisely and to form the several tiers of the arch so that the moldings on each tier match and give the impression of continuity.

Detail of entrance near ramp

The **Westerly Town Hall and Court House** was cut in 1912 by the New England Granite Works. It is made from red granite quarried from the Batterson Quarry on Old Hopkinton Road.

The drum columns are cut in sections, reminiscent of snare drums, with clearly visible joints. These columns are turned on a lathe to a tooled finish and do not require the massive single pieces of granite that are needed for one-piece columns. The challenge with drum columns is cutting and setting them so that they have the appearance and the structural stability of a single column.

Different from Christ Episcopal Church which achieved a contrast by using two different kinds of granite, the Town Hall builders used two different finishes of the same granite. The details around the windows and at the corners are a hammered finish, providing an effective contrast to the rock-face finish of the field.

The columns are topped with Ionic capitals, the scrolls at the top of the columns.

In the heyday of the granite industry, several highly visible buildings were erected in downtown Westerly. The former **Industrial Trust Company** building was cut in 1887 from red granite by the New England Granite Works and served as a major downtown bank for years. Featuring exquisite classical details, the building is now owned by the The Westerly Land Trust.

The fluted columns are not free-standing but are rather engaged i.e. partly embedded in the wall of the building. Each column from the base to the capital was cut out of one piece of stone which was roughed-out and then turned on a lathe. The back of the column was cut off by the stonecutter. Finally, the flutes in the column were cut by hand. Carvers cut by hand the exquisite Corinthian capitals following a model prepared by the sculptor.

The medallion at the peak of the building reflects the industrial focus of the bank. The Industrial Trust Company was founded by Rhode Island politician and industrialist Samuel Pomeroy Colt (1852-1921), who served as president until 1908. In 1901 he became president of the United States Rubber Company, the largest producer of rubber goods in the world.

War Memorials

The **Hiker Memorial**, a tribute to those who served in the war against Spain, is located in Wilcox Park. Designed in 1924 by Allen G. Newman, it features a bronze statue set on a granite boulder by Andrew Low.

The **World War Memorial** at the corner of Grove Avenue and Granite Street is a formal monument that was dedicated on Armistice Day in 1937 and represents the efforts of three local companies. Designed by Arthur A. Shurecliff, it is constructed of Sullivan blue granite. The railings, buttresses, and the base of the railings were cut by the Joseph Coduri Granite Company. The balustrades, round die, round base and points of the star in the platform were cut by the Smith Granite Company. The names of those who served in World War I are on a bronze plaque. This memorial was redesigned in the 1980's to provide easier access to the park and again in 2002 to include bronze plaques on the buttresses with the names of those who served in World War II, the Korean Conflict and the Vietnam War.

On the Pawcatuck side of the river, the **Flag Memorial**, produced by Bonner Monument Company, was erected in 1967.

The **Westerly-Pawcatuck War Memorial** stands next to the bridge on the Westerly side of the Pawcatuck River. It is made from Sullivan blue granite and the statue was cut by Richard Comolli of the Bonner Monument Company. It was erected in tribute to those who gave their lives in World War II, the Korean Conflict and the Vietnam Conflict.

The **Korean War Memorial**, produced by Comolli Granite Company, at the railroad station recognizes those who served during the Korean War.

At the bridge on the Pawcatuck side of the river is the **POW-MIA Monument**, produced by Bonner Monument Company, and dedicated in 1987.

Neighborhood Memorials

The **Oak Street Memorial**, produced by Comolli Granite Company and dedicated in 1997, honors those from the neighborhood who were killed in war and includes a dedication to the people of Oak Street and a promise not to forget.

The **Bradford Memorial**, produced by Columbia Granite Company (Monti) from Sullivan blue granite, honors the men and women of Bradford who gave their lives and those who served in the armed forces of our country.

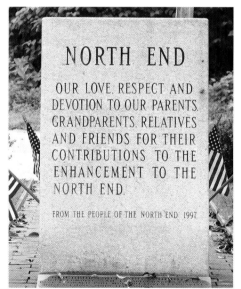

Produced by the Comolli Granite Company and erected in 1997, the **North End Monument** in Columbus Circle recognizes both those from the neighborhood who defended our country and those whose support made the enhancement of the North End possible.

On the corner of Watch Hill Road and Ninigret Avenue, the **Woodruff Exedra** honors the memory of Ensign James Gordon Woodruff, USNR, who was killed in the Battle of Midway on June 16, 1943.

Historical Markers

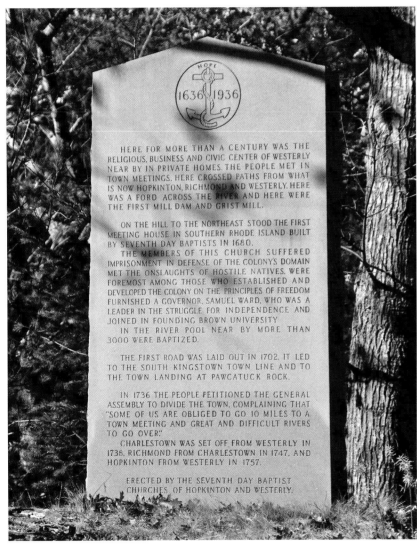

The marker on Route 3 at the **Meeting House Bridge**, erected by the Seventh Day Baptist Churches of Westerly and Hopkinton, marks the business, religious and civic center of the original town of Westerly.

As part of the 300th anniversary of the State of Rhode Island, the Town of Westerly erected five markers to honor significant local events or places in the town's history. These markers were designed by Isaac Smith, Sr. using the state motto "hope" and the state symbol, the anchor, with the dates 1636-1936.The marker on Main Street at the foot of Cross Street designates the dwelling of **Oliver Hazard Perry**, who was later victorious in the battle of Lake Erie during the War of 1812. The design at the bottom depicts Perry in that battle.

The marker in front of the Babcock-Smith House Museum on Granite Street identifies **Joshua Babcock** as the owner of this home, the first physician in town, the first postmaster and chief justice of the Rhode Island Supreme Court of the Colony of Rhode Island. At the bottom of the monument is a caduceus, the symbol of the medical profession.

In front of the present Friendly's Restaurant on Franklin Street, the stone marker indicates the location of town meetings during colonial days and the great buttonwood tree that served as the town **whipping post**. At the bottom of the monument is a buttonwood tree.

On the Watch Hill Road the stone tablet marks the location of the **landing of John and Mary Lawton Babcock**, the first white settlers in Westerly in 1648. At the bottom of the monument is a map of the Pawcatuck River showing Mastuxet Cove, their landing site.

On Margin Street is the marker that indicates the site of a **nineteenth century shipyard**. At the bottom of the monument is a ship under construction.

Downtown Works of Art

Women of Westerly Urn in Wilcox Park was cut by the Smith Granite Company in 1892 to be exhibited in the Rhode Island Building at the Chicago World's Fair in 1893. The carvers were Ededio Bottenelli and Louis Olgetti. Letter cutter was Matthias Wickland. Stonecutters were John Datson, John Hughes, Richard Dower and Mortimer McAvoy.

The **Wilcox Memorial Fountain**, produced by Joseph Coduri Granite Company, and balustrade, produced by the Smith Granite Company, have provided a tranquil space in Wilcox Park since 1929.

The Crandall Urn was "presented to the town by the late Miss Martha Jane Crandall, daughter of Capt. Albert Crandall. 1887." It is a finely detailed urn on an octagonal base. Originally a horse-watering trough at the corner of Grove Avenue and Granite Street, it is now a planter in Wilcox Park.

The **fountain in Dixon Square** is a fairly new addition. It is built from Stony Creek granite which is similar to Westerly red granite in color and texture.

Since granite quarrying had ceased in Westerly, these new **gate posts** at the post office entrance to the park were built from Stony Creek granite because of its resemblance to Westerly granite. The gate posts were designed by Isaac G. Smith, Jr. and cut by the Kenneth Castellucci & Associate, Inc. in 1997.

The statue on the **Columbus monument**, dedicated in 1949, is a tribute to Christoforo Columbo, "the intrepid Italian Explorer who linked the old world of our fathers to the new world of our sons." The fifteen-foot tall monument reflects the profound Italian influence on the town of Westerly. The monument was produced by the Joseph Coduri Granite Company from Sullivan blue granite. Charles H. Pizzano sculpted the model, Charles Gattoni cut the seven-foot statue, Nicholas Verzillo cut the bas relief on the die and Andy Anderson cut the globe.

This monument in Wilcox Park recognizes those who worked in the **Westerly Granite Industry** from 1846 to 1985 and helped to shape the identity of Westerly for more than one hundred years. Donated by Walter Neidel, it was originally a part of a cross that was never shipped. In 1985, Bonner Monument Company used it for this memorial to granite workers.

Several families, individuals and Westerly High School classes have given granite benches to Wilcox Park. The **Class of 1937 bench**, produced by Comolli Granite Company, provides a lovely resting spot.

The polished **red granite urn** at the YMCA was previously located in front of the Tetlow house across the street.

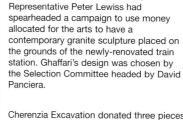

"Misquamicut" was designed by Kam Ghaffari in 2004 to be the first modern sculpture to carry Westerly's granite legacy into the new millennium. In 2004, Representative Peter Lewiss had spearheaded a campaign to use money allocated for the arts to have a contemporary granite sculpture placed on the grounds of the newly-renovated train station. Ghaffari's design was chosen by the Selection Committee headed by David Panciera.

Cherenzia Excavation donated three pieces of Westerly granite—one pink, one blue and one red— as well as services related to the installation. The granite boulders and the bronze fish were cut and cast by the Johnson Atelier firm in New Jersey. One fish and one polished surface are visible from every direction. The sculpture is titled "Misquamicut" which means "place where fish are" and the three bronze fish reflect the three fish on the town seal.

INDEX

C

Calder and Carney: 61

Calvary Catholic Cemetery: 5

Cameron, John: 119

Capizzano, Patsy: vii, 30, 46, 132, 135, 141, 148, 156, 166, 172

Carlson, Carl: 155

Carson: vi, 18, 101

Carver, Joel and Arnold: 22

Castritius balustrade: 185

Celtic cross: 59, 85, 176, 177, 192

Centennial Exposition: 94, 96

Central Park: 14, 188, 191, 193

Chaffee, Linda Smith: i, iii, vi, vii, ix, 80

Champlin, Richard: 50

channels: 136

Chapman: 6, 27, 60, 61, 65, 80, 101, 103, 111, 113, 173, 185, 194, 195

Chapman monument: 173

Charlestown Air Base: 38, 42

Charlottesville, VA: 175

Chattanooga, TN: 183

Cherenzia Excavation: 1, 52, 61, 62, 116, 212

Cherenzia, James: 66

Cherenzia, Jim: 117

Cherenzia, Salvatore: 62

Cherenzia, Sam: 66, 141

Chiappone, Andrew: 51

Chicago World's Fair: 210

Chicago, IL: 187

Chickamauga, GA: 4

Christ Episcopal Church: 196, 201

Civil War: 1, 4, 32, 45, 60, 68, 82, 94, 167, 198

cleaning: 26, 44, 164

Clemens, Samuel Langhorne: 192

Coduri & Marzoli: 6, 27, 32, 61, 82, 177

Coduri mausoleum: ii, ix, 165, 174

Coduri, Albino: 36, 37

Coduri, Giovanni (John): 82

Coduri, Joe: 36

Coduri, John B.: i, iii, vi, vii, ix, 82

Coduri, Joseph: iii, iv, ix, 1, 6, 18, 27, 28, 29, 32, 33, 34, 35, 36, 37, 42, 48, 61, 62, 82, 83, 90, 91, 108, 126, 127, 143, 149, 158, 163, 174, 177, 188, 189, 190, 192, 204, 210, 211

Coduri, Richard: iii, 37, 46

Collins column: 185

Collins, Bill: 141

Colt, Samuel Pomeroy: 202

Columbia Granite Company: 27, 50, 194, 195, 206

Columbia, SC: 48

Columbus monument: 33, 43, 90, 126, 211

Comolli family monument: 51

Comolli Granite Company: iv, 1, 27, 42, 50, 53, 62, 205, 206, 211

Comolli, Adam: 51

Comolli, Ferruccio "Frank": 33, 50, 192

Comolli, Mansuetto: 89

Comolli, Richard: vi, 31, 33, 40, 43, 46, 47, 50, 51, 52, 62, 91, 92, 144, 160, 205

company store: v, 7, 8, 10, 11, 63, 70, 71, 92

Connecticut State Capitol: 14, 17, 60

Conrads, Carl: 95

Continental Divide: 193

Conway, Jim: 117

Coolidge, Calvin: 57

Coon, Charles B.: 89

Craig & Richards Granite Company: 25

Crandall Urn: 210

crane: 10, 22, 50, 117, 153, 160, 166, 188

cross: 176

Cross, James M.: 131

Crumb: 3, 6, 18, 27, 38, 42, 60, 61, 102, 111, 113

Cugini, Dan and Jerry: 118

Cugini, Lisa Guerard: vi, 118

curling: 64, 74, 75

Curwensville, PA: 180

D

Dalbeattie Granite Works: 27, 74

Dalbeattie, Scotland: 18

Darrach monument: 173

Datson, John: 210

Declaration of Independence Plaque: 188

DeFanti: 102, 134

Degler, Melanie Waters: vi, 92

Delivering: 158

Denesha, Robert: vi, 52

DePerry, Peter: vii, 166

DeRocchi monument: 89

DeRocchi, John: 79, 89

Derujinsky, Gleb W.: 187

Designing: 124

Dinwoodie: iv, 18, 21, 22, 25, 40, 102

Dixon: 6, 7, 26, 27, 44, 45, 60, 61, 102, 111, 131, 158, 210

Dixon Square: 158, 210

Dodge, Jerry: 151

Dow, William: 26

Dower, Richard: 210

Drake, Colonel Edwin: 190

Providence and Stonington Railroad: 8

Providence County Courthouse: 22

Providence, RI: 47

Putnam, CT: 85

Putnam, Gen. Israel: 85

Q

Quarries: 111

Quarry Hill: ii, v, 1, 8, 14, 17, 60, 63, 64, 65, 68, 69, 85, 86, 111, 112, 163

Quarry Hill School: v, 8, 63, 64, 65, 68, 69

quarrying: v, 2, 6, 9, 13, 28, 30, 61, 64, 111, 112, 121, 132, 133, 136, 180, 210

Quincy: 3, 40, 44, 57, 58, 72, 174

R

Rae, George: 117

Rainey, Charlie: 46

Recchia, Joseph: 92

Red Stone Quarry: 42

Rezzi, Charles: 5

Rhode Island Granite Works: 2, 7, 14, 24, 27, 60, 111, 131, 151, 162

Rhode Island Redstone Co.: 22, 27

Rhodes Hill: 2, 8, 9, 60

Rhodes, Bill: 120

Richards mausoleum: v, 179

Richards, James: 183

Richards, Robert H.: 179

Richardson monument: 84

Ritacco, Umile: vii, 26

River Bend Cemetery: ix, 4, 18, 40, 56, 58, 59, 84, 85, 88, 89, 91, 93, 164, 165, 168, 173, 174, 182, 184, 196

Robert A. Gray Civil War Memorial: 32, 82

Robinson, Hannah Hill: vii, 76, 141

Rochester, NY: 84

Rock of Ages: 49

Roger Williams monument: 33

Rogers, Randolph: 189

James Romanella and Sons: 40, 62

Roosevelt, Franklin D.: 187

Roosevelt, Theodore: 187

Rosedale Cemetery: 34

Rowe, John: 117

Ruga, Cosmo: 142

Rural Cemetery: 85

S

Saint-Gaudens, Augustus: 187

Salem Field Cemetery: 191

Samuel Maynard monument: 90

San Francisco, CA: 14

Sanders monument: 5, 182

Santaniello, Marian Sposato: vii

Santoro, Thomas: 117

Sarcophagus: 131, 181, 191

Sayles Hall: 193

Scharphler, John: 191

Schlitz, Joseph: 191

Scialabba, Felice Sposato: vii

Scots: v, 18, 63, 64, 74

Second Division Memorial: 33, 190

Segar, Thomas: 16

Serra monument: 51

Setting: 160

Shanks, Alex: 146

Sharpsburg, MD: 14, 94, 98

Shawn Monument Company: 27, 44, 53

Shawn, Roger, Jr.: vii, 44, 52

shear poles: 11, 132, 135, 140, 163

Shelter Harbor: v, 120

Sherman: 18, 106

Shipman monument: 131

Shotwell boulder: 185

Shurecliff, Arthur A.: 204

Slosberg, Harold: 40, 52, 61, 113

Slosberg, Michael: vi, ix

Smalley: 27, 61, 106, 111, 113

Smith Chapman cradle: 185

Smith tablet: 186

Smith, Edward W.: 10, 61, 122

Smith, Emeline Gallup: 8, 68

Smith, Franklin: 9, 173

Smith, Isaac G.: 8

Smith, Isaac G., Jr.: iv, vii, ix, 3, 58, 65, 147, 148, 156, 162, 163, 166, 210

Smith, Isaac G., Sr.: 10

Smith, Jennie Chapman: 80

Smith, Julia: 68

Smith, Julia Chapman: 80

Smith, Orlando: iii, 1, 2, 3, 8, 9, 11, 52, 60, 68, 132, 157, 194

Smith, Orlando R.: vi, 8, 9, 61, 80, 178

Smith, Orlando R., Jr.: 9

Smith, Sarah: 2, 127

Smith, Sarah Chapman: 80

Soldiers and Sailors Monument: 88

Soldiers National Monument: 14, 189

Sotter mausoleum: 124

Spicer: 25

Sposato, Santo: 66

Springfield, MA: 35, 91

St. John's University: 44

St. Pius X Church: 42, 112

St. Sebastian Cemetery: 51, 163